The Emergence of Distinctive Features

OXFORD STUDIES IN TYPOLOGY AND LINGUISTIC THEORY

SERIES EDITORS: Ronnie Cann, *University of Edinburgh,* William Croft, *University of New Mexico,* Martin Haspelmath, *Max Planck Institute Leipzig,* Nicholas Evans, *University of Melbourne,* Anna Siewierska, *University of Lancaster.*

PUBLISHED

Classifiers: A Typology of Noun Categorization Devices
Alexandra Y. Aikhenvald

Auxiliary Verb Constructions
Gregory D.S. Anderson

Pronouns
D. N. S. Bhat

Subordination
Sonia Cristofaro

The Paradigmatic Structure of Person Marking
Michael Cysouw

Indefinite Pronouns
Martin Haspelmath

Anaphora
Yan Huang

The Emergence of Dictinctive Features
Jeff Mielke

Applicative Constructions
David Peterson

Copulas
Regina Pustet

The Noun Phrase
Jan Rijkhoff

Intransitive Predication
Leon Stassen

Co-Compounds and Natural Coordination
Bernhard Wälchli

PUBLISHED IN ASSOCIATION WITH THE SERIES

The World Atlas of Language Structures
edited by Martin Haspelmath, Matthew Dryer, Bernard Comrie, and David Gil

IN PREPARATION

Imperatives and Commands
Alexandra Y. Aikhenvald

Reciprocals
Nicholas Evans

Reference in Discourse
Andrej A. Kibrik

Double Object Constructions
Maria Polinsky

Predicative Possession
Leon Stassen

Sign Languages
Ulrike Zeshan

The Emergence of
Distinctive Features

JEFF MIELKE

OXFORD
UNIVERSITY PRESS

OXFORD
UNIVERSITY PRESS

Great Clarendon Street, Oxford OX2 6DP

Oxford University Press is a department of the University of Oxford.
It furthers the University's objective of excellence in research, scholarship,
and education by publishing worldwide in

Oxford New York

Auckland Cape Town Dar es Salaam Hong Kong Karachi
Kuala Lumpur Madrid Melbourne Mexico City Nairobi
New Delhi Shanghai Taipei Toronto

With offices in

Argentina Austria Brazil Chile Czech Republic France Greece
Guatemala Hungary Italy Japan Poland Portugal Singapore
South Korea Switzerland Thailand Turkey Ukraine Vietnam

Oxford is a registered trade mark of Oxford University Press
in the UK and in certain other countries

Published in the United States
by Oxford University Press Inc., New York

British Library Cataloguing in Publication Data

Data available

Library of Congress Cataloging in Publication Data

Data available

Typeset by SPI Publisher Services, Pondicherry, India
Printed in Great Britain
on acid-free paper by
Biddles Ltd., King's Lynn, Norfolk

ISBN 978–0–19–920791–6 (Hbk)
      978–0–19–923337–3 (Pbk)

1 3 5 7 9 10 8 6 4 2

Contents

Preface

This book represents my attempt to find out where distinctive features come from. I should say that it started with a general uneasiness about the innateness of features. Uneasiness by itself is not helpful, so my goal was to take the issues of innateness and universality seriously, and to assemble data that would help to answer some open questions and evaluate some assumptions. It has never been my intention to discredit or disparage the work that has been done in the framework of innate distinctive features, and most of the questions I have intended to address could not even be formulated without it. Innate feature theory has provided a way to talk about interesting generalizations about sound patterns, and I believe emergent features mean reconsidering the specific mechanisms behind some of these generalizations (history or physiology vs. Universal Grammar), but do not undermine the generalizations themselves. In most cases, evaluating innate feature proposals is not a matter of right vs. wrong but a matter of literal vs. metaphorical, and I understand that for a lot of researchers, it was metaphorical all along. I believe that reinterpreting features as emergent allows feature theory to be better equipped to deal with language, and in this book I have made an effort to illustrate how the insights of innate feature theory can be retained and how new insights are made possible when features are treated as emergent.

The data that are used to examine questions about features are 6000+ classes of sounds involved in several thousand sound patterns pulled from grammars of 600+ language varieties. I am very grateful to the hundreds of linguists who wrote the descriptive grammars that supplied the data for my survey, and also to the folks at SIL for making *Ethnologue*, which made it much easier to keep track of and organize the languages. Mike Armstrong was instrumental in converting my original survey data files into a useful format. The sound patterns database is now publicly available at www.oup.com/uk/companion/mielke. It is being expanded with new languages, and being revised to be more useful for addressing a wider range of questions.

So to summarize so far, dozens of phonologists provided the generalizations and made it possible to formulate the questions, hundreds of linguists provided the language data, and I provided uneasiness about innateness, and free time. The time was actually made possible by the Ohio State University and the people of Ohio, who funded my research. The research was funded largely by a Presidential Fellowship from OSU for my dissertation year, a fellowship that Scott Myers, Keren Rice, and Donca Steriade helped me to get. Attending conferences during graduate school was very important, for getting feedback on ideas and for forming contacts, and for this I (along with all the other linguistics graduate students at OSU) was generously funded by the *Language Files* fund.

My dissertation committee members at Ohio State, Beth Hume, Keith Johnson, and Brian Joseph, were great sources of inspiration and information. I am grateful to them for cultivating my interest in phonological theory, phonetics, and historical linguistics, and inspiring me to try to believe in them all at the same time. Beth and Keith's Perception in Phonology seminars in 1999–2000 were a two-quarter-long watershed moment for me as a linguist. Brian's historical linguistics class in 1999 put some questions in my head that I would later try to answer in this book. Ellen Kaisse attracted me to phonology in the first place, in the Phonology III class at the University of Washington in the spring of 1996, and Kaoru Ohta was very supportive when I decided to go to graduate school in linguistics.

I didn't do this work in isolation, but within a small and a large community. The basic idea came to me while listening to a talk about hypocoristics at the Montréal-Ottawa-Toronto phonology workshop (MOT) at McGill in 2002. Many of the ideas and here and their development came from casual conversations with classmates and colleagues at Ohio State. I know that it was mostly (but not always) just me lugging grammars back and forth between the William Oxley Thompson Library and Oxley Hall (or from and back to the main library at Michigan State during the 2003 summer institute), but just about everything else that happened (thinking etc.) was more collaborative than that. I had the good fortune to be able to discuss this stuff with classmates at OSU, such as Robin Dautricourt, Kathleen Currie Hall, Grant McGuire, Anton Rytting, Tom Stewart, and Steve Winters. Giorgos Tserdanelis was there to help me articulate my dissertation topic on the long drive between Columbus and New Haven for LabPhon 8 in 2002. I have benefited much from talking about features and phonological patterns with Mary Beckman, Doug Pulleyblank, Janet Pierrehumbert, Donca Steriade, and Andy Wedel. Nick Clements and Dave Odden were both very generous to me with their time, and their skepticism helped keep me honest along the way. Chris Brew helped me get the phonetic similarity model on the right track. Juliette Blevins provided great feedback and encouragement, particularly in helping me to clarify some ideas while I was turning my dissertation into this book.

This process of making a book out of my dissertation was made easier by John Davey and three anonymous reviewers, and by feedback from conferences. For this I am grateful to participants of MOT 2003 in Toronto, MCWOP 9 in Urbana-Champaign, LSA 2004 in Boston, VarPhon in Potsdam, NELS 35 at UConn, WECOL' 04 at USC, WCCFL XXIV at Simon Fraser, the

GLOW Phonology Workshop in Geneva, CLS 41, and LASSO 2005 in Lubbock, and audiences at LSCP in Paris, and the Universities of Arizona, Ottawa, Alberta, and Colorado. Chapter 4 contains a lot of content which appeared in *Phonology* 22(2) (Cambridge), and benefited from the review process there. Overviews and related content appear in the proceedings of WCCFL XXIV, NELS 35, WECOL 2004, CLS 41, and a chapter in Variation and Gradience in Phonetics and Phonology edited by Caroline Féry, Ruben van de Vijver, and Frank Kügler (Mouton de Gruyter).

There was more context than that. It's hard to spend six years doing anything (such as a Ph.D.) without a lot of other things happening. In my case, I suddenly became a widower in my first year of graduate school, and probably would have dropped out if not for extraordinary support from people in Columbus whom I had known for less than a year at the time. I am most grateful to Beth Hume for, beyond being a tremendous adviser, somehow knowing what to do with a 22-year-old widowed graduate student. Beth (and Keith) kept me busy working on the ICPhS satellite meeting in 1999, when I needed to be kept busy, got me started on my Turkish /h/ deletion project when I needed a project to work on, and then let me do whatever when it was time for me to do whatever. Pat Hammel, my neighbor and landlord, also went above and beyond the call of duty, and I am particularly grateful to friends like Paul Davis, Vanessa Metcalf, Jason Packer, Andrea Sims, and especially Robin Dodsworth and my dog Hudson.

I must also thank the Remainders, of whom Chad Howe, Grant McGuire, Jason Packer, and I remained for the 2002–2004 "Jangleocity years". The Remainders' third album had about the same starting and completion dates as my dissertation, and the two projects needed each other to provide the right amounts of distraction and urgency. Before that there was also Ken Bame, Paul Davis, Jen Vannest, Patrick Arnold, and Steve Winters. Playing with them was a valuable outlet and source of fun during an otherwise difficult time.

I am most indebted to my parents, Rich and Marilee Mielke, and my sister, Alison, for their love and support, and for putting me in a position where it was possible to go to college and graduate school. I am grateful to Rick, Sheri, Lindsay, Erica, and Kelly Backous, for the same, and Sara, who was my wife when we moved to Ohio so that I could study linguistics, and who died in a car accident seven months later, working for the Ohio Environmental Council. This book is dedicated to her.

List of figures and tables

Figures

Tables

Abbreviations

2a	second person singular
3s	third person singular
AAVE	African-American Vernacular English
acc	accusative
ANOVA	Analysis of variance
ant	anterior
ASL	American Sign Language
ATR	Advanced Tongue Root
C	Consonant
C-pl	Consonant place
Cog Rep	Cognitive Representation
cons	consonantal
constr	constricted
cont	continuant
cor	coronal
Cor	coronal
def	definite
del rel	delayed primary release
del rel 2nd closure	delayed release of secondary closure
distr	distributed
Dor	dorsal
DUP	duplicate
EMA	Electromagnetic Midsagittal Articulometry
F	feminine
F0	fundamental frequency
F2	second formant
F3	third formant
Gen.	genitive
HC	Hand Configuration
hi	high

hi subgl. pres.	heightened subglottal pressure
Hz	Hertz
[I]	Index (signed language feature)
imp	imperative
JFH	Jakobson et al. (1952)
lab	labial
Lab	Labial
LAD	Language Acquisition Device
lat	lateral
lo	low
LS	Lower Southern
[M]	Middle (signed language feature)
masc.	masculine
MDS	Multidimensional Scaling
MEG	Magnetoencephalography
MIT	Massachusetts Institute of Technology
mov glot cl	movement of glottal closure
mov glottal closure	movement of glottal closure
ms	milliseconds
nas	nasal
Nom	nominative
obj	object
[P]	Pinky (signed language feature)
pf	perfect
pl	plural
PL	plural
pp.	past participle
[R]	Ring (signed language feature)
RED	reduplicant
rnd	round
seg	segmental
sg.	singular
SLPC	Sri Lankan Portuguese Creole
son	sonorant

SPE	*The Sound Pattern of English* (Chomsky and Halle 1968)
strid	strident
syl	syllabic
[T]	Thumb (signed language feature)
UCLA	University of California at Los Angeles
UFT	Unified Feature Theory (Clements and Hume 1995)
UG	Universal Grammar
V	Vowel
voc	vocalic
voi	voice
VOT	Voice Onset Time
V-pl	Vowel place

1

Natural classes and distinctive features in phonology

Most large cities in North America have an Ethiopian restaurant called "Blue Nile". A plausible explanation for this fact is that Blue Nile is an Ethiopian restaurant chain with franchises located throughout North America. There would be some evidence to back up this explanation: the restaurants have similar menus, some have similar decor and background music, and there even appear to be other Ethiopian restaurant chains with names such as "Queen of Sheba" and "Abyssinia" and locations across North America.

There is also some counterevidence to this claim. There is no independent evidence of a "Blue Nile Corporation": there is no web page, no publicly traded stock, no national advertising campaigns, and no pamphlet listing locations in other cities. Compared to known chains such as Starbucks®, it is apparent that different Blue Nile restaurants are implemented differently: they don't look the same, they don't use the same fonts on their menus, and their recipes aren't exactly the same. The food, decor, and music which are so similar between the restaurants are all things that are to be expected for an Ethiopian restaurant. Further, "Blue Nile" is a pretty good name for an Ethiopian restaurant, because the source of the Blue Nile is in Ethiopia, and many potential customers in North America have heard of the Nile River. It is not particularly surprising that multiple restauranteurs would choose the name "Blue Nile", so that approximately 7 percent of the Ethiopian restaurants in North America would share the name. In other words, the process by which entrepreneurs choose names for their Ethiopian restaurants favors names like "Blue Nile" over other logically possible names.

Other observations can be accounted for by looking at the factors related to the emergence of restaurant names: For example, the most frequent names are transparently "grounded" in potential patrons' awareness of Ethiopia. Second, even though Eritrean and Ethiopian food are quite similar, there are no Blue Nile Eritrean restaurants, for a very specific reason: the Blue Nile does not pass through Eritrea. The most common name shared by Ethiopian and

Eritrean restaurants is "Red Sea". Eritrea borders the Red Sea, and Ethiopia used to.[1] Concluding that there was an unseen entity Blue Nile Corporation would have prevented a deeper account of the similarities between the restaurants. The fact that "Blue Nile" is such a natural name for an Ethiopian restaurant suggests that it would be a good name for a chain, but the fact that it is such a good name is precisely the reason why it is not necessary to posit the existence of a corporation for which there is no direct evidence. The existence of many coffee shops named "Starbucks®" is better evidence for a Starbucks® Corporation because it is *not* a particularly natural name for a coffee shop, and therefore the corporation (for which there is quite a bit of direct evidence) is the only available explanation.

A parallel situation exists in language. Many languages in different parts of the world have similar sound patterns involving similar groups of sounds. A widely accepted explanation for this fact is that a small set of distinctive features which define these sounds are innate to humans. Theories of innate features have been used to account for many different observations about sound patterns. The purpose of this book is to argue that there are many sound patterns that innate features cannot account for, that there is no direct evidence for innate features, and that observations about sound patterns are better accounted for by emergent feature theory, a theory of how the development of sound patterns leads to the recurrence of particular groups of sounds, or natural classes.

1.1 Natural class behavior

Speech sounds in spoken languages do not always act independently. Instead, multiple sounds often participate in the same sound patterns. When a group of sounds exhibits the same behavior, it is often the case that these sounds are phonetically similar to each other. This type of grouping of sounds has been termed a "natural class", and the observation that phonological alternations often involve groups of sounds which share phonetic properties has led to the proposal that phonological alternations act upon specific properties of sounds, or "distinctive features", rather than on the sounds themselves. If a particular feature is targeted by an alternation, then all sounds bearing that feature are involved. Because many of the same groupings of sounds are observed in unrelated languages, it has been proposed that distinctive features are part of Universal Grammar, the innate and uniquely human capacity for

---

[1] Although there is no obvious synchronic motivation for naming an Ethiopian restaurant "Red Sea", there is a historical explanation: Ethiopia bordered the Red Sea before Eritrea gained independence in 1991, and Red Sea Ethiopian restaurants may all have been named at a time when there *was* synchronic motivation.

language. It follows from this that possible natural classes are those which can be characterized using the innate distinctive features. This has been a standard assumption in phonological theory since the 1960s.

For example, Turkish final devoicing applies not just to one type of sound, but to all of the non-nasal voiced consonants in the language, some of which are shown in (1). Consonants which are voiced word-medially are devoiced word-finally. Because devoicing is something that happens to all of these consonants in Turkish, it is claimed that the process applies not to segments, but to the feature [voice]. Final devoicing is observed in many unrelated languages, and this is taken as evidence that [voice] and other features are innate.

(1) Turkish final devoicing
      a. Root-final nonnasal voiced consonants occur before vowel-initial suffixes.
         kitabɨm   'my book'
         kadɨm   'my floor'
         fɛzim   'my fez'
      b. These consonants are voiceless when word-final.
         kitap   'book'
         kat   'floor'
         fes   'fez'

Distinctive features have been widely assumed to be part of Universal Grammar since the mid-twentieth century. While the theory of innate features predicts that a small set of distinctive features can describe most if not all natural classes, this prediction has never been explicitly tested. The usefulness of distinctive features in phonological analysis is clear from decades of research, but demonstrating that features are innate and universal rather than learned and language-specific requires a different kind of evidence. This book presents the results of the first large-scale crosslinguistic survey of natural classes. Based on data from 628 language varieties, the survey reveals that unnatural classes are widespread: among 6,077 unique classes of sounds which are targets or triggers of phonological processes in these languages, analyzed in three popular feature theories (*Preliminaries to Speech Analysis*, Jakobson et al., 1952; *The Sound Pattern of English* (*SPE*), Chomsky and Halle 1968; and Unified Feature Theory, Clements and Hume 1995), no single theory is able to characterize more than 71 percent of the classes, and over 24 percent are not characterizable in *any* of the theories. While other theories are able to account for specific subsets of these classes, none is able to predict the wide range of classes which actually occur and recur in the world's languages.

This book argues that the natural classes and distinctive features found in human languages can be accounted for as the result of factors such as phonetically based sound change and generalization, which can be described without reference to a feature system. A feature system can be constructed (by a language learner or a linguist) on the basis of the results, but the feature system critically does not need to be a driving force behind sound patterns. Facts which have been attributed to innate features are accounted for by independently needed concepts (such as language change and similarity). It follows that phonological distinctive features no longer need to be assumed to be innate.

It is no secret that there are phonological patterns which do not conform to models of innate features, and a common approach is to treat these as marginal processes which are beyond the purview of innate feature models. One example is palatalization in the Chi-Mwi:ni dialect of Swahili (Kisseberth and Abasheikh 1975, Clements 1985), in which certain consonants undergo palatalization before the perfect suffix -iːɬ-. The only place feature these consonants retain their value for is *SPE*-era [anterior]. [g] is an exception, because it loses its value to change to [z], instead of the expected [ʒ] (2).

(2)   p ṭ t   →   s
      k   →   ʃ   / [+nasal]__
      bḍdgɬ   →   z

This is problematic for innatist approaches which hold that all place features are expected to spread as a constituent. Rules such as the one in (2) appear to be the result of telescoping (the merging of independent rules), and Clements (1985: 246) draws a distinction between this type of rule and those which are captured simply using innate features and feature organization:

We will not relax the empirical claims of our theory in order to provide simple descriptions of rules such as these, since if we did so we would fail to draw a correct distinction between the common, widely recurrent process types that we take as providing the primary data for our theory, and the sort of idiosyncratic phenomena whose explanation is best left to the domain of historical linguistics.

The strongest versions of innate feature theory might require the relationship between attested or attestable phonologically active classes and featurally natural classes to be identity. However, many phonologists may not expect features to predict all of the classes that occur, because many of the classes are the historical residues from millennia of diachronic changes that may interfere with naturalness. The telescoping of multiple natural changes may result in seemingly arbitrary unnatural-looking synchronic patterns. While these idiosyncratic classes might be treated as fundamentally different from natural classes, there is also a relationship between natural changes and natural classes. Recurrent natural classes may also be understood as simply the most common types of historical residue.

In accounting for unnatural classes, it makes sense to separate the classes into two categories: those which are phonetically natural and may have a transparent phonetic basis, but have the misfortune of being natural according to a set of properties for which a distinctive feature has not been proposed, and those which are phonetically unnatural, and likely arose via a series of changes, each of which may have been natural but whose end result is a phonetically unnatural class. One approach is to aggressively expand the innate feature set to account for all phonetically natural classes while forsaking unnatural classes. Anderson (1981) argues that this can be a very difficult distinction to make, because many classes which appear to have a transparent basis in phonetically natural changes turn out to have very different origins. Further, a vast theory of innate features which attempts to capture all phonetically natural classes without adopting an independent gradient notion of naturalness would need to draw a distinction between the most marginally natural (but perhaps unattested) classes which are admitted and classes for which there is no apparent phonetic basis (but which may be attested nonetheless) which are rejected.

Another approach, taking into account the experimental evidence that natural and unnatural classes may be processed the same way synchronically, is to treat all classes as historical residues, and to explore phonologically active classes in terms of their historical development, to understand the types of class a learner may be called upon most frequently to acquire. In this view, natural classes are a special case of idiosyncratic historical residues, i.e. they are the ones which most transparently reflect their phonetic origins and which therefore occur most frequently and are most likely to be encountered and embraced by phonologists.

While historical explanations are often invoked within innate feature approaches in order to account for problematic cases, it is unclear how often such an explanation can be invoked. Is it a coincidence that a model of synchronic phonology such as innate features is well suited to modeling processes which commonly arise from phonetic motivations (and for which a straightforward phonetic explanation exists) and ill-equipped to model less common phonological processes (for which only a more complicated phonetic explanation exists)?

Suppose that explanation from innate distinctive features is a medium-sized rectangle, and that explanation from phonetics and language change is a large triangle. The argument that phonological processes can be explained by innate distinctive features (phonetically grounded or not) amounts to the statement represented in Fig. 1.1.

Suppose that a sample of phonological processes includes examples (such as the one from Chi-Mwi:ni Swahili) that fall outside the rectangle (Fig. 1.2). The rectangle has already been placed very carefully by many bright linguists, on the basis of observed patterns and phonetic considerations, but counterexamples persist. Counterexamples that appear to defy innate features are often argued to be beyond the purview of the feature system, and have been accounted for by invoking external factors such as language change and physiology. Accounting for these by invoking external factors amounts to adding extensions (small triangles) to account for problem cases (Fig. 1.3).

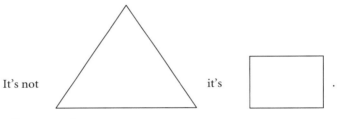

FIGURE 1.1 Factors vs. features

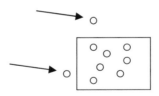

FIGURE 1.2 Innate feature theory with exceptions

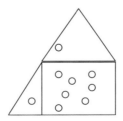

FIGURE 1.3 Innate feature theory with extensions

Adding small triangles to the rectangle causes it to look more and more like the triangle that was rejected in the first place, and the distinction between the modified rectangle and the larger triangle is less useful. It is argued in this book that sound patterns can be accounted for more effectively by dispensing with the rectangle/triangle distinction, i.e. by treating recurrent, natural classes as a special case of historical residues (the residues favored by the factors relevant to the development of residues) rather than a separate privileged category.

1.2 Emergent feature theory

In showing that innate distinctive features are unnecessary to explain the existence of natural classes, it is not necessary to deny that features are a relevant part of a phonological system. Features which arise in the way proposed here are just as well suited as innate ones for defining phonological patterns, forming contrasts, and doing everything else that features have been claimed to do. Emergent feature theory simply offers a different explanation for the existence of phonological features, one which is more compatible with knowledge of genetic and linguistic change, and with known synchronic phonological patterns.

Emergent feature theory is at least partially consistent with and/or inspired by a good deal of work previous work on:

- the emergence of linguistic patterns and structure (e.g. Martinet 1968, Lindblom 1983, 1984, 1986, 1990a,b, 1999, 2000, Ladefoged 1984, Bybee 1985, 1998, 2001, Corina and Sagey 1989, Port 1996, Steels 1997, Mac-Whinney 1998, Pierrehumbert 2001, 2003, Beckman and Pierrehumbert 2003, Pulleyblank 2003, and Wedel 2004);
- the unnaturalness of some synchronic patterns (e.g. Bach and Harms 1972, Anderson 1981, Ladefoged and Everett 1996, Buckley 2000, and Hale and Reiss 2000);
- the explanation of synchronic observations in terms of diachrony (e.g. Andersen 1972, 1973, Anttila 1977, Ohala 1981, 1983, 1992, 1993a,b, 2003, Labov 1994, 2001, Newmeyer 1998, Blevins and Garrett 1998, Garrett and Blevins 2004, Dolbey and Hansson 1999, Janda 1999, 2001, 2003, Hyman 2001, Janda and Joseph 2001, 2003, Myers 2002, Vaux 2002, Guy 2003, Hale 2003, Kiparsky 2003, Blevins 2004, and Culicover and Nowak 2004);
- the explanation of synchronic observations in terms of external factors (Beddor 1991, de Boer 2000, Hume and Johnson 2001a, Kochetov 2002, and Hume 2004a, b); and

- approaches to morphology as a distinct component of grammar (e.g. Maiden 1992, Aronoff 1994, Carstairs-McCarthy 1994).

There is a general trend in the field toward narrowing the scope of the uniquely human language faculty, typified by Hauser et al. (2002). The idea that phonological classes are language-specific is consistent with language development-based arguments that phonological (Vihman and Croft 2007) and grammatical classes (Croft 2001, Tomasello 2003) are emergent. Innatist and emergentist approaches both posit relationships between phonetic substance, abstract features, and the phonological patterns found in human languages. The difference lies in the nature of these relationships. For innate features (Figure 1.4a), abstract features are grounded directly in phonetics, and phonological patterns reflect both the features and the phonetic substance because features are the building blocks of phonological patterns. The relationship between phonological patterns and phonetics (bypassing features) is less direct, but necessary in order to provide the phonetic or historical accounts for "idiosyncratic" phenomena which are difficult or impossible to analyze with the given features. For emergent features (Figure 1.4b), this loose relationship between phonetics and phonological patterns is the sole connection between phonological patterns and phonetic tendencies. Just as grammar-external factors (including external phonetic factors) can be used to account for idiosyncratic phenomena in an

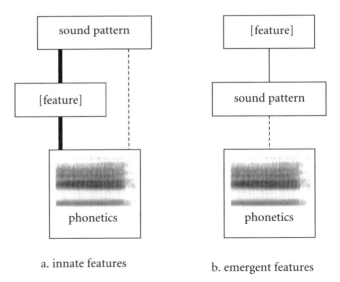

a. innate features   b. emergent features

FIGURE 1.4 Relationships between phonetics, features, and phonological patterns

approach which otherwise depends on innate features, phonetics can account for these unusual phonological patterns, and *also* for more common patterns, which tend to reflect more common phonetic tendencies. In this way, emergent feature theory employs a single mechanism to account for common and rare phonological patterns, in contrast with innate feature theory, which employs two.

In emergent feature theory, features are abstract categories based on generalizations that emerge from phonological patterns. In innate feature theory it is typically the other way around: phonological patterns emerge (at least in part) from the effects of features. Whereas innate features are typically grounded directly in phonetics, this relationship is different for emergent features: recurrent phonetically defined features reflect phonetics *via* the phonetically grounded phonological patterns they are motivated by. Because features are abstract, there need not always be a connection between phonetics and phonological patterns, and features do not necessarily always refer to phonetically natural classes.

A more detailed view of the relationship between features, phonological patterns, and external factors is given in Chapter 5. The environment in which language is used includes the anatomy used to produce and perceive speech, the laws of physics this anatomy is governed by, the social context in which language is used, and the cognitive mechanisms employed in learning and using language. The factors audition, attention, categorization, aerodynamics, coordination, and social identity contribute to the development of the phonological patterns found in language, making some patterns more common than others. The influence of these factors on sound patterns is illustrated in Fig. 1.5. The features which learners use to define these sound patterns reflect the factors that influence them, and have the potential to influence the patterns (the reason for the bidirectional arrow). The role of speech production and perception is not to be interpreted as simply ease of articulation and ease of perception, but as the physiological and cognitive realities in which language exists. The external factors in Fig. 1.5 and their relationships with each other, sound patterns, and features will be discussed in more detail in Chapters 5 and 8.

Emergent feature theory holds that phonetic factors shape the phonological patterns of the world's languages, and these patterns can be internalized by speakers in terms of features which are necessary to describe them, rather than in terms of predetermined innate features. These external influences lead to classes which tend to involve phonetically similar segments. The use of phonetically defined distinctive features is just one way to describe classes of phonetically similar segments. While these types of explanation are often invoked to account

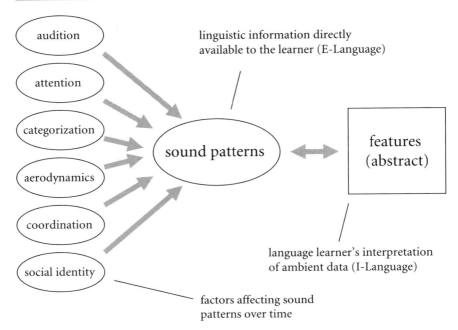

FIGURE 1.5 Abstract features from concrete external factors

for "idiosyncratic" unnatural classes, it will be shown that they are even better at accounting for "natural" classes, and the result is a unified account of what have previously been considered to be natural and unnatural classes.

1.3 Incorporating insights of innate features into emergent feature theory

Innate feature theory has captured many different insights about phono-logical patterns over the years. Because it abandons the assumption of in-nateness, emergent feature theory needs to account for these observations in other ways. One important observation is that there are a limited number of phonetic parameters available for use in language. Jakobson et al. (1952) suggest that all languages can be described using the twelve oppositions vocalic/non-vocalic, consonantal/non-consonantal, interrupted/ continuant, checked/unchecked, strident/mellow, voiced/unvoiced, compact/diffuse, grave/acute, flat/plain, sharp/plain, tense/lax, and nasal/oral. It will be seen below how well these features are represented in the phonologically active classes of 628 language varieties. To the extent that there is a crosslinguistic preference for these oppositions, emergent feature theory accounts for them in roughly the same way Jakobson et al. account for them, by observing that there are a limited number of phonetic parameters available to language, and that phonological patterns reflect that. Jakobson et al.'s features are stated in acoustic terms, but they observe also that the acoustic parameters associated with these features correspond to specific articulatory parameters, and they account for typological observations in terms of these parameters. For example, they account for the apparent absence of languages which contrast pharyngealization and labialization separately by noting the acoustic similarity of the two types of articulatory gesture, and consequently allow the feature [flat] to represent the acoustic property that is produced by two different articulatory means. It is now known that there are languages such as Tamazight Berber (Abdel-Massih 1968) with contrastive pharyngealization and labialization, but the finding that the coexistence of these contrasts is much rarer than the coexistence of many other contrasts still stands.

Emergent feature theory attributes the *rarity* of such languages to acoustic *similarity*, and attributes the *possibility* of coexistence to the articulatory difference and acoustic *non-identity*. Because it uses similarity to predict the likelihood of phonological patterns, emergent feature theory is better equipped to distinguish between similarity and identity than is innate feature theory. In formulating linguistic theories, it is very tempting to identify similarity with identity. The upside of confusing similarity with identity is that it allows more sweeping generalizations to be made. The downside is that they are often wrong.

Another observation is that articulatory parameters are relevant to phonology. It has been proposed (e.g. Chomsky and Halle 1968, Sagey 1986) that all phonological patterns can be accounted for with an innate set of articulatory features. In *The Sound Pattern of English* (*SPE*), the features themselves, rather than phonetic parameters, are the explanation for observed phonological patterns. Emergent feature theory accounts for the same observations on the basis of language change, phonetic similarity, and the cognitive process of generalization. As shown in Chapter 7, the classification of phonologically active classes involves many of the articulatory parameters identified by Chomsky and Halle, as well as parameters they do not identify.

A third observation to be accounted for is that some phonetic parameters are interdependent on each other, and some act independently. This is represented in Feature Geometry (e.g. Clements 1985, Sagey 1986) and Dependency Phonology (Anderson and Ewen 1987, Harris 1994) by a feature hierarchy with constituents which correspond to features that pattern together. Features which are linked under the same node tend to be features which are linked articulatorily. In this way, Feature Geometry is an abstract model of some of the phonetic parameters relevant to phonology. In abstracting away from the phonetic basis for phonology, the different versions of Feature Geometry highlight some of the phonetic parameters which are most important for determining phonological patterns as well as the ways in which they interact with each other.

1.4 Definitions

The term "natural class" is used to mean different things, and it will be necessary to be precise about how the term is used in this book. The traditional definition has two parts, as in (3).

(3) Natural class (traditional two-part definition)
    i. A group of sounds in an inventory which share one or more distinctive features, to the exclusion of all other sounds in the inventory.
    ii. A group of sounds in an inventory which may participate in an alternation or static distributional restriction, to the exclusion of all other sounds in the inventory.

These two definitions are often assumed to be equivalent, and if it can be demonstrated that phonological alternations do indeed act only upon distinctive features, then these definitions would be equivalent. Because one of the goals of this study is to find out if the two definitions really are equivalent, this is not something that will be assumed. When the term "natural class" is used in the rest of this book, it will be used in terms of a particular feature theory, using the theory-dependent definition in (4).

(4) Natural class (feature theory-dependent definition)
    A group of sounds in an inventory which share one or more distinctive features *within a particular feature theory*, to the exclusion of all other sounds in the inventory.

It is often assumed that that phonological natural classes are phonetically natural, as defined in (5). In cases where this is the intended interpretation, the term "phonetically natural class" will be used instead.

(5) Phonetically natural class
    A group of sounds in an inventory which share one or more phonetic properties, to the exclusion of all other sounds in the inventory.

Note that this definition is broader than the one in (4), because not all phonetic properties have features assigned to them in each theory. An "unnatural class" is a class that does not meet a particular set of criteria for being natural. What has been dispensed with in the definitions in (4, 5) is any reference to phonological patterning, which is crucially not *assumed* to be identified with phonetic similarity or shared features. To refer to classes which participate in phonological patterns, the term "phonologically active class" will be used. This term is defined in (6). It is a crucial point that while any phonologically active class is, by definition, naturally occurring, there is no guarantee that it is a "natural class" with respect to any given feature theory (4) or "phonetically natural" with respect to any interpretation of phonetic similarity (5).

(6) Phonologically active class (feature theory-independent definition)
     A group of sounds in an inventory which do at least one of the following, to the exclusion of all other sounds in the inventory:
     • undergo a phonological process,
     • trigger a phonological process, or
     • exemplify a static distributional restriction.

It is useful to give some examples of these different types of class. For example, Japanese has a well-known sound pattern in which unaccented high vowels are devoiced between voiceless consonants and word-finally after the same consonants, as in (7).

(7) Japanese vowel devoicing (Vance 1987, Shibatani 1990)[2]
     /kɯtsɯ'/   →   [kɯ̥tsɯ]   'shoes'
     /haʃi/   →   [haʃi̥]   'chopsticks'
     /sɯsɯki'/   →   [sɯ̥sɯ̥ki]   'eulalia'

Because the the vowels /i ɯ/ are targeted by this sound pattern and the consonants /p t k s ʃ h/ trigger it, both of these are phonologically active classes, and provide data points for the survey. Additionally, both of these are featurally natural classes with respect to the feature system of *The Sound Pattern of English* (Chomsky and Halle 1968), among others, because they can be represented with the conjunction of one or more features, in this case [+high, +tense] and [−voice]. Finally, they are both phonetically natural classes as well, because they can be described, to the exclusion of all other sounds in the inventory, in terms of measurable phonetic parameters such as second formant frequency, duration, and vocal fold vibration.

The consonants /t k s ʃ h/ are another phonologically active class in Japanese, because they are voiced when they appear initially in the second

---

[2] Note that the final vowels in 'shoes' and 'eulalia' are not devoiced because they are accented.

part of compounds, a pattern known as "sequential voicing" or *rendaku* (8a). /p/ is alone among the voiceless consonants in not participating in sequential voicing (8b).

(8) Japanese sequential voicing (Vance 1987, Shibatani 1990: 173–4, McCawley 1968: 187)

a. [ama]   + [teɾa]   → [amadeɾa]
   'nun'   'temple'   'nunnery'

   [ɯwa]   + [tsɯmi]   → [ɯwadzɯmi]
   'over'   'piling'   'upper load'

   [oo]   + [same]   → [oozame]
   'big'   'shark'   'big shark'

   [to]   + [ʃimaɾi]   → [todʒimaɾi]
   'door'   'closing'   'locking of a house'

   [tabi]   + [hito]   → [tabibito]
   'travel'   'person'   'traveler'

   [iroha]   + [kaɾɯta]   → [irohagaɾɯta]
   'Japanese   'cards'   'playing cards with
   syllable counting'   *hiragana* on them'

b. [genmai]   + [pan]   → [genmaipan]
   'whole rice'   'bread'   'whole rice bread'

While this is a phonologically active class, it is not a featurally natural class in *SPE*, because there is no conjunction of *SPE* features which can describe the set of all voiceless consonants except /p/. It is a phonetically natural class, though, because it can be described in terms of measurable properties such as lip closure, constriction degree, and vocal fold vibration. An analysis of this sound pattern in *SPE* features requires devices beyond the scope of the feature system, such as rule ordering or antagonistic constraints or conjunction of feature bundles (i.e. bracket notation).

Finally, the consonants /b d z n m ɾ/ are a featurally natural class in Japanese with respect to *SPE*, because they can be described with a conjunction of features such as [+voice, +anterior], and a phonetically natural class, because they can be described in terms of measurable properties such as stricture location and vocal fold vibration. However, this is not a phonologically active class in Japanese, because there is no reported sound pattern which targets or is triggered by specifically these segments.

With these definitions in hand, it is now possible to proceed to investigating the connections between these different types of class, and how they might be accounted for. The concepts "phonologically active class", "featurally natural

class", and "phonetically natural class" have often been conflated in phonological theory as the monolithic "natural class". There is obviously a considerable
amount of overlap because featurally natural classes tend to be phonetically natural (because most if not all widely accepted features are phonetically
defined) and because many phonologically active classes are natural both
featurally and phonetically. It is clear that there are many phonetically
and featurally natural classes which are not phonologically active in a given
language or perhaps any language, and the survey results will show that many
possible phonologically active classes are also not featurally or phonetically
natural, and others are phonetically natural without being featurally natural.
Due to the considerable overlap between phonetic and featural naturalness, it is
difficult to assess how much responsibility each bears for the nature of phonologically active classes.

1.5 General arguments against innate features

Beyond phonological evidence which is the subject of Chapters 4, 6, and 7,
there are many reasons to be suspicious of the idea that distinctive features are
innate. In this section, arguments from signed languages and from phonological theory are presented, pointing to the conclusion that features are not
universal or innate. The purpose of this discussion is not to underestimate the
contribution of innate feature proposals to our understanding of phonological systems, but to examine the specific proposal that distinctive features
are innate. While innate features are central to the way most of these
approaches to phonology are implemented, the insights about phonological
patterning which have been cast in terms of innate features in the past fifty
years stand on their own, and emergent feature theory could not proceed
without them.

1.5.1 *Signed language features*

Most work in feature theory focuses on spoken languages, and typological
surveys, markedness generalizations, and hypothetical universals are generally
made on the basis of only spoken language data. While substantial work has
been conducted in the area of sign language features and feature organization
(e.g. Stokoe 1960, Liddell 1984, Liddell and Johnson 1989, Sandler 1989,
Brentari 1990, 1995, 1998, Perlmutter 1992, van der Hulst 1995, Uyechi 1996),
there are obvious practical reasons for focusing on a single modality (and the
survey in this book only includes spoken language data). Focusing on spoken
language allows modality-specific questions to be addressed (such as the role

of the vocal tract and auditory system in phonology), but questions about phonological universals cannot ignore the existence of sign language phonology.[3]

The hypothesis that there is a small set of innate distinctive features which are defined in terms of the articulation and/or audition of spoken language and which are the only features available to the phonologies of the world's languages is incompatible with signed language phonology, because signed languages involve an entirely different set of articulators and rely primarily on vision rather than on audition. Consequently, the claims about an innate feature set must be qualified with the acknowledgement that this universality is really only applicable to languages of one modality, even though UG purportedly applies to all languages.

There are a number of ways to reconcile the universalist claims with the existence of signed language phonology: (1) relax the requirement that features are defined in phonetic terms and interpret each innate feature as having both spoken language and signed language phonetic correlates, (2) posit additional innate features which apply to signed language, and claim that humans are hardwired with two sets of innate features for two different modalities, or (3) consider that features and their phonetic correlates are learned during acquisition, according to the modality of the language being acquired.

If signed and spoken languages use the same innate features but with different phonetic correlates, it is expected that there would be some evidence that they are otherwise the same features. This evidence could include feature geometries for signed languages that look like Feature Geometries for spoken language. Research in signed language features offers no such evidence (see Brentari 1995, 1998 for reviews). In fact, Liddell (1984) reports that evidence from American Sign Language suggests that signed languages have significantly larger numbers of contrastive segments than spoken languages, and many other analyses are consistent with this. Stokoe (e.g. 1960) produced the first phonemic analysis of signed language, using 12 distinctive places of articulation, 18 distinctive handshapes, and 24 distinctive aspects of movement. The Hold-Movement Model (e.g. Liddell and Johnson 1989) involves 299 distinctive features. Brentari (1990) reorganizes Liddell and Johnson's feature system and reduces the number of features to 20, a number more comparable to that proposed for spoken languages; but Brentari's analysis achieves this by using seven features with more than two values, in addition to other binary and privative features.

---

[3] The importance of considering sign languages when formulating linguistic universals is discussed further in Blevins (2004: 301–4) and Sandler and Lillo-Martin (2006, esp. 272–8). Haspelmath et al.'s (2005) *World Atlas of Language Structures* includes a survey of morphosyntactic properties of signed languages (Zeshan 2005).

Sandler's (e.g. 1989) Hand Tier model was the first to incorporate a hierarchical organization of features, placing hand configuration and location on separate trees, as shown in Figs. 1.6 and 1.7, and bears little resemblance to any spoken language Feature Geometry proposals. Similarly, other feature organizations such as the Dependency Phonology model (e.g. van der Hulst 1995), Visual Phonology (e.g. Uyechi 1996), or the Moraic Model (e.g. Perlmutter 1992) do not resemble proposed spoken language Feature Geometries.

The similarities between the feature organizations for different modalities are limited to very general statements, such as the observation that both have a place node. Just as spoken language feature organization reflects the physiology of the vocal tract, signed language feature organization (e.g. as seen in Figs. 1.6 and 1.7) tends to reflect the anatomy that is relevant for signed language. For example, the organization of features in the Hand Configuration tree, such as the features [T], [I], [M], [R], [P], representing fingers, corresponds to the organization of body parts. Beyond the representation of physiology in feature hierarchies (as is seen in spoken language), Brentari (1998) draws parallels between the structure of signed language phonology and the human visual system, just as many sound patterns in spoken languages reflect the human auditory system. If features are driving phonology, and these are the same features, there should be observations that are attributable only to the features and their organization, rather than to commonalities between the physiological facts they represent.

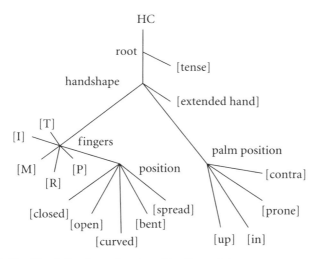

FIGURE 1.6 The Hand Configuration tree (Sandler 1989)

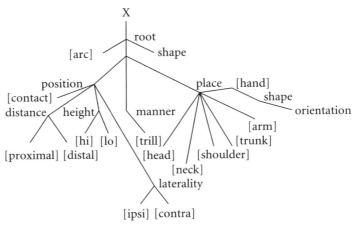

FIGURE 1.7 The Location tree (Sandler 1989)

Positing separate feature sets for signed and spoken languages runs into specific problems, namely that even if spoken language features could have evolved through natural selection, it is not very plausible that signed language features did as well, because most humans are not deaf, and because deafness is rarely hereditary. It is not clear how a genetic mutation introducing an innate signed language distinctive feature could have been advantageous before Deaf communities became established in fairly recent times (e.g. the first Deaf school was established in the 1500s).

If phonetic correlates, and perhaps feature organization, are assigned by the language learner in acquisition, then what is shared by signed language and spoken language phonology may simply be cognitive categories. In other words, categories/features emerge as a result of contact with language data, and they naturally reflect the modality of the language being learned. A child learning a signed language will develop features associated with the production and perception of signs, and a child learning a spoken language will develop features associated with the production and perception of speech. This is essentially the position taken by Brentari (1998: 313) regarding differences between signed and spoken language: that the formal role of distinctive features and other primitives is the same for both modalities, but that the substantive definitions of them depend on modality and experience.

The idea that signed language features, and thus perhaps all features, must be learned, is not new. Corina and Sagey (1989) analyze phonological alternations in ASL using a feature-geometric framework. They note that the proposed Feature Geometry for signed languages is clearly related to anatomy and very different from the Feature Geometry models proposed for spoken languages (e.g. Sagey 1986), which are also clearly related to anatomy (but different parts). Finding it implausible that signed language features are in UG, they try to reconcile the differences between the two:

An alternative [to putting them in UG] is to say that sign language hierarchies are learned or derivable from some language external facts. Since the features and the feature hierarchy are closely tied to articulation, this is not an implausible result. In fact, their being learned could explain why they are clearly tied to articulation. But we are left with a peculiar state of affairs. We posit an innate feature system for spoken language, but a derivable one for signed languages. Once again this seems inconsistent. Could it be the case that spoken language features and hierarchies too are derivable or learned constructs rather than innate? If we adopt this position that features and feature hierarchies are learnable and not given in UG, we open up the possibility that they are not completely universal. That is there could be slight differences between languages, the particular language influencing the feature set and the hierarchy. The vast differences in the feature hierarchy proposed here simply represent the extreme end of this continuum, due to the radically different mediums in which they are conveyed. The puzzle to be explained would now become why hierarchies are so similar among languages. If features are in UG, then any variations must be explained; if features are not in UG, then any universals among languages must be explained. (Corina and Sagey 1989: 81–2)

During the past half-century, phonologists have generally taken UG as the explanation for crosslinguistic similarities, and sought special explanations for apparent exceptions. Emergent feature theory takes the opposite approach. The fact that features and feature hierarchies appear to be so similar may not be so much a puzzle as a result of the *assumption* that features and feature hierarchies are so similar. In fact, as will be seen in later chapters, most languages do not have phonological phenomena to motivate most features. There is no reason to believe that these languages have particular features except for the assumption that all languages must have the features which are motivated by other languages. The differences between the features which are useful for analyzing signed and spoken languages demonstrate how much the similarities are dependent upon modality.[4]

---

[4] It is worth noting that the survey data presented in subsequent chapters of this book is from spoken languages. In the discussion, the term "sound pattern" is generally used in contexts which for some reason do not apply to signed languages. The term "phonological pattern" is used in more general contexts where exclusion signed languages is not intended.

1.5.2 *No evidence that unattested = impossible*

The goal of many theories of phonology is to distinguish possible phono-logical phenomena from impossible ones. Often the only evidence given for the impossibility of a phonological pattern is that it is unattested in the fraction of existing spoken languages which have been described; for example, Sagey (1986: 9) writes: "It should be possible to represent within the theory any phonological process or form that is possible in human language, and it should be impossible to represent phonological forms and processes that do not exist in human language."

The ability to represent all and *only* the phonologically active classes which recur is described by McCarthy (1994: 191) as the most import criterion for an adequate theory of distinctive features (emphasis mine):

An adequate theory of phonological distinctive features must meet four criteria: (i) it must have a relatively consistent and direct relation to the phonetic properties of speech sounds; (ii) it must be able to describe *all and only the distinctions* made by the sound systems of any of the world's languages; (iii) it must be able to characterize *all and only the natural classes of sounds* that recur in the phonological phenomena of different languages; and (iv) it must correctly characterize the subgroupings of features by recurrent phonological phenomena. The third criterion is the most important one and probably the hardest to achieve.

At least two questions are relevant here: First, how confident are we that phonological patterns which are unattested in today's documented languages are impossible? The number of languages which have been documented are a small sample of the languages which exist, and the number of languages which are currently living are just a small sample of the languages which have existed and will exist in the future. When there are so many linguistic phenomena found in only a handful of attested languages, how can we be certain that *any* phonological pattern never existed in the past, never will exist in the future, and doesn't exist currently in an understudied language?

Chomsky and Halle (1968: 4) contrast linguistic universals and accidental universals. To illustrate accidental universals, they construct a hypothetical scenario in which only inhabitants of Tasmania survive a future war. In this scenario, it would be a true generalization to say that no existing language uses pitch to distinguish lexical items; but Chomsky and Halle argue that this would be useless information to linguistic theory, because this generalization is only true by virtue of the elimination of most of the world's population by a non-linguistic event.

War, genocide, and other events have already destroyed entire language families. Phonological patterns that were unique to these languages are unattested in today's languages, and making it impossible to represent them inevitably rules out possible forms that the human language faculty is capable of dealing with (and has dealt with before). Theories of representations which exclude unattested patterns are valued in many approaches to feature theory and phonetically driven phonology, and this is a common assumption in Optimality Theory (factorial typology).

Whether or not the phonological formalism should rule out unattested phonological patterns is a very important issue. While it is clearly important to have a theory of possible and impossible or likely and unlikely phono-logical phenomena, there is no reason to believe that the formalism for the cognitive representation of phonological patterns is the only appropriate place for such a theory.

One of the reasons for positing a *small* set of innate features is to keep the theory from overgenerating, i.e. being able to represent phonological patterns which have not been observed. The languages which have been documented give a picture of what types of phonological pattern are expected; it is justified to conclude that phonological patterns which occur frequently in the sample are common crosslinguistically. However, if a pattern is unattested in documented languages, it is not justified to conclude that it is impossible. This is because there are so many phenomena which are attested only once, and which the same criteria would likely deem impossible if a different sample were selected. While it may be justified to conclude on the basis of a sample that a pattern is rare, there is a major difference between rare and impossible when the issue is whether the language faculty should be capable of dealing with the pattern at all.

1.5.3 *No null hypothesis and no large-scale survey*

While most feature theories are supposed to cover all spoken languages, the arguments in favor of particular versions of innate feature theory generally consist of examples from a handful of languages which are dealt with in an elegant fashion by the theory being advocated. The success of a given feature theory, combined with the assumption that features are innate, is taken to support the assumption that features are innate and to validate the model in question. The fact that a variety of feature theories are able to account for different phonological phenomena using phonetically defined features is consistent with the idea that a variety of phonetic facts are relevant for accounting for phonological phenomena. Even if they conflict, it is not surprising that there are many different competing theories of innate features, since each one is valid for some set of data but lacks the ability to account for data that some other theory is better suited for. The claim that one theory in particular is innate and universal is a leap that requires the evidence that would be provided by a large-scale survey. In addition to competing feature theories, it is quite common for feature systems to be tweaked slightly in specific cases in order to better fit the data. Not considering all of these tweaks at once gives the false impression that conventional feature systems are handling all of the data. Considering a wide array of languages all at once suggests that phonological theory should recognize a feature system which is officially as malleable as feature theory has been in practice all along.

McCarthy (1994: 191, quoted above) describes the ability to characterize all recurrent natural classes as the most important criterion for an adequate theory of distinctive features (and the most difficult to achieve), and it will be seen in the survey results that all universal feature theories fail to meet this criterion.

Aside from the optimistic goal of accounting for everything, there is no theory of *how much* phonological patterning should be accounted for by a feature theory in order to motivate the innateness of its features. Arguments for innate feature models do not involve a theory of the extent to which phonetic factors would be expected to influence phonology *anyway*, without the existence of an innate feature set. A possibility that is generally ignored is that the successes of a given model of features can be taken as evidence that the model is correct in its choice of articulatory and acoustic facts to recapitulate, but in itself unnecessary precisely because these phonetic explanations already exist.

Innate feature are often treated as though they are the primary explanation for the fact that sound systems in different languages tend to resemble each other, as though they would be in chaos without being regimented by innate features. For example, Clements and Hume (1995: 245) state that feature theory "explains the fact that all languages draw on a similar, small set of speech properties in constructing their phonological systems" and "has provided strong confirmation for the view that languages do not vary without limit". In the view that features explain why sound systems do not vary without limit, the similar patterning of speech sounds is taken as evidence that there are universal features. It is probably uncontroversial, though, that sound patterns would not really be in complete chaos without innate features, that the null hypothesis is not that all logically possible phonological patterns should be equally likely in human language. For example, "/car horn/ → [60 Hz hum] / __fruit bat chirp" is a logically possible phonological pattern. Even without innate features, the absence of this pattern can easily be attributed to the fact that the human vocal tract is not well suited to producing these sounds, the human auditory system cannot detect them all, and that even if the sounds were producible and perceivable, it is unclear what diachronic changes would lead to such an alternation. The null hypothesis must take into account the fact that the speech sounds of human spoken languages are limited by human physiology and general cognitive capacity, and that natural languages are not invented by their speakers but descended along sometimes familiar paths from earlier languages. Given this, the case for an innate feature set could be strengthened by specifying the minimum amount of similar patterning that must be found, and what its nature must be, in order to conclude that an evolutionary leap has created an innate feature set. The same applies to extragrammatical features of language use which are presented as arguments for an innate feature set. What would we expect language acquisition, disablement, and change to look like in a world without innate features but with familiar tangible constraints on possible languages?

In addition to the lack of a null hypothesis with which to compare innate feature theories, there have been no large-scale typological studies examining the predictions of various models. This book provides the results of a large-scale typological survey in order to examine the extent to which innate feature theories and the phonetic factors they are grounded in are able to account for phonological patterning in a wide range of languages.

1.5.4 *New theories without new evidence*

In the history of phonological theory, new theories have often been preceded by new types of evidence. For example, the use of spectrography to examine the acoustic properties of speech led to Jakobson et al.'s (1952) acoustically defined feature system, and the use of Electromagnetic Midsagittal Articulometry (EMA) and X-ray microbeam technology led to Articulatory Phonology (e.g. Browman and Goldstein 1992). In other cases, the connection between new theories and new evidence is less overt. The claim that distinctive features are innate is one of these. Early feature theories did not claim innateness, but innateness is now a fairly standard assumption, and it is not clear what if any evidence brought about this shift.

In the early years of modern phonological theory, Trubetzkoy (e.g. 1939) and Jakobson stressed the importance of describing languages on their own terms. Jakobson (1942: 241) writes that "[t]he description of a system of values and the classification of its elements can be made only from that system's own perspective". Later, Jakobson takes more universalist views, but the evidence that leads to this conclusion is unclear. In part II of *Fundamentals of Language* (Jakobson and Halle 1956: 39), Jakobson claims that "[t]he study of invariances within the phonemic pattern of a given language must be supplemented by a search for universal invariances in the phonemic patterning of language in general". Further, Jakobson reports implicational relationships between phonological distinctions, which are reportedly found in acquisition and in aphasia (Jakobson and Halle 1956: 38). While studying aphasia and acquisition would be expected to shed light on the structure and universality of distinctive features, none of the examples of aphasia given by Jakobson provides evidence for this. This work must be taken as an explication of the *predictions* of the theory, rather than empirical evidence in support of it. It is acknowledged more recently (by proponents as well as critics of his later universalist views regarding language acquisition) that Jakobson's model of language acquisition is based on his general theory of phonology rather than on actual language acquisition data (Menn 1980, Rice and Avery 1995). What is troubling about Jakobson's change of view is that unlike other developments, it is not accompanied by new evidence, but has nevertheless been widely accepted by phonologists who followed in his path.

Recent work on language acquisition has shown that children are highly individualistic in their order of acquisition of sounds and words (see Vihman 1993, 1996 for summaries). This is unexpected if a set of innate features is at the core of phonological acquisition. Research has shown that similarities between children acquiring language reflect the languages the children are learning, rather than universal tendencies (e.g. Ingram 1978, Pye et al. 1987, de Boysson-Bardies and Vihman 1991, Vihman 1996, Beckman, et al. 2003, Vihman and Croft 2004).

Another theoretical development which is not accompanied by any new evidence is the criterion that simplicity of representation should reflect the phonetic naturalness of a process, and that (according to Sagey 1986: 9–11) the phonological representation "should lead to explanation, where possible, of why the facts are as they are, and of why the representation is structured as it is". For example, the simplicity of the representation of a phonological pattern is argued to explain why it is more frequent than one with a more complex representation. The assumption that representations are explanatory in this way was not present in the bulk of early work on distinctive features (e.g. Jakobson 1942, Jakobson et al. 1952, Jakobson and Halle 1956, Chomsky and Halle 1968: chs. 1–8), but is assumed, apparently without any motivation, in many approaches to Feature Geometry. This has the effect of adding another dimension to the claim of distinctive feature universality (the need for the representation of one language to reflect markedness generalizations about language in general) without any argument for why such a representation is desirable, beyond aesthetic reasons (see e.g. Lass 1975 and Hume 2004b for counterarguments).

It is often assumed (e.g. Sagey 1986) that a representation that can be explained on the basis of factors such as vocal tract anatomy, acoustics, and knowledge of the world is more highly valued than a representation which accounts for the same phonological facts arbitrarily. Not discussed, however, is the possibility that the phonological representation does *not* need to explain the non-occurrence of non-occurring segments, precisely because they do *not* occur. Sagey argues that segments such as doubly articulated palatal/velar stops should be unrepresentable because they are extremely difficult to produce as segments distinct from both palatal and velar stops. The hypothetical cognitive representation may be the last line of defense keeping doubly articulated palatal/velar stops out of human languages, but it is by no means the first. If no language ever develops them (for production-based reasons), then there is no need for the cognitive representation of phonological patterns to rule them out.

Sagey explicitly argues against including the Well-Formedness Condition (No Line-Crossing) in Universal Grammar, because it follows from knowledge about the world. This argument could also be leveled against phonetically grounded Feature Geometry as a whole, because the requirements it derives from are extralinguistic (physiological).

The role of features in acquisition and aphasia and the role of representations in reflecting the naturalness and frequency of phonological patterns are both relationships that are often treated as evidence for innate features. But these, like the ability of innate features to account for most if not all phonological patterns, are hypotheses. Acquisition and aphasia are the subject of much ongoing research, and the ability of feature theories to predict the frequency or possibility of sound patterns is challenged by the results of the crosslinguistic survey reported in later chapters.

1.5.5 *Dogs, fish, chickens, and humans*

Phonological features are sometimes treated as a uniquely human endowment which explains in part why humans acquire language but other animals do not. This is contrary to some of the early arguments for features, which involved evidence from the behavior of other animals to motivate key aspects of features. For example, in "The concept of phoneme", Jakobson (1942) treats distinctive features as a manifestation of the fundamental relationship between meaningful contrast and the ability to distinguish sounds. Jakobson observes that all native speakers of a given language can accurately perceive even the most minute phonetic differences as long as they perform a discriminative role, while foreigners, even professional linguists, often have great difficulty perceiving the same differences if they do not distinguish words in their own native languages. Jakobson's point is that there is a fundamental relationship between meaningful contrast and the ability to distinguish sounds, not that this has anything to do with universality in the sense of Universal Grammar. Indeed, Jakobson notes that dogs and fish possess a similar faculty. The important distinction is between meaningful and non-meaningful differences, rather than between innately provided and non-innately provided differences. Jakobson gives examples of dogs being trained to recognize a particular pitch that signals the arrival of dog food, and to distinguish it from other, very similar pitches, as well as certain species of fish being trained to associate a certain acoustic signal with receiving food, and to associate another slightly different acoustic signal with "something nasty", so that the fish surface upon hearing one signal, hide upon hearing another, and ignore other signals. Jakobson (1942: 233) writes that the fish "recognize the signals according to their meanings, and only because of their meanings, because of a constant and mechanical association between signified and signifier".

Another parallel between the proposed nature of distinctive features and animal behavior is observed by Jakobson and Halle (1956: 26), involving relational rules. The opposition [compact] vs. [diffuse] (acoustic correlates of low vs. high vowels) characterizes the relation between [æ] and [e] and also the difference between [e] and [i]. Jakobson and Halle observe that the ability to understand such relations as instances of a single property is not unique to humans. They cite experiments in which chickens were trained to pick grain from a gray field, but not from a darker one, and when presented with a gray field and a *lighter* one, the chickens transferred the relation and picked grain only from the lighter field.

Much like the hypotheses involving aphasia, acquisition, and naturalness, the notion that features are part of the uniquely human ability to acquire language arose without direct evidence. Innate distinctive features are cognitive categories with built-in phonetic correlates. As shown by Jakobson, Halle, and others, cognitive category formation is shared with other members of the animal kingdom. Meanwhile, the phonetic correlates of features are not even shared by all human languages; spoken languages lack the correlates of signed language features, and vice versa. It is hard to imagine how a uniquely human capacity for language could involve innate distinctive features, when one aspect of supposedly innate features is too widespread and the other is too restricted. The use of innate distinctive features in phonology can be contrasted with syntax, which was the original motivation for Universal Grammar, and whose uniquely human innate component Hauser et al. (2002) have reduced to the operation of recursion.

1.5.6 *Innate features recapitulate independently observable facts*

Innate features have been used to account for a variety of observable facts about language. Often there are other explanations available for these facts, and it may be the case that the feature theories are simply restating what is accounted for by other factors. Two ways in which this occurs are when synchronic formulations of phonological patterns appear to recapitulate historical changes, and when the feature organization which accounts for affinities between articulators appears to repeat explanations which are available simply from observing the physical relationships between them. For example, the model proposed in *SPE* accounts for a very wide range of sound patterns in modern English, often drawing on diachronic changes known to have occurred in the history of English. This approach has been criticized (e.g. by Pinker 1999: 100) as a recapitulation of the history of long-dead rules whose remnants can be memorized by modern speakers.

It is in large part because phonologists have had, over the past forty-odd years, an opportunity to build upon the groundwork laid by Chomsky and Halle that it is possible now to re-evaluate their claims. A critical re-evaluation of their assumptions about innate distinctive features would have seemed natural, but this is a path that mainstream phonological theory has not explored yet. Criticisms of the framework set forth in *SPE* are largely limited to Chomsky and Halle's choices of features and their organization, but do not address the basic assumption that there is a universal set of distinctive features. Chomsky and Halle's *assumption* that distinctive features are innate is treated in subsequent literature as if it were a *conclusion*.

While derivations often recapitulate historical changes, innate feature organization also encodes information that is independently observable. In motivating constituency among distinctive features, Clements (1985: 229) observes that at least four articulatory parameters show considerable independence from each other: (1) laryngeal configuration, (2) degree of nasal cavity stricture, (3) degree and type of oral cavity stricture, and (4) pairing of an active and a passive articulator. Oral tract configuration can be held constant while the state of the vocal folds or velum changes, and vice versa. However, within each category, it is difficult or impossible to vary one gesture while maintaining another.

There are external explanations for affinities between features and the properties they represent. For example, the claim (on the basis of patterning) that features such as [anterior] and [distributed] are dominated by the [coronal] node does not make particularly interesting predictions as long as these features are only used for coronal segments and are defined in terms of the coronal articulator. The organization recapitulates anatomical information which is built into the definitions of the features. A more compelling case for innate feature organization could be made on the basis of features which pattern in a certain way *in spite of* their phonetic definitions.

The incorporation of physiological information into formal phonology is taken to the extreme by Articulator Theories (Sagey 1986, Halle 1988, 1989, 1992, Halle et al. 2000), which directly incorporate anatomical adjacency as a criterion for feature organization. By incorporating anatomical adjacency rather than basing the model on phonological phenomena, Articulator Theories construct a model of the physiological facts which lead, via the phonologization of phonetic effects, to articulatorily driven phonological alternations. Drawing on physiological facts as a means of accounting for phonological patterns is not the same as including physiological facts in the representation of synchronic phonology. Including these facts in the representation is justified if it is motivated by observed phonological patterns that cannot be accounted for by other known factors.

Recent phonological theory has placed emphasis on explaining phonological patterns in terms of independent observations about phonetics and other factors. While this is a worthwhile pursuit, identifying these factors does not require repeating them in Universal Grammar. It may be true that these factors really are in the grammar, but motivating this requires more than just evidence that there is a pattern, because the pattern is already predicted by the external facts.

1.5.7 *Summary*

As seen in this chapter, there is substantial independent evidence calling innate features into question. The fact that quite a bit of what they account for may have other explanations anyway makes abandoning innateness quite reasonable. The formal model of the cognitive representation of phonology is often treated as if it is the only way to account for the nonexistence of unattested phonological patterns. This issue is particularly important when ruling out unattested phenomena compromises the ability of the formalism to capture some attested phenomena (such as unnatural classes), especially when there is no independent evidence that "unnatural" phenomena are treated any differently by speakers vis-à-vis common phenomena (see Buckley 2000, Onishi et al. 2002, and Peperkamp and Dupoux 2007 for additional discussion).

The notion of innate distinctive features clearly would not have remained popular for so long if there were not many correlations between phonological patterns and the phonetically grounded features that have been proposed to account for them. The question is this: When we study sound patterns, are we looking at something that innate features do that manifests itself in sounds, or are we looking at something sounds do that can be described with features?

The strongest position in support of innate features is one that perhaps has no proponents. This is what phonological patterns might be expected to be like, given literal interpretation of the idea that features are the building blocks of phonological patterns (9).

(9) Innate features (strong position)
   - All phonological patterns in spoken and signed languages can be reduced to operations on a small set of innate features.
   - The role of phonetics in phonology can be reduced to the phonetic basis of distinctive features.
   - A wide range of observations about phonological patterns can be attributed to facts about features themselves (e.g. their organization in the brain), with no interpretation in phonetics, language change, or anywhere else.

The weaker position in (10) is more widely held but harder to falsify. This position is informed by the observation that some phonological patterns are not easily interpretable as the manifestation of innate features. External factors are invoked to account for problem cases.

(10) Innate features (weak position)
   - Most if not all *recurrent* phonological patterns in spoken and signed languages can be reduced to operations on a small set of innate features.
   - The role of phonetics in phonology can *often* be reduced to the phonetic basis of distinctive features.
   - Some observations about phonological patterns may be attributed to facts about features themselves (e.g. their organization in the brain), with no interpretation in phonetics, language change, or anywhere else.

The emergent features position in (11) dispenses with innate features as a means of accounting for observations about phonological patterns, and appeals directly to influences on phonological patterns.

(11) Emergent features
   - Phonological patterns occurring with greater than chance frequency in spoken and signed languages can be accounted for in terms of external factors affecting them.
   - The role of phonetics in phonology can be reduced to external factors (relating to vision, audition, articulation, etc.).
   - No observations about phonological patterns may be attributed to facts about features themselves (e.g. their innate organization in the brain), with no interpretation in phonetics, language change, or anywhere else.

It should be clear that the strong version of the innate features position is not tenable. The purpose of this book is to motivate the emergent features position over the weak version of the innate features position. There are already many widely recognized external explanations for the existence, absence, or rarity of certain phenomena among the world's languages, and many of these are invoked in the weak version of the innate features approach. Two goals of emergent feature theory are (1) to show that when these external factors are taken seriously, there is nothing left for innate features to account for, and (2) to formalize the role of external factors in phonological patterns without including them in Universal Grammar or otherwise building them into the cognitive representation of phonology.

1.6 Original motivations for distinctive features

While there are many reasons to suspect that distinctive features are not innate, there are also many facts which distinctive features have been used successfully to account for. The approach in this book focuses on re-evaluating the insights of distinctive feature theory and recasting them in a framework that does not assume innateness, rather than discounting the contributions of innate feature theories to the study of phonology. This section summarizes some of the motivations for features and some of their typical properties.

1.6.1 *Motivations for features*

Features were proposed as a part of phonological theory long before they were argued to be innate. Early motivations for distinctive features focused on minimizing demands on memory and perception. Based on assumptions about a correlation between meaning and strain on perception and memory, Jakobson hypothesizes about a constraint on the number of phonological contrasts in a language:

Differences which have differentiating value are, as we have seen, more accessible to perception and to memory than differences which have no value at all, but on the other hand differences between phonemes—since they lack particular meanings— strain perception and memory and necessarily require a great deal of them. We would expect, therefore, that the number of these primordial and unmotivated values would be relatively small for any given language. (1942: 235)

Because Jakobson assumes that the differences between phonemes, being "unmotivated", tax perception and memory, he argues that the number of oppositions should be minimized. If binary oppositions between phonemes

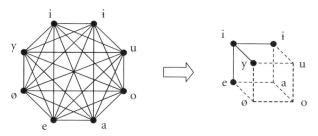

FIGURE 1.8 Reducing twenty-eight binary relations to three

are taken to be the "primordial" values, then twenty-eight (7+6+5+4+3+2+1) binary relations are necessary to characterize the eight vowels of Turkish. By introducing the notion of distinctive features, Jakobson reduces twenty-eight binary relations to three, as in Fig. 1.8.

For Jakobson, the argument for a minimal number of distinctive features in any given language is the same as the argument for the *existence* of distinctive features: It is assumed that primitives which have no inherent meaning are costly to perception and memory, and that their numbers in any given system are therefore minimized. Universality of distinctive features is limited to the claim that features in two languages which refer to the same acoustic feature are fundamentally the same. Thus, the feature [high] in Turkish is fundamentally the same as the feature [high] in Russian. In this sense, the set of possible phonological distinctive features is limited only by acoustic and articulatory phonetics, and the universality of the distinctive features (in spoken languages) is a direct consequence of the universality of the human vocal tract.

1.6.2 *Motivations for binarity*

The conclusion that distinctive features are binary was supported by Jakobson et al., on the basis of the observation that the distinctions between some pairs of words, such as *bill/pill* and *bill/dill*, can be characterized by a difference of one feature. Others are distinguished by more than one feature, such as pairs like *bill/fell*, which involve a duple distinction in initial segments and a minimal distinction in their middle segments. In essence, the fact that differences between words *can* be represented by a series of binary decisions is taken as evidence that this is actually how information is encoded in language. Jakobson et al. assert that Information Theory (e.g. Shannon and Weaver 1949) provides a sequence of binary selections as the most reasonable way to analyze communication, and that in the special case of language, this is not simply the best analysis to impose on the data, but how it is inherently structured. While there is a continuous range of possible degrees of voicing and lip-rounding and other articulatory movements, only two polar points are picked out as distinctive features. Jakobson and colleagues argue that the dichotomous scale is the optimal code, and therefore there is no reason to suppose that speakers would use a more complicated system. However, they provide no evidence to show that this is limited to language rather than more general cognitive patterns of human beings (and perhaps also dogs, fish, and chickens). They report that binary relations are imprinted in children's early cognitive development (citing Wallon's 1945 study of gradual binary fissions in child development and Parsons and Bales' 1955 study of socialization), and note that almost all distinctive features are dichotomous at the articulatory and acoustic levels, and that applying the dichotomous scale makes the analysis of phonological patterns so clear that it must be inherent in language.

1.6.3 *Motivations for innateness*

The assumption of innate primitives in linguistic theory did not originate in the study of phonology. Chomsky's transformational grammar program, starting in the 1950s, crucially involved a universal, innate human language faculty containing formal and substantive linguistic universals. Formal universals correspond to the formalisms of linguistic theory, which are believed to be unlearnable, and therefore innate. The central component of linguistic competence in Chomsky's (e.g. 1957, 1965) program is syntactic, and so are the arguments for formal and substantive universals. *The Sound Pattern of English* (Chomsky and Halle 1968) represents a move to extend some of the formal universals of Chomsky's account of syntax, such as the transformational cycle, to the study of phonology. The claim set forth in Jakobson et al. (1952) that all the phonemes of the world's languages can be described in terms of twelve features is quite compatible with Chomsky's program. However, since many of the formal universals of syntax are no longer assumed (see e.g. Hauser et al. 2002), it is reasonable to reconsider some of the formal universals proposed for phonology on the basis of 1960s syntactic theory.

In contrast to previous accounts by Trubetzkoy (1939), Jakobson (1942), and Jakobson et al. (1952), Chomsky and Halle (1968) assume a cognitive, rather than physiological, basis for the universality of distinctive features. Distinctive features are provided by Universal Grammar, rather than determined by, for example, the universal vocal tract. While they acknowledge the role of the universal vocal tract in phonological patterns, Chomsky and Halle (1968: 14) propose that a phonetic representation is a feature matrix with rows corresponding to a small set of features and columns corresponding to segments, and that "such representations are mentally constructed by the speaker and the hearer and underlie their actual performance in speaking and 'understanding'".

According to Chomsky and Halle (1968: 164), distinctive features "must be determined absolutely, within general linguistic theory, and independently of the grammar of any particular language". This argument is based on the assumption that it is necessary for the functioning of their model and therefore necessary to the extent that their model works to explain English phonology. Because conditions such as the principle of the transformational cycle and the principles of organization of grammar do not seem to be learnable, these universals are hypothesized to be innate (Chomsky and Halle 1968: 43).

Phonology has never been central to the motivations for Universal Grammar, but many theories of phonology assume that primitives such as features are part of UG. Recently there have been a number of challenges to some of the more fundamental motivations for UG.[5] The more questionable the foundations of UG as well as the relationship between these foundations and phonology become, the more precarious the innate features position becomes.

This section examines the connections between arguments for Universal Grammar and the application of Universal Grammar in phonology. Many of the arguments for UG in other domains do not hold for phonology. For example, there is little evidence of a learnability problem in phonology (see Blevins 2004 for discussion).

Chomsky (1968: 124) considered the theory of universal phonetics to be much more fully established than the theory of universal semantics. This asymmetry could have been the result of the comparatively large amount of crosslinguistic work in phonetics and phonology (e.g. Trubetzkoy 1939, Jakobson et al. 1952, Chomsky and Halle 1968, and many others). Another possibility is that language sound systems seemed much more straightforwardly restricted in a way that could be attributed to Universal Grammar. Phonetics is well known to be constrained by physiology, and Jakobson found that a large number of sound systems can be described with a very small number of distinctive features. If the former is not treated as the cause of the latter, then Jakobson's distinctive features look like evidence for Universal Grammar. But if physiology is what constrains phonetics in such a way that it can be described with a small set of features, then neither observation is suggestive

---

[5] See Steels (1997) for a summary of some arguments against Universal Grammar.

of Universal Grammar. The fact that phonetics observations can be expressed with a small set of features has nothing to do with language-specific capabilities of the human brain, except perhaps that the human brain is usually in close proximity to the human vocal tract.

Jakobson observes that no language uses both labialization and velarization for distinguishing words, and that these could be variants of one abstract feature, and Chomsky (1968: 123) claims that such generalization can be proposed as laws of universal phonetics. Abstract generalizations are consistent with the notion of Universal Grammar as proposed for syntax, but the abstractness of the labialization/velarization feature is less clear when acoustics is considered in addition to articulatory phonetics. The acoustic correlate of both gestures is a lowering of F3, and the antagonistic relationship between labialization and velarization can be explained by the fact that they are perceptually indistinct. Invoking Universal Grammar is not necessary to explain Jakobson's observation.

The notion of universal phonetics can be stated in two ways: as a set of cognitive constraints in Universal Grammar, or as observations about the human vocal apparatus. The approach which would most strengthen Chomsky's (1968) position in general is the former, exemplified by the reference to an abstract feature responsible for labialization and velarization. But universal phonetics is often defined in the more trivial way, as in Chomsky and Halle (1968: 294–5), where it is the set of "phonetic properties that can in principle be controlled in speech". This definition is unassailable, but entails no cognitive explanation whatsoever for phonetic universals. Indeed, the phonetic motivation for Universal Grammar is extremely weak. Perhaps the most compelling case that can be made is that phonetics, like semantics, is part of the grammar, and that there is an implicit assumption that if syntax is rooted in Universal Grammar, the rest should be too. Most of the evidence for UG is not related to phonology, and phonology has more of a guilt-by-association status with respect to innateness.

1.7 Outline of the book

This chapter has raised a number of issues casting doubt on innate distinctive features. Emergent feature theory is developed as an alternative to innate features in Chapter 5. The three intervening chapters provide a little more background and some phonological evidence for emergent features. Chapter 2 reviews phonetic and psycholinguistic evidence that relates to distinctive features and/or their universality. Chapter 3 describes the methods of the crosslinguistic survey of phonologically active classes, and Chapter 4 gives a first look at the results, focusing on "ambivalent" segments, which provide a means to separate the predictions of innate and emergent features. Chapters 5 and 6 present the results of the survey generally and in terms of three feature theories (Jakobson et al. 1952, *SPE*, and Unified Feature Theory). A general model of the emergence of linguistic structure is described in Chapter 8.

2

Phonetic and psycholinguistic evidence

The existence and innateness of distinctive features has been argued on the basis of phonological and esperimental evidence. The experimental literature contains a wide variety of results which are often presented as evidence for distinctive features and their universality. Three mitigating factors are common to many phonetic and psycholinguistic studies involving features. First, some of these studies *assume* that distinctive features are innate, and test the predictions of different theories of universal distinctive features without considering the possibility that distinctive features are *not* innate. Second, some studies find evidence that segments sharing distinctive features are processed similarly but do not rule out the possibility that this may result from phonetic similarity, which is usually positively correlated with the number of shared features. Third, some studies find evidence for abstract features but do not find evidence that these features are innate rather than learned. In short, a variety of studies produce data that is relevant for answering questions about the existence of distinctive features, but there is no experimental evidence that distinctive features are innate.

Finding evidence that distinctive features are innate would mean finding evidence that a feature for which there is no motivation in a subject's native language (and which thus could not have been learned) accounts for some aspect of their behavior that cannot be accounted for by other factors such as phonetics. For example, if it is found that subjects in a phoneme recognition task or a memory task confuse segments which are featurally similar more than they confuse segments which are phonetically similar, this would be evidence that features are somehow at the root of these errors, although these features could be learned rather than innate. If subjects make the same errors involving features not active in their native language (e.g. [lateral] for Japanese speakers or [constricted glottis] for Standard American English speakers), then this would be better evidence that the features are innate. If there is motivation for the feature in the subject's native language, then the feature could be learned rather than innate. If what the feature seems to account for can be accounted for equally well (or better) by independently motivated facts such as the production and perception of speech, then there is no need to posit innate features as an additional/redundant source of explanation. The next sections deal with some of the phonetic and psycholinguistic evidence related to distinctive features, and it will be seen that none of these studies provides the type of evidence needed to show that features are innate.

2.1 Phonetic evidence

Phonetic evidence related to distinctive features has come from production and perception errors, from quantal relations between different phonetic parameters, and from crosslinguistic differences in inventories, coarticulation, and phonetic realization. Some of this evidence has been used to argue for innate features, some of it has been used to argue against innate features, some of it does not bear on innateness at all.

2.1.1 *Speech errors*

Speech errors would be expected to betray the organization of the phonological component of the grammar, and errors appearing to involve features have been cited as evidence for distinctive features. Fromkin (1973, 1988) reports 55 feature errors from a corpus, and argues that there would be no explanation for speech errors such as *metaphor → menaphor* without a theory of distinctive features, but concedes that many errors are ambiguous as to whether they involve features or segments. Shattuck-Hufnagel and Klatt (1975: S62) analyze 1,500 spontaneous phonetic errors and report that consonant substitutions are significantly more likely to preserve a feature value than would be expected by chance, "suggesting that at some point in the production process, segments are represented psychologically in terms of features". But speech sounds can be similar in many ways, and features are only one of these. The fact that consonants are substituted for more similar consonants and not substituted at random is not surprising. Therefore, to conclude that features are behind these substitution errors, there would need to be evidence that featural similarity is a better predictor than, for example articulatory and perceptual similarity, and that gestural overlap (e.g. perseveratory nasalization in "metaphor → menaphor") is not responsible. In an analysis of a larger data set, Shattuck-Hufnagel and Klatt (1979) report that distinctive features and markedness appear to play little if any role in articulatory control during speech production, and that most phonetic speech errors involve manipulating segments rather than features. In the combined UCLA (Goldstein 1977) and MIT error corpora, containing 2,989 substitution errors, fewer than a dozen examples appear to involve a feature being exchanged between two segments.

2.1.2 *Quantal relations*

Acoustic evidence cited for distinctive features includes evidence from the quantal relations between different parameters of speech. Stevens (e.g. 1972, 1989) proposes that the sound inventories of languages are determined by the nonlinear mapping between articulatory and acoustic parameters and between acoustic and auditory parameters. The articulatory and acoustic attributes which occur within the plateau-like regions of the relations, where articulatory changes result in comparatively small acoustic changes, are the correlates of the distinctive features. When languages exploit these stable regions, variability in production results in minimal confusion, as opposed to the areas where the mapping is steeper, and minor changes have more drastic acoustic consequences. The same is true of the mapping from acoustics to audition. These nonlinearities allow phonetic continua to be divided into two or more regions, and Stevens argues that this provides evidence for innate features with values corresponding to these regions. The features would have emerged in human evolution in response to nonlinearities in articulatory/acoustic/auditory mapping.

An alternative is that the nonlinearities may account more directly for the nature of common phonological patterns (see e.g. Beckman and Pierrehumbert 2003). In this view, the naturally occurring discretization of phonetic space is exactly why innate features are unnecessary. The human vocal tract and auditory system both favor particular regions of stability that are naturally exploited by the world's spoken languages, and speech sounds which involve stable regions are less likely to change than those which are in unstable regions. This results in sound systems that resemble each other, because they all settle in stable regions, as defined by the anatomical parts used for spoken language, which under most circumstances are common to all humans. If the similarities between languages were caused by innate features associated with quantal regions rather than the quantal regions themselves, they would be expected to extend, for example, into sign language, a linguistic domain where the vocal tract and auditory system are largely irrelevant, but Universal Grammar ostensibly is relevant. Not surprisingly, signed languages show no evidence of the facts that innate features corresponding to acoustic/articulatory quantal relations are intended to account for. Instead, signed language phonology reflects the anatomical parts that are used in signed languages. Sandler and Lillo-Martin (2006) discuss in more detail modality effects in signed and spoken language.

2.1.3 *Perception*

Studies reported to involve perceptual evidence for distinctive features include Miller and Nicely (1955), who find that different attributes of speech sounds are affected differently when the speech signal is degraded by the application of noise or high-pass or low-pass filtering. Miller and Nicely adopt voicing, nasality, affrication, duration, and place as features to distinguish the sixteen consonants used in their study. Differences in the way these features of sounds are affected by signal degradation are attributed to their acoustic correlates. For example, nasality and voicing are more resistant to random masking noise than the other features because random noise across the frequency spectrum is more likely to weaken the already weaker high-frequency cues to the other features than the more robust low-frequency cues for nasality and voicing. The features imposed on the consonants by Miller and Nicely are describable in phonetic terms, and the explanations given for the clear differences in confusion rates between consonants distinguished by different features are all found in the acoustic signal. This does not motivate more abstract or innate feature representations. It simply motivates the important claim that speech sounds have attributes that are affected differently by different types of noise.

Studdert-Kennedy and Shankweiler (1970) find that subjects in a dichotic listening experiment are better at identifying segments in both ears simultaneously when the segments share phonetic features. Studdert-Kennedy et al. (1972) replicate the experiment with the purpose of determining whether auditory similarity is at issue rather than more abstract phonetic features. In order to vary auditory similarity without varying phonetic features, Studdert-Kennedy et al. compare the identification of stop consonants (which differ in terms of voicing and place) in cases where the following vowels are identical with cases where the following vowels are different. The formant transitions which provide cues to the place of articulation of identical consonants are acoustically different when the following vowels are different, but the abstract representations of the place of articulation of the consonants are expected to be the same.

The results show that the ability of English-speaking subjects to recognize the place of articulation and voicing of stop consonants in both ears simultaneously is no better when the following vowels are identical than when they are different. This indicates that an abstract notion of place of articulation is relevant, rather than simple acoustic similarity. So this study, unlike many others, teases apart features and acoustic similarity. However, it does not address the questions of universality or innateness. In order to determine whether the features are innate or learned, it would be necessary to examine features which are claimed to be innate but which are not motivated by the subjects' native languages. The study involves only voice and place distinctions among the stops [p t k b d g]. Both of these abstract distinctions are well motivated in the phonology of English, the language spoken by the subjects in the study. Therefore, innate features and emergent features make the same predictions about these features. Thus, the study does not bear on the question of whether features are innate or emergent, and it does not claim to.

2.1.4 *Crosslinguistic differences*

While there is some phonetic evidence for distinctive features (but not for their universality), there is some phonetic evidence against the notion of innate distinctive features. Ladefoged (1984: 85) observes that many facts of phonetic realization, while consistent within a given speech community, cannot be explained by universal principles (i.e. universal phonetics, Chomsky and Halle 1968) or a universal set of distinctive features:

Speakers of every language have to use exactly the right vowel and consonant qualities, intonations, rhythms, etc. on pain of being wrongly labeled if they do not. There can be very subtle phonetic differences among languages resulting from this drive to be correctly identified as part of a group; but these phonetic phenomena are important to speakers and listeners. They cannot be ascribed to any general universal principles; they are due to the vagaries of local history and personal desire. But their maintenance can be regarded as ascribable to the behavior of individuals.

As an example, Ladefoged (1984: 85) describes Disner's (1983) study involving the similarities and differences between the vowel systems of Yoruba and Italian. The similarities between the way the vowels of Yoruba and the vowels of Italian are organized are attributable to the human drive for communicative efficiency (see e.g Lindblom 1983). This accounts for why the two systems of vowels are fairly evenly spaced in articulatory and perceptual space and more fully exploit contrast along the F2 dimension in the high vowels than in the low vowels. Ladefoged attributes the *differences* between Yoruba and Italian in part to the biological drive for group identification. While both vowels systems are largely similar, the Yoruba vowels are less evenly distributed than the Italian vowels. For example, the low vowel [a] is considerably lower with respect to the low mid vowels than Italian [a] is in relation to

Italian low mid vowels. These patterns are consistent across speakers of Yoruba and speakers of Italian, and they are consistent because speakers want to show their group identity, not because any universal laws of language have caused these vowels to manifest themselves in such a way. Likewise, while coarticulation can be attributed to forces acting upon speakers of all languages, it manifests itself differently in different languages.

Many phonetic facts about language can be explained in terms of universal physiological and physical constraints, but many phonetic facts cannot be explained by universal constraints, be they functional or hardwired. A theory of innate distinctive features is consistent with many observations that can be made based on universal functional considerations (e.g. Lindblom's work), but neither universal theory can account for the subtle phonetic differences between languages, even though these subtle phonetic differences are used by language users to form contrasts. Port (1996: 503) similarly reports that experimental observations show that there are "subtle context effects" (e.g. language-specific coarticulation facts), most of which are language-specific and cannot be language universals, and that these subtle variables can be employed by listeners in speech perception.

Further evidence against the notion of universal phonetics and the idea that phonological categories are defined in terms of universal distinctive features comes from studies which show that phonology influences speech perception and/or that speech perception influences phonology. Huang (2001) finds that tone sandhi in Chinese Putonghua can be attributed to the perceptibility of differences between different tonal patterns, and further that the perception of similarity between tones is not universal but instead differs between Chinese and American English listeners. If phonological processes are subject to perceptual constraints, and perception is not universal, it is difficult to see how these phonological processes can be explained by means of a universal set of distinctive features. Similarly, Seo (2001), Tserdanelis (2001), and Mielke (2001, 2003) find that segmental processes of assimilation, dissimilation, and deletion, respectively, can be accounted for in terms of perceptibility, and that perceptibility of segmental differences varies from language to language in accordance with language-specific phonetic and phonological patterns. Makashay (2001) finds that consonant clusters with more salient cues are more common in English than consonant clusters with less salient cues. While proposals by Chomsky and Halle (1968) were made in terms of articulatory features, the notion of distinctive features has also been invoked to account for observations that involve perceptibility (see e.g. Flemming 2002). While the role of perception in phonology can indeed be cast in terms of distinctive features, perception has been demonstrated to be non-universal (see also

Vihman 1996). Consequently, an account of perceptually grounded phonological alternations that is laid out in terms of perceptibility or generalizations about perceptibility cannot be reduced to features which are universal.

2.1.5 *Incomplete neutralization*

Port (1996) claims that incomplete neutralizations also present a problem for a theory of universal distinctive features. For example, German final devoicing is generally considered by phonologists to result in phonological neutralization, but the neutralized forms are measurably different, and native speakers can distinguish them about 75 percent of the time. Labov (1994) discusses near mergers in more detail, including cases where speakers produce a contrast they cannot hear. The strongly held belief that speech sounds are either the same or different (having the same features vs. differing in one or more features) has prevented partial neutralization data from being taken seriously in phonological theory (Labov 1994: 367–9).

Studdert-Kennedy et al.'s study stands out because it does point to abstract place features as being superior to acoustic cues in accounting for dichotic listening results. This means that phonological features appear to be motivated as a part of phonology that is distinct from phonetics, but the study does not demonstrate or attempt to demonstrate universality. Stevens' interpretation of quantal relations as evidence for innate features would predict that the patterns observed by Studdert-Kennedy et al. will be found for speakers of other languages and for other features, including speakers with features that are not active in their language. Emergent feature theory predicts that the effects would only exist for features which would have emerged during the speaker's acquisition of language.

2.2 Psycholinguistic evidence

This section deals with evidence for and against a universal set of distinctive features from areas such as infant perception, development, and memory. Much of this evidence originally appeared to support innate distinctive features, but further research has indicated that some of the conclusions may have been premature.

2.2.1 *Infant perception*

The results of early experiments on infant speech perception (e.g. Eimas et al. 1971) suggested that the ability of infants to discriminate a wide range of phonetic contrasts is a part of the innate human capacity for language, and that perhaps neural atrophy during childhood is responsible for the inability of adults to distinguish many non-native contrasts. This conclusion is very compatible with the idea of universal phonetics proposed by Chomsky and Halle (1968). However, the results of further studies (many of which are summarized in Aslin and Pisoni 1980) indicate that it is not so simple.

For example, Kuhl and Miller (1975, 1978) find that chinchillas can be trained to distinguish synthetic voiced and voiceless labial stop stimuli, and that the perceptual boundary of chinchillas (who, as Aslin and Pisoni point out, do not use distinctive voicing) is very close to the boundary found for the voiced/voiceless stop contrast in (presumably American) English adults. If Chinchillas show human-like categorical perception, it seems less plausible that the same observations in the perception of infants can be attributed to innate linguistic processing abilities that are unique to humans.

Aslin and Pisoni (1980: 85) argue that the ability of infants to detect Voice Onset Time (VOT) contrasts is the result of general constraints on the mammalian auditory system which cause detection of the onset of the first formant relative to higher formants to be easiest at ± 20 ms, especially when the lower-frequency component begins first (positive VOT). This can also be extended to explain the crosslinguistic preference for VOT contrasts with boundaries in the region of ± 20 ms (especially +20 ms).

Many of the results reported by Aslin and Pisoni support an "attunement theory" which states that infants start life much like chinchillas, with the ability to make distinctions between acoustic stimuli, and that human infants' distinction-making abilities are "tuned" in response to exposure to linguistic stimuli. While infants may start with a vowel space that is processed most efficiently by the auditory system, it can then be rearranged to match the phonological categories in the language being learned. Aslin and Pisoni (1980) conclude that the question of how infants learn to perceive language as adults do is complicated, and can likely be best characterized by a combination of various mechanisms. Such a combination is generally incompatible with a hardwired system of "universal phonetics".

Also casting doubt on the neural atrophy hypothesis is the finding of Werker and Tees (1984) that under the right conditions, adult subjects are able to distinguish non-native contrasts. Therefore, earlier results implicating neural atrophy can more adequately be explained in terms of different processing strategies used by adults. While adults appear to have the sensory-neural abilities to distinguish non-native contrasts, they simply do not use them to perform many tasks, such as discriminating syllables.

Best et al. (1988) report evidence that the apparent loss of sensitivity to contrasts which are not present in the native language is the result of assimilation to native contrasts, and that the ability to discriminate non-native contrasts which are not perceptually similar to native phonemic categories remains into adulthood. If assimilating sounds to native categories facilitates speech perception by eliminating redundant and irrelevant information, then the differences between adult and infant perception under many circumstances is evidence of the adults' successful acquisition of language rather than the decay of UG-endowed speech perception abilities. Adults essentially enhance quantal relations by warping the perceptual space according to learned phonological categories.

2.2.2 *Developmental evidence*

Among the developmental evidence sometimes cited in favor of distinctive features is Graham and House (1971), who examine the ability of English-speaking girls aged 3–4½ years to perceive differences between seventeen English consonants. They find that the results "fail to support the idea that the descriptive labels used to specify speech sounds (that is, linguistic descriptive features) identify the perceptual parameters used by the listener in categorizing the speech sounds" (p. 565). While segments which differ with respect to only one *SPE* feature (and are somewhat similar phonetically) are more confusable to children than segments which differ with respect to more than one feature, the set of features they consider makes no more specific correct predictions about the perceptibility of contrasts. For example, the two most confusable pairs of segments ([f] vs. [θ] and [r] vs. [w]) differ in more than one feature ([coronal] and [strident] and [vocalic], [consonantal], [coronal], and [rounded], respectively). Graham and House conclude that the set of distinctive features they consider "may have no psychological reality for the group of children studied" (p. 564), and that traditional articulatory descriptions also fail to account for their results.

Another study cited as providing evidence for features is Gierut (1996), although apparently it is not intended to. Gierut assumes innate features and tests the predictions of two different versions of underspecification. The study examines the ability of monolingual English-speaking children aged 3–5 to categorize stimuli containing an assortment of English stops and fricatives, with the goal of testing two different approaches to underspecification. According to Gierut, the children group segments according to features that they share, and the representations the children appear to use are to be less specified than those assumed for adults. Some portions of the results which are inconsistent with this premise that features are innate (e.g. the grouping of [t] with [f] instead of [s]) are simply ignored. This study provides no evidence for an innate set of distinctive features.

Studies involving the interaction of speech sounds with short-term memory have also been presented in favor of distinctive features. Wickelgren (1965, 1966) examines errors in recalling English vowels and consonants, looking for evidence of what system of features corresponds best to the way speech sounds are stored in short-term memory, assuming that individual features of sounds may be forgotten, causing sounds which are more similar to be substituted for one another more frequently. For vowels, Wickelgren (1965) finds that the features of Chomsky and Halle's (1968) systematic phonetic level (given certain assumptions), which as of 1965 were stated in acoustic terms, works as well as conventional (articulatory) phonetic analysis for predicting the rank order of replaced vowels. Chomsky and Halle's phonemic level and Jakobson et al.'s (1952) features are both found to be less adequate.

Cole et al. (1973) conducted a similar experiment involving both consonants and vowels, using predictions made by Halle's (1962) feature system. They find that Halle's feature system predicts the frequency of segment substitutions quite accurately, and that consonants and vowels seem to be replaced in identical ways. However, since it does not consider any other feature systems or any less abstract articulatory or acoustic descriptions, this study does not demonstrate that an abstract feature system is necessary. As Wickelgren (1965, 1966) shows, Chomsky and Halle's abstract feature system does predict errors with greater than chance accuracy, but not as accurately as feature systems based on the articulatory or acoustic descriptions that the features are grounded in.

2.2.3 *MEG studies*

In a study parallel to Studdert-Kennedy et al.'s (1972) dichotic listening experiment, Phillips et al. (2000) report magnetoencephalography (MEG) evidence of an abstract feature [voice] in the left-hemisphere auditory cortex. Phillips et al. also control for acoustic similarity, and thus provide evidence for abstract features. Since the feature [voice] is motivated by the language of the subjects (like place of articulation in Studdert-Kennedy et al.'s study), these abstract features could be innate or learned from experience (emergent). Obleser et al. (2004) report MEG evidence of the extraction of abstract vowel features, and Eulitz and Lahiri (2004) report MEG evidence of featural underspecification in an abstract mental lexicon. Ongoing research involving infants is suggestive, and is critical with regard to the question of whether these abstract representations are innate or the result of experience with language.

2.3 Summary

While there is psycholinguistic evidence for abstract features, there is no clear experimental evidence in support of a universal features set, meaning that these abstract features could be innate or could be emergent. The bulk of the generally accepted arguments for features and their innateness are phonological, but work in phonology has not converged on a single feature set, and the feature sets which are argued for have not been tested against a large set of data.

The past two chapters have reviewed arguments involving distinctive features, and if one thing should be clear from this review it is that innateness in phonological representations is by no means a conclusion, but is instead an assumption that has not been rigorously tested with a large amount of phonological data. This leaves open the question of whether phonological patterns can be learned inductively, and whether the patterns themselves are not manifestations of Universal Grammar but generalizations involving phonetic factors and language change. The next chapter describes the survey intended to address many of the relevant questions.

3

Survey methods

The idea that features are innate and able to describe most if not all phonologically active classes has been reinforced by phenomena reported in the phonology literature. Data which are difficult or impossible to analyze in innate feature theories tend not to get analyzed and therefore tend not to end up in theory-oriented publications. For this reason, the phonology literature is not the best place to find a random sample and to assess the ability of phonological features to account for phonological data. Assessing the ability of features to account for data requires a survey of a large sample of classes which are not selected according to their compatibility with any particular theory. However, no large-scale survey of phonologically active classes has previously been available to determine whether or not assumptions about innate features are valid, or to answer many different questions about distinctive features and their universality. This chapter describes the survey of phonologically active classes in 628 language varieties which is intended to address questions about distinctive features.

3.1 Data collection

The survey is based on the language grammars (written in English) available in the Ohio State University and Michigan State University library systems. These grammars were found in Library of Congress subclasses PA (Greek and Latin), PB (Celtic), PC (Romance), PD (Germanic), PE (English), PF (West Germanic), PG (Slavic, Baltic, and Albanian), PH (Uralic and Basque), PJ (Near Eastern languages), PK (Indo-Iranian), PL (other languages of East Asia, Africa, and Oceania), and PM (languages of the Arctic and North and South America, and pidgins and creoles), for a total of 628 language varieties. For the purposes of this survey, two varieties are considered to belong to the same language if they share an entry in *Ethnologue* (Grimes et al. 2000), and the 628 language varieties correspond to 549 languages. Grammars were located by manually checking the shelves, in order to avoid any potential bias related to the questions the survey is intended to address. For this reason no attempt was made to seek out any particular language or languages for theoretical reasons. This sampling method favors the better-studied languages families; but if anything, this bias favors the universal feature approach, because the features which have been argued to be universal are based in large part on well-studied families such as Indo-European.

The survey was limited to living spoken languages and languages which have died recently (as long as the grammar of the language is based on data collected while the language was still living). The 628 language varieties languages of the survey represent 549 languages, or 7.69 percent of the world's languages, based on the 7,139 listed in *Ethnologue*. The 549 languages include members of 51 language families (number of languages in parentheses): Niger-Congo (109), Afro-Asiatic (54), Austronesian (51), Indo-European (49), Australian (32), Sino-Tibetan (21), Trans-New Guinea (18), Dravidian (17), Nilo-Saharan (16), Uto-Aztecan (15), Algic (10), Altaic (10), Mayan (9), Austro-Asiatic (8), Chibchan (8), Quechuan (8), Na-Dene (7), Mixe-Zoque (6), North Caucasian (6), Uralic (6), Hokan (5), Salishan (5), Iroquoian (4), Oto-Manguean (4), Penutian (4), Arawakan (3), Carib (3), Eskimo-Aleut (3), Siouan (3), Tacanan (3), Tucanoan (3), Aymaran (2), Caddoan (2), Muskogean (2), South Caucasian (2), Tai-Kadai (2), Torricelli (2), West Papuan (2), Barbacoan (1), Basque (1), East Papuan (1), Japanese (1), Khoisan (1), Kiowa Tanoan (1), Lower Mamberambo (1), Mataco-Guaicuru (1), Panoan (1), Sepik-Ramu (1), Totonacan (1), Wakashan (1), and Yanomam (1), as well as creole (18), isolate (3), and unclassified (1) languages.

Of the 49 spoken language families reported in *Ethnologue* and not represented in the survey, only seven contain enough languages that a random sampling of 7.69 percent would be more likely than not to include one of them. These are Tupi, Geelvink Bay, Macro-Ge, Choco, Arauan, Left May, and Sko. The fact that some families are better represented in the survey than others is not expected to skew the results in any way that is related to the predictions being tested. Indo-European is somewhat overrepresented (11.06 percent), but less so than 31 other (smaller) families. The complete list of languages and references can be found in Appendix A.

The grammars of all of these languages were mined for what are referred to here as "phonologically active classes". The term "phonologically active class" is used instead of "natural class" in order to exclude the assumption that classes are inherently "natural" either phonetically or according to any particular feature theory, because this is an assumption that the survey is designed to test. A phonologically active class is defined as any group of sounds which, to the exclusion of all other sounds in a language's inventory, do at least one of the following:

- undergo a phonological process;
- trigger a phonological process; or
- exemplify a static distributional restriction.

Classes were notated as a subset of the phoneme inventory of each language. Classes with only one member and classes including all of the phonemes in the language were omitted. Assumptions about phonology were minimized where possible, but certain assumptions were necessary in order to make the survey more feasible. These assumptions include the existence of phonemes and an a priori distinction between consonants and vowels. To the extent possible, these assumptions are taken into account during the analysis, and if any of these assumptions should prove problematic, this survey lays the basis for follow-up work which can abandon them.

3.2 Analysis

Each of the classes in the database was given a characterization in the feature systems of *Preliminaries to Speech Analysis* (Jakobson et al. 1952), *The Sound Pattern of English* (Chomsky and Halle 1968), and Unified Feature Theory (Clements 1990, Hume 1994, Clements and Hume 1995), if such a feature specification was possible. The features assumed for each of these theories are shown in Table 3.1. These feature systems were selected to be representative of distinctive feature theory in general. The feature system of *Preliminaries* is rooted in the acoustic properties of speech sounds, and the feature system of *SPE* is rooted in articulatory properties. Unified Feature Theory is also rooted in the articulatory properties of speech sounds, building upon previous articulatorily based feature theories, and differs from *SPE* in many important respects. More recent approaches involving auditory features (e.g. Flemming 2002) would be desirable to include, but the *Preliminaries* system was selected because it makes more explicit predictions about possible natural classes. Only segmental features are included, but the feature theories are not held accountable for the absence of tone and other suprasegmental features.

Distinctions which are intended by the theories' authors to be beyond the scope of the feature system (length in all three systems, and syllabicity in UFT) were allowed to define classes. The features used in each of these systems are listed in Table 3.1. All of *SPE*'s features and most of *Preliminaries'* features are binary, having two values (+ and −). The *Preliminaries* feature system also includes the equipollent feature [compact/diffuse], which effectively has three values (compact, diffuse, and neither). For the feature analysis, this is formally equivalent to a pair of binary features, and it is treated as such. No

TABLE 3.1 Primary feature systems

Theory	Features
Preliminaries to Speech Analysis (Jakobson et al. 1952)	*11 binary acoustically defined features* (1) vocalic/non-vocalic, (2) consonantal/non-consonantal, (3) interrupted/continuant, (4) checked/unchecked, (5) strident/mellow, (6) voiced/unvoiced, (7) grave/acute, (8) flat/plain, (9) sharp/plain, (10) tense/lax, (11) nasal/oral *1 equipollent acoustically defined feature* (12) compact/diffuse
The Sound Pattern of English (Chomsky and Halle 1968)	*10 binary articulatorily defined features* (1) consonantal, (2) vocalic, (3) sonorant, (4) continuant, (5) voice, (6) nasal, (7) coronal, (8) anterior, (9) strident, (10) lateral, (11) back, (12) low, (13) high, (14) round, (15) distributed, (16) covered, (17) syllabic, (18) tense, (19) delayed primary release, (20) delayed release of secondary closure, (21) glottal (tertiary) closure, (22) heightened subglottal pressure, (23) movement of glottal closure
Unified Feature Theory (Clements 1990, Hume 1994, Clements and Hume 1995)	*17 binary features (effectively)* (1) sonorant, (2) approximant, (3) vocoid, (4) nasal, (5) ATR, (6) strident, (7) spread, (8) constricted, (9) voice, (10) continuant, (11) lateral, (12–14) anterior (C-place/V-place/either), (15–17) distributed (C-place/V-place/either) *18 unary features (effectively)* (18) C-place, (19) vocalic, (20) V-place, (21–23) pharyngeal (C-place/V-place/either), (24–26) labial (C-place/V-place/either), (27–29) lingual (C-place/V-place/either), (30–32) dorsal (C-place/V-place/either), (33–35) coronal (C-place/V-place/either) *Potentially unlimited binary aperture features* (36) open1 [, (37) open2 [, ...]]

segment is both [compact] and [diffuse], and this is equivalent to the absence of segments which are both [+high] and [+low] in *SPE*-style feature systems. Unified Feature Theory has a set of binary features related to manner of articulation, as well as a set of unary features mostly related to place of articulation. These unary features have only one value (present). For instance, this means that while *SPE*'s [coronal] feature can define [+coronal] and [−coronal] classes, Unified Feature Theory's [coronal] features can only define classes of segments which bear the feature, i.e. there is no class of non-coronal segments. Unified Feature Theory's list of features includes place features which may be referred to in three ways: as dependents of the C-place node, as dependents of the V-place node, or either. For the purpose of defining natural classes, this amounts to three different features for each place feature.

The languages in the database contain a total of 1,040 distinct segment transcriptions. Each of these segments was assigned a feature specification according to each of the feature theories, resulting in a large feature matrix. Not all the features were possible to specify outside the context of the inventories in which the segments occur. [ATR], [tense], and [open] features were assigned as needed in order to maximize contrast in each inventory. For example, SPE's [tense] feature was assigned reactively in languages with tense or lenis consonants. Plain consonants were specified as [+tense] in languages such as Ibilo which contrast plain and lenis consonants, and specified as [−tense] in languages such as Korean which contrast plain and tense consonants. Language-specific feature specification was performed only in the interest of contrast. No features were assigned according to phonological patterning. Features which were specified identically (or unspecified) for all segments in the inventory were excluded from the analysis. For each phonologically active class, shared feature values were identified, and compared with the feature specifications of segments not participating in the class.

A feature matrix was built for each language, containing all of the segments in its inventory. Table 3.2 shows a feature matrix for Japanese in terms of *SPE* features. Features which do not distinguish segments in the inventory (such as [delayed primary release]) are omitted. The phonologically active class shown in this table is the class of segments which trigger high vowel devoicing (i.e. /p t k s ʃ h/). These segments have the same values for six features: [−vocalic, −nasal, −voice, −round, −syllabic, −LONG]. The feature values shared by the segments in the class are shaded. LONG is a feature added in order to account for length distinctions which are not intended to be accounted for by segmental features in theories such as *SPE*. No segments in the complement (/b d g z m n ɾ j ɰ i i: ɯ ɯ: e e: o o: a a:/) share all of these values, so the class is natural according to SPE. The analysis of a similar class is shown in Table 3.3. None of the segments in the complement is [−voice], so the description involving five features can be reduced to one. This is the class of [−voice] segments which are subject to rendaku "sequential voicing", i.e. they are voiced at the start of a non-initial morpheme which does not contain a voiced obstruent. These segments also share six feature values, but there is a segment in the complement (/p/) which also shares all of these feature values. As a result, there is no way to distinguish the phonologically active class from the other segments in the language in terms of a conjunction of *SPE* features, so it is unnatural in the *SPE* system.

TABLE 3.2 A natural class in Japanese: [−voice]

	p	t	k	s	ʃ	h	b	d	g	z	m	n	ɾ	j	ɥ	i	iː	ɯ	ɯː	e	eː	o	oː	a	aː
consonantal	+	+	+	+	+	−	+	+	+	+	+	+	+	−	−	−	−	−	−	−	−	−	−	−	−
vocalic	−	−	−	−	−	−	−	−	−	−	−	−	−	+	−	−	+	+	+	+	+	+	+	+	+
sonorant	−	−	−	−	−	+	−	−	−	−	+	+	+	+	+	+	+	+	+	+	+	+	+	+	+
continuant	−	−	−	+	+	+	−	−	−	+	−	−	−	+	+	+	+	+	+	+	+	+	+	+	+
voice	−	−	−	−	−	−	+	+	+	+	+	+	+	+	+	+	+	+	+	+	+	+	+	+	+
nasal	−	−	−	−	−	−	−	−	−	−	+	+	−	−	−	−	−	−	−	−	−	−	−	−	−
coronal	−	+	−	+	+	−	−	+	−	+	−	+	+	−	−	−	−	−	−	−	−	−	−	−	−
anterior	+	+	−	+	−	−	+	+	−	+	+	+	+	−	−	−	−	−	−	−	−	−	−	−	−
strident	−	−	−	+	+	−	−	−	−	+	−	−	−	−	−	−	−	−	−	−	−	−	−	−	−
lateral		−		−	−			−		−		−	−												
back	−	−	+	−	−	−	−	−	+	−	−	−	−	−	−	−	−	+	+	−	−	+	+	+	+
low	−	−	−	−	−	+	−	−	−	−	−	−	−	−	−	−	−	−	−	−	−	−	−	+	+
high	−	−	+	−	+	−	−	−	+	−	−	−	−	+	+	+	+	+	−	−	−	−	−	−	−
round	−	−	−	−	−	−	−	−	−	−	−	−	−	−	−	−	−	−	−	−	−	+	+	−	−
distributed	+	−		−	+		+	−		−		+	−												
covered																−	−	−	−	−	−	−	−		
syllabic	−	−	−	−	−	−	−	−	−	−	−	−	−	−	−	+	+	+	+	+	+	+	+	+	+
tense																+	+	+	+	+	+	+	+	−	−
del rel	−	−	−				−	−			−	−													
LONG	−	−	−	−	−	−	−	−	−	−	−	−	−	−	−	−	+	−	+	−	+	−	+	−	+

TABLE 3.3 An unnatural class in Japanese: no features shared to the exclusion of all other segments

	t	k	s	ʃ	h	p	b	d	g	z	m	n	ɾ	j	ɥ	i	iː	ɯ	ɯː	e	eː	o	oː	a	aː
consonantal	+	+	+	+	−	+	+	+	+	+	+	+	+	−	−	−	−	−	−	−	−	−	−	−	−
vocalic	−	−	−	−	−	−	−	−	−	−	−	−	−	+	−	−	+	+	+	+	+	+	+	+	+
sonorant	−	−	−	−	+	−	−	−	−	−	+	+	+	+	+	+	+	+	+	+	+	+	+	+	+
continuant	−	−	+	+	+	−	−	−	−	+	−	−	−	+	+	+	+	+	+	+	+	+	+	+	+
voice	−	−	−	−	−	−	+	+	+	+	+	+	+	+	+	+	+	+	+	+	+	+	+	+	+
nasal	−	−	−	−	−	−	−	−	−	−	+	+	−	−	−	−	−	−	−	−	−	−	−	−	−
coronal	+	−	+	+	−	−	−	+	−	+	−	+	+	−	−	−	−	−	−	−	−	−	−	−	−
anterior	+	−	+	−	−	+	+	+	−	+	+	+	+	−	−	−	−	−	−	−	−	−	−	−	−
strident	−	−	+	+	−	−	−	−	−	+	−	−	−	−	−	−	−	−	−	−	−	−	−	−	−
lateral	−		−	−				−		−		−	−												
back	−	+	−	−	−	−	−	−	+	−	−	−	−	−	−	−	−	+	+	−	−	+	+	+	+
low	−	−	−	−	+	−	−	−	−	−	−	−	−	−	−	−	−	−	−	−	−	−	−	+	+
high	−	+	−	+	−	−	−	−	+	−	−	−	−	+	+	+	+	+	−	−	−	−	−	−	−
round	−	−	−	−	−	−	−	−	−	−	−	−	−	−	−	−	−	−	−	−	−	+	+	−	−
distributed	−		−	+		+	+	−		−		+	−												
covered																−	−	−	−	−	−	−	−		
syllabic	−	−	−	−	−	−	−	−	−	−	−	−	−	−	−	+	+	+	+	+	+	+	+	+	+
tense																+	+	+	+	+	+	+	+	−	−
del rel	−	−					−	−			−														
LONG	−	−	−	−	−	−	−	−	−	−	−	−	−	−	−	−	+	−	+	−	+	−	+	−	+

In the event that a class was not describable as a conjunction of distinctive features, additional attempts were made to describe it using disjunction of feature bundles (union of natural classes) and subtraction of classes. The class which was unnatural in Table 3.3 is expressible as the disjunction of two classes in Table 3.4: all the segments in Japanese which are either voiceless coronals or voiceless non-anterior segments.

This class is also describable as one natural class subtracted from another, as seen in Table 3.5. It is the class of all voiceless segments which are not anterior non-coronals. The class can be described formally as the class [−voice] minus the class [−coronal, +anterior]. This might also be described more straightforwardly in phonetic terms as the class of nonlabial voiceless segments, but since there is no feature [labial] in *SPE*, the class of labials is described using the features [coronal] and [anterior]. Three of the four possible combinations of these two binary features already appear in segments in the class, and so these features cannot be used to rule out the fourth combination without explicitly subtracting segments specified as [−coronal, +anterior].

TABLE 3.4 Disjunction of natural classes: [−voice, +coronal] (lighter shading) ∨ [−voice, −anterior] (darker shading)

	t	s	ʃ	k	h	p	b	d	g	z	m	n	r	j	ɥ	i	iː	ɯ	ɯː	e	eː	o	oː	a	aː
consonantal	+	+	+	+	−	+	+	+	+	+	+	+	+	−	−	−	−	−	−	−	−	−	−	−	−
vocalic	−	−	−	−	−	−	−	−	−	−	−	−	−	+	−	−	+	+	+	+	+	+	+	+	+
sonorant	−	−	−	−	+	−	−	−	−	−	+	+	+	+	+	+	+	+	+	+	+	+	+	+	+
continuant	−	+	+	−	+	−	−	−	−	+	−	−	−	−	+	+	+	+	+	+	+	+	+	+	+
voice	−	−	−	−	−	−	+	+	+	+	+	+	+	+	+	+	+	+	+	+	+	+	+	+	+
nasal	−	−	−	−	−	−	−	−	−	−	+	+	−												
coronal	+	+	+	−	−	−	−	+	−	+	−	+	+												
anterior	+	+	−	−	−	+	+	+	−	+	+	+	+	−	−	−	−	−	−	−	−	−	−	−	−
strident	−	+	+	−	−	−	−	−	−	+															
lateral	−	−	−			−	−		−																
back	−	−	−	+	−	−	−	−	+	−	−	−	−	+	−	−	−	+	+	−	−	+	+	+	+
low	−	−	−	−	+	−	−	−	−	−	−	−	−	−	−	−	−	−	−	−	−	−	−	+	+
high	−	−	+	+	−	−	−	−	+	−	−	−	−	+	+	+	+	+	+	−	−	−	−	−	−
round	−	−	−	−	−	−	−	−	−	−	−	−	−	−	−	−	−	−	−	−	−	+	+	−	−
distributed	−	−	+			+	+	−			−	+	−	−											
covered															−	−	−	−	−	−	−	−	−	−	−
syllabic	−	−		−		−	−	−	−	−	−	−	−	−	−	+	+	+	+	+	+	+	+	+	+
tense														−	−	+	+	+	+	+	+	+	−	−
del rel	−		−	−		−	−	−	−		−	−													
LONG	−	−		−		−	−	−	−	−	−	−	−	−	−	−	+	−	+	−	+	−	+	−	+

TABLE 3.5 Subtraction of natural classes: [−voice] (lighter shading) − [−coronal, +anterior] (darker shading)

	t	s	ʃ	k	h	p	b	m	d	g	z	n	r	j	ɥ	i	iː	ɯ	ɯː	e	eː	o	oː	a	aː
consonantal	+	+	+	+	−	+	+	+	+	+	+	+	+	−	−	−	−	−	−	−	−	−	−	−	−
vocalic	−	−	−	−	−	−	−	−	−	−	−	−	+	−	−	+	+	+	+	+	+	+	+	+	+
sonorant	−	−	−	−	+	−	−	+	−	−	−	+	+	+	+	+	+	+	+	+	+	+	+	+	+
continuant	−	+	+	−	+	−	−	−	−	−	+	−	−	+	+	+	+	+	+	+	+	+	+	+	+
voice	−	−	−	−	−	−	+	+	+	+	+	+	+	+	+	+	+	+	+	+	+	+	+	+	+
nasal	−	−	−	−	−	−	−	+	−	−	−	+	−	−	−	−	−	−	−	−	−	−	−	−	−
coronal	+	+	+	−	−	−	−	−	+	−	+	+	+	−	−	−	−	−	−	−	−	−	−	−	−
anterior	+	+	−	−	−	+	+	+	+	−	+	+	+	−	−	−	−	−	−	−	−	−	−	−	−
strident	−	+	+	−	−	−	−	−	−	−	+	−	−	−	−	−	−	−	−	−	−	−	−	−	−
lateral	−	−	−					−	−	−	−														
back	−	−	−	+	−	−	−	−	−	+	−	−	−	+	−	−	−	+	+	−	−	+	+	+	+
low	−	−	−	−	+	−	−	−	−	−	−	−	−	−	−	−	−	−	−	−	−	−	−	+	+
high	−	−	+	+	−	−	−	−	−	+	−	−	−	+	+	+	+	+	+	−	−	−	−	−	−
round	−	−	−	−	−	−	−	−	−	−	−	−	−	−	+	−	−	−	−	−	−	+	+	−	−
distributed	−	−	+			+	+	+	−	−	−	−													
covered															−	−	−	−	−	−	−	−	−	−	−
syllabic	−	−	−	−	−	−	−	−	−	−	−	−	−	−	−	+	+	+	+	+	+	+	+	+	+
tense								−				−				+	+	+	+	+	+	+	−	−	
del rel	−		−			−	−		−																
LONG	−	−	−	−	−	−	−	−	−	−	−	−	−	−	−	−	+	−	+	−	+	−	+	−	+

Subtraction was attempted if disjunction with two classes did not work. If neither approach worked, feature disjunction was attempted with an increasing number of classes. If the inventory of a language is fully contrastive (and this is not the case for every theory/language combination), then every segment is its own trivial natural class. This means that the worst-case scenario is to account for a class with one natural class for each of its segments. There are about 200 classes with only two members which cannot be accounted for as a conjunction of features in any of the three theories; but as long as the segments are contrastive, every theory can deal with them with disjunction, using one class for each segment. A case where three classes are needed to describe a three-segment class is found in Runyoro-Rutooro. /t r j/ is the class of segments which turn into alveolar fricatives before certain suffixes starting with /j i/ (Table 3.6). This class can only be described in *SPE* as the union of three classes: [−voice, +coronal, +anterior] ∨ [+heightened subglottal pressure] ∨ [−consonantal, −vocalic, +voice, −back].[1]

---

[1] The union of multiple classes is the set of sounds which match at least one of the feature bundles for these classes, so union is indicated by the disjunction (∨) of one or more feature bundles.

TABLE 3.6 Worst-case scenario: one class for each segment

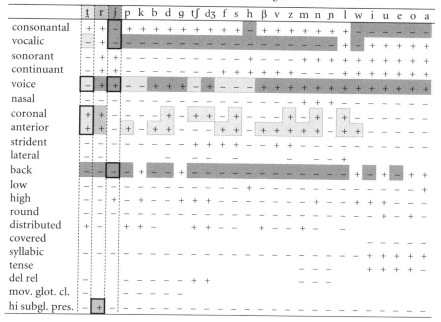

Each of the 6,077 phonologically active classes was analyzed in this way in terms of each of the three feature theories. The results of this analysis are presented in the following chapters. Chapter 7 presents the results in terms of the feature theories, after Chapter 6 presents the survey results in more general terms. Chapter 4 is the first to look at the results, considering what appears to be a special case: segments which are ambivalent in their phonological patterning.

4

Ambivalent segments

It has long been known that some speech sounds have less predictable phonological patterning than others. While some sounds have attracted a broad consensus concerning their appropriate representation, the phonological ambivalence of others has led to disagreements in how they should be represented, and the precise nature of their phonological specification has remained murky. The feature [continuant] is involved in a number of cases of representational murkiness. Since its introduction, there has generally been agreement that fricatives and vowels are most definitely [+continuant], and that oral stops are certainly [−continuant], but flaps, trills, and lateral liquids have been observed patterning as continuants with fricatives and also patterning as non-continuants with stops. The feature specification of these liquids has been appropriately controversial. The analysis in this chapter will account for ambivalent phonological behavior in terms of phonetic ambiguity. While ambivalent segments appear to be exceptions in innate feature theories, in emergent feature theory the phonologically consistent segments are special, owing to their phonetic unambiguity.

Focusing just on the voiced alveolar lateral liquid /l/, diverse phonological patterning and phonological analyses may be observed. For example, Jakobson et al. (1952) group laterals with [continuant] sounds (as opposed to [interrupted]), and Chomsky and Halle (1968) similarly group /l/ with [+continuant] sounds, but Halle and Clements (1983), among others, group laterals with [−continuant] sounds. Kaisse's (2002) informal survey of eleven phonology texts from 1968 to present finds that six of them (55 percent) treat /l/ as [+continuant], three (27 percent) treat it as [−continuant], and two (18 percent) treat it as variable from language to language. Two of the most recent texts disagree on the [continuant] specification of /l/. It will be seen in the following pages that the actual crosslinguistic patterning of /l/ matches these percentages fairly closely.

The difficulty of categorizing /l/ and other liquids on the basis of a phonetic definition of [continuant] is noted by Chomsky and Halle (1968: 318; their emphasis):

The characterization of the liquid [l] in terms of the continuant-noncontinuant scale is even more complicated [than the characterization of other liquids]. If the defining characteristic of the stop is taken ... as total blockage of air flow, then [l] must be viewed as a continuant and must be distinguished from [r] by the feature of 'laterality.' If, on the other hand, the defining characteristic of stops is taken to be the blockage of air flow *past the primary stricture*, then [l] must be included among the stops. The phonological behavior of [l] in some languages supports somewhat the latter interpretation.

In treating /l/ as a non-continuant, Halle and Clements (1983) accordingly adopt a definition that refers specifically to the *mid-sagittal* region of the vocal tract, which is obstructed in the production of laterals (see also McCawley 1968: 26n.). Kaisse (2000) summarizes the lateral/[continuant] issue as follows: the status of laterals hinges on whether [continuant] is defined in terms of occlusion in the oral tract ("vowel tract", in *SPE*, p. 318) or occlusion in the *mid-sagittal* region of the oral tract. But conversely, the proper definition can only be determined by examining the *phonological patterning* of laterals. Kaisse examines seventeen languages in which [continuant] is relevant for characterizing a phonological pattern involving /l/, and concludes that sonorant laterals are [−continuant], because they pattern that way in the great majority of the languages. Kaisse argues that the apparent counterexamples among the languages she analyzes in depth are cases in which continuancy is not at the heart of the sound pattern, and therefore these cases may not provide information on continuancy at all. Van de Weijer (1995) deals with the murkiness of liquids' patterning with stops and fricatives by proposing that liquids are not specified for [continuant] at the same level of the feature hierarchy as obstruents.

Kenstowicz and Kisseberth (1979: 21) summarize the broader state of affairs: phonological patterning motivates the partitioning of speech sounds according to manner features that may be very difficult to define phonetically:

There are no truly satisfactory articulatory or acoustic definitions for the bases of these two different partitions [consonant and sonorant]. Nevertheless, they are crucial for the description of the phonological structure of practically every language.

Taking this as a starting point for an investigation into the behavior and representation of lateral liquids and other seemingly ambivalent segments, there are basically two observations. On the one hand it is clear, on the basis of phonological patterning, that spoken languages exploit an opposition between segments with phonetic properties characterized as "continuant" and "interrupted"; on the other hand, it is not clear where the boundary lies, and /l/ is somewhere in the middle. It will be seen below that nasals also exhibit ambivalent behavior, similar to what has been observed for lateral liquids.

The debate over whether /l/ or any other segment is [+continuant] or [−continuant] presupposes that it must be one or the other. This presupposition follows from the claim that distinctive features are universal, innate, and explanatory (e.g. Chomsky 1968, Chomsky and Halle 1968, Clements 1985), summarized by Clements and Hume (1995: 245):

[S]ince features are universal, feature theory explains the fact that all languages draw on a similar, small set of speech properties in constructing their phonological systems... Feature theory... has provided strong confirmation for the view that languages do not vary without limit, but reflect a single general pattern which is rooted in the physical and cognitive capacities of the human species.

Taken seriously, this claim means that the behavior of /l/ is attributed to whether or not it possesses the specification [+continuant]. The indecision of the past half-century may be attributed to a lack of data points or to the incorrect analysis of certain counterexamples. To understand the relationship between the feature [continuant] and segments such as lateral liquids and nasals, we can ask two questions: (1) Are /l/ and other segments truly cross-linguistically ambivalent in their phonological patterning? And (2) If so, is there a way to predict the flexibility of a given partition and the behavior of segments along the boundary?

To address these questions, this chapter presents some results of the survey of the patterning of segments in classes. Section 4.1 examines the results of the survey of phonological patterning in 628 language varieties, showing how lateral liquids, nasals, and other consonants pattern with other segments. Section 4.2 discusses various approaches to dealing with phonological ambivalence within phonological theory. After reviewing various ways in which innate feature theory could be altered in order to be compatible with these sound patterns, an account will be proposed which draws upon the phonetic dimensions that the feature [continuant] is grounded in. This approach to accounting for the observations which have been attributed to innate features, as well as the apparent counterexamples, has broader implications for the general notion of natural classes, discussed in Chapter 5.

4.1 Some survey results

4.1.1 *Prototypically non-prototypical segments: lateral liquids*

The phonological ambivalence of lateral liquids is assessed on the basis of the 928 phonologically active classes (out of a total of 6,077) which contain at least one lateral liquid. These 928 classes were categorized according to their apparent specification for the feature [continuant], which is based on the specifications of other segments in the classes.

The three feature theories differ in their treatment of the continuancy of lateral liquids. In *Preliminaries* and *SPE*, lateral liquids are [continuant] and [+continuant], respectively, while UFT treats them as [−continuant]. To negate the effects of differences between these feature theories that are unrelated to [continuant] but affect their ability to define classes, all the feature analyses were duplicated with each feature theory's [continuant] specification for lateral liquids reversed. For example, this approach prevents Unified Feature Theory's restrictive use of unary place features from resulting in a relative underrepresentation of [−continuant] classes. This added a few classes which were otherwise unspecifiable.

All possible feature characterizations of the 928 classes were computed, and 644 classes (69.4 percent) are characterizable by a conjunction of features within at least one of the three feature systems (i.e. they are featurally natural classes according to one or more theories). The remaining 284 (30.6 percent) are featurally unnatural according to every one of the feature theories. This means they are not characterizable by a conjunction of features without ad hoc modifications such as the addition of new features tailor-made to account for specific classes which were not predicted to occur. This rate is slightly higher than the survey's overall featural unnaturalness rate of 24.7 percent (i.e. 1,498 of the 6,077 classes are featurally unnatural in all three feature theories).

The criteria for the [continuant] specification of these classes are as follows. A class is necessarily [+continuant] or [−continuant] if it is characterizable using the feature [continuant]/[interrupted] in one or more of the feature systems, and it is *not* characterizable within any of these feature systems without using the *same* value of the feature [continuant]. These criteria exclude a number of classes which a phonologist might analyze using the feature [continuant], but which have alternative analyses that do not require the feature. These classes are excluded because they do not provide crucial evidence about the continuancy status of lateral liquids. For example, in the Mande language Boko/Busa (Jones 1998), the segments /t d l/ cause a preceding nasal to assimilate in place to [n], but /s z j/ do not. The trigger class can be defined straightforwardly in Unified Feature Theory as [Coronal, −continuant], but it does not *require* [continuant] in order to be featurally natural. This can also be achieved using the features [strident] and [vocoid], and defining the class as [Coronal, −strident, −vocoid]. The class is definable in a parallel fashion in *Preliminaries* ([acute, mellow, consonantal]) and *SPE* ([+coronal, −strident]), where [−continuant] is not an option for a class containing a lateral liquid. Because of these alternate analyses, this class does not provide crucial evidence about the [continuant] specification of /l/.

Of the 644 classes with lateral liquids which are featurally natural in at least one feature theory, the vast majority (578) can be defined without the feature [continuant], and therefore cannot provide crucial evidence for either value of the feature. Sixty-six classes *do* require one value of the feature [continuant], and among these, 36 are necessarily [+continuant] and 30 are necessarily [−continuant]. The composition of the classes in these two categories is shown in Fig. 4.1. Each bar represents a characterization of the segments with which lateral liquids pattern. Light bars represent traditionally [+continuant] segments, while dark bars represent traditionally [−continuant] segments.

In the [+continuant] and [−continuant] classes that they participate in, lateral liquids occur most commonly with fricatives and nasals. Among the [+continuant] classes, lateral liquids occur in thirteen classes with at least one fricative in twelve languages (Arapesh, Agulis Armenian, Central Outer Koyukon, Ecuador Quichua, Ehueun, Epie, Lumasaaba, Manipuri, Yecuatla variety of Misantla Totonac (twice), Navajo, Shambala, and Ukue), with at

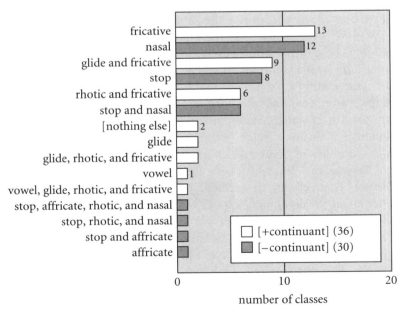

FIGURE 4.1 The other members of necessarily [+continuant] and [−continuant] classes containing lateral liquids

least one glide and one fricative in nine classes in eight languages (Ehueun, Epie, Lumasaaba, Mising, an innovative variety of Bearlake Slave, Temne (twice), Tswana, and Umbundu), and with at least one rhotic and one fricative in six classes in five languages (Doyayo, Finnish (twice), Greek, Onti Koraga, and Runyoro-Rutooro). Two or more lateral liquids occur with no other segments in two classes which are only characterizable in theories where they are [+continuant] (in Arabana and Dunquin Irish). Lateral liquids occur with at least one glide in two classes (in Okpe and Wiyot), with at least one rhotic, one glide, and one fricative in two classes (in Doyayo and Estonian), with vowels in one class (in Yucatan Maya), and with vowels, glides, fricatives, and a rhotic in one class (in Catalan). This is not an exhaustive list of classes in the database which contain these segments, but an exhaustive list of the classes containing these segments which are featurally natural if and only if the feature [continuant] is involved.

On the [−continuant] side, lateral liquids occur with at least one nasal in twelve classes in ten languages (Alyawarra, Basque, Dieri (twice), Gooniyandi, Koromfé, Libyan Arabic, Yucatan Maya, Spanish, Toba, and Yir-Yoront (twice)), and with at least one oral stop in eight classes in seven languages (Catalan, Dholuo, the Kolkuma dialect of Ijo, Koromfé (twice), Tsakhur, Tswana, and Turkish). Lateral liquids occur with at least one nasal and one oral stop in six classes (in Anywa, Arabana, Catalan, Nangikurrunggurr, Wangkangurru, and Yir-Yoront), and there is one example each of lateral liquids occurring in classes with an affricate (in Guatuso), with affricates and oral stops (in Mishmi), and with oral stops, a nasal, and a flap (in Agn Armenian).

Examples of laterals patterning with continuants and noncontinuants are shown in (12) and (13). One of the languages in which Kaisse (2002) argues that laterals pattern as non-continuants is Basque. In Basque (Saltarelli et al. 1988, Hualde 1991), nasals and laterals (i.e. /n ɳ ɲ l ʎ/), to the exclusion of rhotics (/r ɾ/), undergo place assimilation to a following consonant (12). This is the class [+sonorant, −continuant] in Unified Feature Theory. In Finnish, the lateral liquid patterns with continuants. /t s n r l/ are possible stem-final consonants in Finnish (Sulkala and Karjalainen 1992), and of these, /s r l/ trigger total assimilation of a following suffix-initial /n/ (13a). In the same environment, /t/ *undergoes* total assimilation to /n/ (13b). Further examples of laterals patterning with continuants and noncontinuants are given below.

(12)   /l/ patterning with noncontinuants in Basque (Hualde 1991: 96)
       egu[m] berri   'new day'
       egu[ɱ] fresku   'cool day'

egu[n] denak   'every day'   ata[l̪] denak   'every section'
egu[ɲ] ttiki   'small day'   ata[ʎ] ttiki   'small section'
egu[ŋ] gorri   'red day'

(13)   /l/ patterning with continuants Finnish (Sulkala and Karjalainen 1992: 87–8)

		active potential /+nUt/	*2nd participle active* /+nee/	
a.	/pur/	[purrut]	[purree]	'bite'
	/nous/	[noussut]	[noussee]	'rise'
	/tul/	[tullut]	[tullee]	'come'
b.	/avat/	[avannut]	[avannee]	'open'

Recall that classes only supply crucial evidence if none of the three feature theories can account for them without using the feature [continuant]. A full twenty-nine classes are characterizable without the feature [continuant] only by virtue of *SPE*'s little-used [heightened subglottal pressure], which distinguishes /l/ from /r/. These are primarily cases where lateral liquids pattern with nasals and/or unaspirated oral stops, which are [–heightened subglottal pressure], to the exclusion of /r/, which is [+heightened subglottal pressure]. In the absence of this feature, these classes would join the ranks of the [–continuant]. There are also several classes which would need to be [+continuant] if not for Unified Feature Theory's [+/–vocoid] and/or [+/–approximant] features. If one feature system were to be selected as the correct one, the number of alternative analyses would be reduced, resulting in an increase in the number of classes requiring [+continuant] or [–continuant] and also an increase in the number of classes with no possible feature specification.

The most general observation to be made from these results is that lateral liquids do indeed pattern with continuants as well as non-continuants, and with surprising even-handedness, patterning 55 percent of the time with continuants and 45 percent of the time with non-continuants. Before accounting for the ambivalence of lateral liquids, these results are put into context with the patterning of other segments, to explore whether this kind of ambivalent behavior is unique to lateral liquids.

4.1.2 *Other continuants and non-continuants*

In order to learn whether lateral liquids are unique in their patterning as [+continuant] as well as [–continuant], the same analysis was conducted with voiced oral stops, voiced fricatives, and nasals, produced at places of articulation found in lateral liquids in the survey, from dental to palatal (i.e. /d̪ d ɖ ɟ/, /z̪ z ʒ z̢ ʝ/, /n̪ n ɳ ɲ/ and closely related segments). This comparison was limited to voiced coronals in order to eliminate confounds due to the fact that all lateral liquids in the sample are coronal and nearly all are voiced. While all of the feature theories in Table 3.1 treat oral and nasal stops as non-continuants and fricatives as continuants, variants with [continuant] specifications for each of the relevant classes of segments inverted were tried as well, to duplicate the analysis of lateral liquids and detect cases where a class containing one or more of these segments would be natural only in case the segment(s) had a [continuant] specification which is opposite its traditional specification, i.e. to find evidence that they too may be ambivalent.

Fig. 4.2 shows a summary of the lateral liquid class data (36 [+continuant] vs. 30 [−continuant]) along with the same data for the other coronal consonants. Voiced coronal nasals show ambivalent behavior comparable to lateral liquids, occurring in seventeen classes which are necessarily [+continuant] and nine classes which are necessarily [−continuant]. The patterning of nasals is taken up in more detail below. It needs to be pointed out here that the number of nasals patterning as [+continuant] will increase when all nasals are considered, because considering only coronal nasals prevents all nasals from patterning together as continuants, because non-coronal nasals are still [−continuant].

The voiced oral stops occur in forty-three classes which are necessarily [−continuant], and in just one class which is natural only if they are treated as continuants. This class is in the Dravidian language Koya Gondi (Subrahmanyam 1968). In this case, [d] is inserted between /ɖ v r j/ and /k'/ or a vowel (14). /p b m l k ŋ/ also occur finally, and do not trigger insertion. The class /ɖ v r

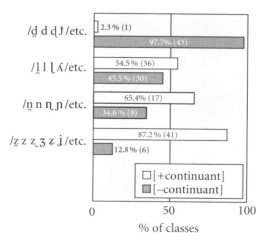

FIGURE 4.2 The patterning of four groups of coronal consonants with respect to [continuant]

j/ can be treated as [+voice, –syllabic, –lateral, +continuant] in *SPE* features if /ɖ/ is treated as [+continuant]. In reality, there are countless analyses of this pattern which are less dubious than treating /ɖ/ as a continuant. The point is that this is the *only* example where patterning motivates the analysis of a voiced coronal stop as a continuant, while there is ample evidence from the patterning of laterals for their analysis as both [+continuant] and [–continuant].

(14)   Koya Gondi [d] insertion (Subrahmanyam 1968: 109)

/uɖ-is/	→ [uɖd-is]	'to cause to plough'
/uɖ-it-aːna/	→ [uɖd-it-aːna]	'I will plough'
/uɖ-kʼoː-nu/	→ [uɖd-kʼoː-nu]	'I would have ploughed'
/koj-a/	→ [kojd-a]	'to plough'
/nor-a/	→ [nord-a]	'to wash'
/kav-a/	→ [kavd-a]	'to laugh'

The voiced fricatives occur in forty-one classes which are necessarily [+continuant], but also in six classes which are natural only if the fricative is treated as a non-continuant. In Ndyuka (Huttar and Huttar 1994), /z/ appears to be straightforwardly patterning with stops instead of fricatives; word-initial nasals become syllabic before stops /b d g p t k/ and /z/, but not before /v f s h/ or any other consonants. In the other cases, the ambivalence appears to be best attributed to another segment. These are all classes of voiced obstruents which are subject to devoicing and/or trigger the voicing of voiceless obstruents. They involve /z/ and/or /ʒ/, along with any voiced affricates or stops occurring in the language (in Bulgarian, Cres Čakavian, Hungarian, Pengo, and Slovene). In all five cases, the segments involved comprise all voiced obstruents except /β/ (in Pengo) or /v/ (in the rest). As traditionally analyzed, these cases are less about the ambivalence of /z/ and /ʒ/ with respect to [continuant] and more about the ambivalence of /v/ and /β/ with respect to [sonorant], an analysis which is more consistent with other sound patterns in some of the languages.

This section has shown that oral stops and fricatives, which are expected to be prototypical [–continuant] and [+continuant] consonants, pattern as expected with respect to [continuant] in nearly all cases. Thus, the ambivalent behavior of lateral liquids is indeed special. However, it is not limited just to lateral liquids. Rather, /v/ patterns with sonorants, and nasals pattern with continuant consonants in numerous cases. While ambivalence for any of these segments, including oral stops and fricatives, is formally equivalent, there is a phonetic account: The segments which exhibit ambivalent behavior are phonetically ambiguous with respect to the feature involved. Fricatives and oral stops are more prototypical (non-)continuants, and they are also much more consistent crosslinguistically in their phonological patterning with continuants and non-continuants.

4.1.3 *The ambivalence of nasals*

The investigation of consonants in 4.1.2 was intended to provide comparison for the lateral liquids produced at the same places of articulation, so the [continuant] specifications of only coronal nasals were manipulated. While useful for comparing nasals to lateral liquids, controlling for place of articulation is misleading with regard to questions about the continuancy of nasals; but on the basis of this limited evidence, it appears that nasals can pattern as [+continuant]. This subsection analyzes nasals for the sake of analyzing nasals, considering all places of articulation in order to explore the possibility that all the nasals in a particular language might pattern as [+continuant]. Including nasals with continuants would require only a minor rewording of the definition of [continuant] (changing "vowel tract" to "vocal tract" or "oral and nasal tracts"). Jakobson et al. (1952) do not specify nasals for the feature [continuant], and in their analysis of English, Chomsky and Halle (1968) make very little use of the fact that they define nasals as [−continuant], so this is not implausible.

Anderson (1976) argues that nasals are [−continuant], on the basis of a sound pattern in Finnish in which /n/ patterns with /t d/ to trigger spirantization of /k/ to /h/, and a mutation pattern in Brythonic Celtic languages whereby /m/ (although not /n/) is spirantized along with the voiced oral stop series. Anderson notes that it is possible to define [continuant] in terms of continuous airflow (as opposed to the traditional definition, which refers to a blockage in the oral cavity), and states, like Kaisse, that evidence for the correct definition must come from observing the patterning of nasals in particular languages, and determining whether they pattern with stops or fricatives. The Finnish and Brythonic Celtic cases are both included in the survey, but neither meets the criteria to be included in the current analysis, the Finnish case because it does not require the feature [continuant], as /t d n/ are the only non-strident nonvocalic consonantal coronals in Finnish, and the Celtic case because it does not involve a natural class in any of the feature theories (because /n/ does not participate). Further, [voice] could be used to define the Celtic class instead of [continuant]. While there are obviously many examples of nasals patterning with stops (as seen below in Figs. 4.2 and 4.3), the problem is with the assumption that if nasals pattern with stops, then they must not pattern with continuants.

The results of the analysis of nasals at all places of articulation are shown in Fig. 4.3, alongside the results for lateral liquids from Figs. 4.1 and 4.2. Considering nasals at all places of articulation shows nine cases where nasals pattern with non-continuants (the same as in Fig. 4.2, because [−continuant] is the normal specification for nasals in all three feature systems), and twenty-five cases where nasals pattern with continuants. This is an increase in the number of [+continuant] nasal cases, because this approach counts instances where all the nasals in a language (not just the coronals examined above) pattern with continuants. Among the nine cases are five with stops and/or affricates and lateral liquids (in Arabana, Capanahua, Nangikurrunggurr, Wangkangurru, and Yir-Yoront), and four with stops and/or affricates (in Catalan, Comanche, Higi, and Tiv).

Among the twenty-five instances of nasals patterning with continuants are ten cases where nasals pattern with one or more fricative (in Abun, Boraana Oromo, Bukusu, Korean, Lower Grand Valley Dani, Macuxi, Navajo, Russian, Uneme, and West Greenlandic Inuktitut), five with fricatives and lateral liquids (in Amele, Faroese, Kalispel, Kukú dialect of Bari, and Onti Koraga), three with one or more lateral liquid (in Arabana, Wangkangurru, and Warlpiri), two with a fricative, rhotic, and a lateral liquid (in Finnish and Mokilese), and five with some other combination of fricatives, glides, rhotics, lateral liquids, and vowels (in Jacaltec, Samish, Northern Tepehuan, Tuvaluan, and Wangkangurru. Taking all nasals into consideration reveals that they pattern as continuants a full 73.5 percent of the time.

An example from Bukusu is shown in (15). Nasals delete before fricatives and nasals (15a), but not before other consonants (Austen 1974: 53–7). Nasals assimilate in place before a stop (15b) except when that stop is /k/ (15c). Of interest here is the patterning together of fricatives and nasals.

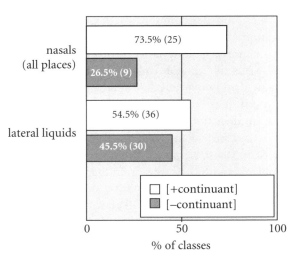

FIGURE 4.3 The patterning of nasals and lateral liquids as continuants and non-continuants

(15) Bukusu nasal deletion and assimilation

a.
/i-n-ḟula/	→	[e:fula]	'rain'
/in-s̱om-ij-a/	→	[e:somia]	'I teach'
/i-n-x̱ele/	→	[e:xele]	'frog'
/in-ṉuun-a/	→	[e:nuuna]	'I suck'
/in-m̱eel-a/	→	[e:meela]	'I am drunk'
/i-n-ṉaɲa/	→	[e:ɲaɲe]	'tomato'
/i-n-ṉuaŋua/	→	[e:ŋwaŋwa]	'camel'

b.
/in-wulil-a/	→	[embulila]	'I hear'
/in-pim-a/	→	[empima]	'I measure'
/in-bon-a/	→	[embona]	'I see'
/in-ùʃex-a/	→	[eɲèʒexa]	'I laugh'
/ùʃi-n-ɟu/	→	[ùʃiɲèʒu]	'houses'
/ùʃi-n-jimb-o/	→	[ùʃiɲimbo]	'songs'
/i-n-goxo/	→	[eŋgoxo]	'hen'

c.
/in-kanakana/	→	[enkanakana]	'I think'

Another example of nasals patterning with continuants is found in the Samish dialect of Straits Salish (Galloway 1990: 3). In Samish, geminate stops and affricates are rearticulated (16a), while geminate fricatives and nasals are simply realized as long consonants (16b).

(16) Samish geminate realization (Galloway 1990: 3)

a.
[ʔəmatʰtʰxʷ]	'seat somebody'	[sn̥ɛtʃtʃ]	'lagoon'
[ʔitʰtʰ]	'to sleep'	[ʃn̥ɛʔtʃʃatʃ]	'any bay'
[kʷɬ ʔiʔtʰtʰ]	'still sleeping now'		

b.
[tʰsas:ən]	'I'm poor'	[pʰən:ʊxʷəŋ]	'Matia Island'
sʔasəs: tən' seləs	'palm of your hand'		

From a theory-design standpoint, it does seem prudent to include nasals with non-continuants, if they must be universally either continuant or non-continuant. This allows the partitioning of the sonorants (which, with the exception of glottal stop, are otherwise all [+continuant] in *SPE*) without referring to nasality, and a precise articulatory definition is possible (segments produced with a blockage of airflow in the "vowel tract"). However, if the goal is for phonologically active classes to be featurally natural, then the most important question is whether the partition which groups nasals with non-continuants is supported by phonological patterning. The non-continuancy of nasals appears to be relevant for only one rule in *SPE*, namely rule 56 in Chapter 4, shown in (17). This rule inserts [u] to break up word-final stop+[l]

clusters in derivable words exemplified by such paradigms as *table–tabular–tabulate, constable–constabulary, angle–angular–triangulate* (Chomsky and Halle 1968: 196).

(17)
$$\emptyset \;\rightarrow\; u \,/\; \begin{bmatrix} -\,\text{cont} \\ -\,\text{voc} \\ +\,\text{cons} \end{bmatrix} \;\text{—l} + \text{VC}\;[-\,\text{seg}]$$

As this rule is formulated, nasals are subject to it as well, and although no such examples are given, Chomsky and Halle (1968: 196 n.) do suggest that the presence of [u] in words such as *formula* may be attributable to the same rule. If nasals were intended to trigger this rule, there would have been no way to make a featurally natural class out of oral stops and nasals in the *SPE* system without nasals being [–continuant]. Pairs such as *tremble–tremulous* indicate that Chomsky and Halle are correct to posit this class; but in view of all of the contrary evidence that is available from other languages, this single example does not warrant concluding that nasals are *universally* [–continuant]. The evidence presented in this section indicates that not only are nasals not exclusively non-continuant, but they are actually *more likely* to pattern with continuants to the exclusion of non-continuants than vice versa. The grouping of nasals with continuants is intuitive to many, and this intuition is indeed backed up by phonological evidence.

4.1.4 *Lateral ambivalence in action*

Cases where /l/ has been argued to be [+continuant] or [–continuant] are well documented, and this subsection give examples of each which illustrate another aspect of the ambivalence of /l/. If laterals are ambivalent because they are non-prototypical with respect to continuancy, they might be predicted to play a "last-in"/"first-out" role in classes based on continuancy—something that would be reflected in differences between related varieties or related sound patterns. That is, by being in the middle, they have the opportunity to be incorporated by reanalysis into existing classes of more extreme (non-)continuants or to be jettisoned from classes that retain their more extreme members. As "swing continuants" they are expected to come and go more freely than stauncher "base" continuants and non-continuants. This section gives an example from Hungarian where a palatalization pattern which affects more prototypical non-continuants also affects the lateral liquid in some cases and for some speakers, and an example from Catalan where spirantization is triggered by classes of continuants which in some cases contain lateral liquids and in other cases do not.

In Hungarian, /t d n/ coalesce with a following [j] across a morpheme boundary to form a geminate palatalized consonant, which Abondolo (1988: 63–5) treats as a combination of palatalization ("adpalatalization") of the consonant preceding [j] (which may be underlying /i/) and j-assimilation, which totally assimilates the [j] to the preceding (now palatalized) consonant. Other non-palatalized coronal consonants (e.g. /s z/) trigger total assimilation of [j], but do not undergo palatalization, resulting in a geminate unpalatalized consonant. /l/ undergoes palatalization for some speakers (particularly in the verb inflection), meaning that it patterns with the non-continuants for some speakers and with the continuants for others (Abondolo 1988: 64). Abondolo (1988:107) reports that non-palatalized forms (surfacing as [lj]) are disparaged by prescriptivists but seem to be gaining ground.

As seen in (18a), inflectional suffix-initial /i/ coalesces with a root-final /t d n/ (fairly prototypical non-continuants) to form a palatalized geminate version of the root-final consonant. Root-final coronal fricatives become non-palatalized geminates in the same environment (18b), while root-final /r/ also does not undergo palatalization, and does not form geminates either (18c). Root-final /l/ (18d) patterns with /t d n/ for many speakers, especially in verbs, producing [jj], the geminate version of the palatal counterpart of [l]. The palatalized counterpart of [l] in most modern varieties of Hungarian is [j], but it was widely pronounced [ʎ] until the late eighteenth century, and continues to be [ʎ] in some regions (Kálmán 1972: 70). For other speakers, and particularly in nouns, /l/ does not palatalize, patterning with /s z/ and /r/. Palatalization and j-assimilation fail to occur with suffixes that do not begin with /i/ (19).

(18) Hungarian palatalization and j-assimilation with /i/-initial suffixes ([j] is the palatal counterpart of /l/ in Hungarian) (Abondolo 1988)

a.	/ad + ia/	→ [ɔdʲdʲɔ]	'he gives him'
	/lakat + ia/	→ [lɔkɔtʲtʲɔ]	'padlock 3s'
	/lat + iatok/	→ [latʲtʲatok]	'you (pl) see it'
	/fon + iak/	→ [fonʲnʲak]	'they braid it'
	/køkørtʃin + ia/	→ [køkørtʃinʲnʲɛ]	'anemone 3s'
b.	/is + ia/	→ [issɔ]	'he drinks it'
	/nez + iuk/	→ [nezzyk]	'we behold it'
c.	/var + ia/	→ [varjɔ]	'he awaits him'
d.	/dobal + ia/	→ [dobalja] ~ [dobajja]	'he throws it around'
	/enekel + iuk/	→ [enɛkɛjjyk]	'we sing it'
	/hotel + ia/	→ [hoteljɔ]/[hoteljɛ]	'hotel 3s'

(19)   Palatalization and j-assimilation fail to occur elsewhere (Abondolo 1988)

/ad + od/	→	[ɔdod]	'you give him'
/lakat + od/	→	[lɔkɔtod]	'padlock 2s'
/lat + od/	→	[latod]	'you see it/him/her'
/fon + ala/	→	[fonal]	'twine'
/is + od/	→	[isod]	'you drink it'
/var + od/	→	[varod]	'you await him'

Imre (1972: 315) reports also that /i/-conditioned palatalization of /l/ in addition to /t d n/ is particularly prevalent in parts of the northern Palóc region (again, to the exclusion of fricatives and other continuants), where /t d n l/ also palatalize within morpemes before /i/ (and sometimes other high vowels): [dʲio] "nut", [dʲinjnje] "melon", [tjykør] "mirror", and more rarely [djisno] "pig",[tjino] "young ox", [jiba] "goose"; cf. Standard Hungarian [dio], [dinjnje], [tykør], [disno], [tino], and [liba].

A similar type of case is found in Catalan, where spirantization of the voiced stops /b d g/ is triggered by preceding vowels, glides, liquids, and fricatives, but not by oral stops, nasals, or word boundaries. While there are also conditions on which following segments trigger spirantization, these differences among preceding contexts are apparent in environments where the stop/spirant precedes a vowel, shown in (22–24) (Wheeler 1979, Angelo Costanzo p.c.). This pattern has been analyzed as [continuant] spread, similar to patterns in Spanish and Basque (e.g. Mascaró 1984, Hualde 1991, Kaisse 2002). The voiced stops are spirantized (i.e. become continuants) after vowels, glides, and fricatives (traditional continuants), as well as rhotics (20), but not after stops or nasals, which are traditional non-continuants, or word-initially (21).

(20)   Vowels, glides, fricatives and rhotics induce sprirantization of a following /b d g/ in Catalan.

    a. *acaba*   [əkaβə]   'ends'

        gaubança   [gəwβansə]   'rejoicing'

        bisbe   [bizβə]   'bishop'

        barba   [barβə]   'beard'

    b. *ferida*   [fəɾiðə]   'wound'

        avui dia   [aβujðiə]   'nowadays'

        absurda   [əpsuɾðə]   'absurd (F)'

        agost de 1914 [eɣozðə . . .]   'August 1914'

    c. *he guanyat* [eɣwəɲat]   'I've won'

        aigua   [ajɣwə]   'water'

        amarga   [əmaɾɣə]   'bitter (F)'

        els guants   [əɫzɣwans]   'the gloves'

(21) Oral stops and nasals do not condition spirantization of following
      voiced stops, which also do not spirantize word-initially.

a. *canvi*   *[kamβi]   [kambi]   'change'
    advent   *[abβen]   [əbben]   'advent'
    Basta!   *[βastə]   [bastə]   'enough'

b. *gendre*   *[ʒɛnðɾə]   [ʒɛndɾə]   'son-in-law'
    un xic difícil *[unʃigðifisil] [unʃigdifisil] 'a bit difficult'
    Déu meu!   *[ðeumew]   [deumew]   'Good God!'

c. *sangonós*   *[saŋɣunos]   [saŋgunos]   'bloody'
    drap gastat *[dɾabɣəstat]   [dɾabgəstat]   'used cloth'
    Guaita!   *[ɣwajtə]   [gwajtə]   'look!'

As in Hungarian, the lateral liquids are ambivalent in their behavior,
patterning with continuants to condition the spirantization of /b g/, but
patterning with non-continuants in not conditioning spirantization of /d/
(22). The fact that it is the lateral liquids which pattern both as continuants
and non-continuants even within a sound pattern is consistent with the
attribution of their ambivalent behavior to their phonetic ambiguity.[1]

(22) Lateral liquids pattern with continuants to condition spirantization
      of /b g/, but pattern with non-continuants to fail to condition
      spirantization of /d/.

a. *estalvis*   [əstalβis]   'savings'
    molt bèstia   [moɫβestiə]   'very stupid'

b. *vol demanar*   *[bɔlðəmənə]   [bɔldəmənə]   'wants to ask'
    gall dindi   *[gaʎðindi]   [gaʎdindi]   'turkey'
    caldre   *[kaɫðɾə]   [kaɫdɾə]   'to be necessary'

c. *colgar*   [kulˠɣa]   'to bury'
    el gual   [əɫɣwaɫ]   'the ford'

Interestingly, affricates display ambivalence in a different way. The stop and
spirant realizations of /b d g/ are both acceptable after affricates (20). Being
composed of stop and fricative components phonetically, affricates are potentially ambiguous with respect to continuancy. The observation that affricates

---

[1] The fact that /l/ and /d/ are homorganic may be related to the fact that it is specifically /d/ which
fails to be spirantized after /l/, and Harris (1984) makes this point for a very similar pattern in Spanish.
However, /d/ is also homorganic with other segments such as /z ɾ/ which *do* trigger its spirantization.
What is important is that it is /l/, not a more prototypical continuant like /z/, that exhibits this
behavior.

may pattern as stops to the left and as fricatives to the right ("edge effects") has led to the proposal that they are in fact contour segments at the feature level, bearing ordered [–continuant] and [+continuant] specifications (e.g. Hoard 1971, Sagey 1986). Others have argued, on the basis of anti-edge effects, that affricates possess both values of the feature [continuant] (or equivalent), but that the two values are not ordered (e.g. Hualde 1988, Lombardi 1990, Schafer 1995). Still others have argued that affricates are not contour segments at all, but strident stops (e.g. Jakobson et al. 1952, LaCharité 1993, Rubach 1994, Kim 1997, Szigetvári 1997, Clements 1999). See Szigetvári (1997) for a review of these positions. The fact that various phonological phenomena have been observed and used to motivate various (mutually incompatible) representations for affricates suggests that they are parallel to laterals and other featurally ambiguous segments, and that a variety of representations may be needed to describe the sound patterns that affricates participate in. It is consistent with previously reported edge effects that affricates are ambiguous between stops and fricatives in their interaction with segments to their right rather than to their left. This is an interesting difference between two types of ambiguity: lateral liquids and nasals are ambiguous throughout, but the ambiguity of affricates is one of scope. If the affricate is a single segment, then a segment that follows it is adjacent to a phonetically continuant interval, and also adjacent to a segment containing a phonetically noncontinuant interval. The spirantization pattern in Catalan is consistent with this fact. Again, it is important that this ambivalence occurs to the right of affricates, where the ambiguity lies, rather than to the left, where affricates are more unambiguously noncontinuant phonetically.

(23)   Voiced stops and their spirantized counterparts both may appear after affricates.

vaig voler	[badʒβulɛ]	~ [badʒbulɛ]	'I wanted'
grapats de sorra	[grəpadzdðə…]	~ [grəpadzdə…]	'handfuls of sand'
vaig gosar	[badʒɣuza]	~ [badʒguza]	'I dared'

4.1.5 *Summary of results*

It has been seen in this section that lateral liquids pattern with continuants about as often as they pattern with non-continuants. Nasals, which have generally been treated as non-continuants, actually pattern with continuants in the majority of cases. One thing that laterals and nasals have in common is that they are phonetically ambiguous with respect to the continuancy dimension. Fricatives and oral stops, which are phonetically prototypical continuants and non-continuants, are much more consistent in their patterning with respect to [continuant]. It has also been seen that lateral liquids may behave ambivalently within sound patterns in Hungarian and Catalan. Further, [v] can be ambivalent with respect to [sonorant], and affricates may manifest scope ambiguity as phonological ambivalence as well. There are many more cases of recurrent ambivalent behavior to be explored.

4.2. Discussion

It was shown in 4.1 that the phonological patterning of lateral liquids and even nasals is quite variable from language to language. Segments such as fricatives and oral stops are prototypical continuants and non-continuants, and are consistent crosslinguistically in their phonological patterning with respect to [continuant], but nasals and lateral liquids are phonetically ambiguous with respect to the letter and/or the spirit of the feature [continuant]. It will be argued in this section that this phonetic ambiguity can account for their phonological ambivalence.

The ambivalence facts are problematic for a strict interpretation of innate feature theory in which phonological patterning is to be predicted by innate features, but there are ways to allow this type of behavior without abandoning innate features. One is to say that segments in different languages realized phonetically as [l] may result from two distinct feature bundles, namely one that contains [+continuant] and one that contains [−continuant]. This raises the question of whether these segments could also have two distinct phonetic realizations, and the appearance of one ambivalent lateral liquid instead of two unambivalent ones is an illusion perpetuated by the use of a single IPA symbol to represent them. While a tendency for phonetic details to correlate with phonological patterning would not be surprising, a systematic correlation between details of phonetic realization and patterning with respect to [continuant] has not been suggested. In the absence of this evidence, the phonological patterning would need to be known before the feature specifications of [+continuant] and [−continuant] liquids could be determined, and so the phonetic properties and phonological patterning would not actually be predicted by a universal set of distinctive features. Further, this does not address the question of why [continuant] ambivalence happens with /l/ but not with /d/, /z/, or other segments, if the ambivalence is permitted by formal rather than phonetic factors. While voiced obstruents can exhibit ambivalent behavior in other ways (e.g. with respect to [voice] and [sonorant]), individual voiced stops and fricatives do not pattern ambivalently with continuants and non-continuants in the way that laterals and nasals do.

Two common responses to problems with innate features are to argue that some of the current features are wrong, or that one of the right features is missing. The feature [continuant] has been assigned different phonetic definitions in order to account for different sets of data, so one possibility for accounting for both sets of data within the same theory is to split [continuant] into two features, perhaps [continuant$_{mid-sagittal}$], which would require unrestricted airflow in the *mid-sagittal* region of the oral cavity for a [+] value (following e.g. Halle and Clements 1983) and [continuant$_{classic}$], which would merely require unrestricted airflow through some part of the oral cavity for a [+] value (following e.g. Jakobson et al. 1952). With this addition, laterals would be specified [+continuant$_{classic}$, −continuant$_{mid-sagittal}$], as shown in (24). Classes of stops and laterals would be featurally natural ([−continuant$_{mid-sagittal}$]), and so would classes of fricatives and laterals ([+continuant$_{classic}$]). However, nasals would still present a problem under this regime, requiring an additional feature [continuous airflow] which would group them with fricatives, vowels, and glides, while they could still be grouped with stops and clicks by [continuant$_{mid-sagittal}$] and [continuant$_{classic}$]. See McCawley (1968: 26n.) for related discussion on different interpretations of the feature [continuant].

(24)	[continuant$_{mid-sagittal}$]	[continuant$_{classic}$]	[continuous airflow]
stops	−	−	−
nasals	−	−	+
lateral liquids	−	+	+
fricatives	+	+	+

The situation depicted in (24) has been something of a *de facto* reality in phonological theory, because multiple feature systems have been in use for nearly the entire history of distinctive features. This type of gradience is also built into certain feature theories. For example, in Dependency Phonology and Element Theory (Harris 1994, Harris and Lindsey 1995), many intermediate segments are represented with a combination of the material that defines more extreme segments. In Element Theory, the role of [continuant] is largely filled by the elements [h] and [?], and this allows a gradience in the representation that is not available with *SPE*-style features.

Features like [continuant], which appear to involve bundles of closely related phonetic dimensions, or dimensions that can easily partition segments in more than one place, are the ones which are expected be involved in the most cases of ambivalence. Unambivalent segments are the ones which are on the same end of each dimension in the bundle or are on the same side of all the reasonable boundaries (e.g. oral stops are on the [−] side no matter how continuancy is defined or where the line is drawn). Ambivalent behavior occurs in segments which are not extreme enough phonetically that they pattern the same in each case.

Each value of each of [continuant$_{classic}$], [continuant$_{mid\text{-}sagittal}$], and [continuous airflow] corresponds to a clear set of phonetic properties, and each one is involved in sound patterns. Continuous airflow in the vocal tract, the oral cavity, and the mid-sagittal region of the oral cavity are all phonetic dimensions that are relevant for speech, and various intermediate definitions probably are as well. To many phonologists, a phonetic dimension that is relevant for speech is precisely the definition of a distinctive feature. For example, Jakobson et al. (1952) documented the twelve phonetic oppositions they "detected" in sound patterns, not a subset that they believed to be tied to innate features. In the last fifty years, more properties have been found to be relevant for sound patterns. Particular feature theories rule out particular properties (such as the phonetic properties associated with the "other" definitions of [continuant]), but evidence from sound patterns shows that this makes incorrect predictions, and that a wide variety of phonetic properties are relevant. To encode all of these relevant phonetic properties in an innate feature set would require a huge increase in the number of features. Expanding the set of innate features to cover all phonetic properties is equivalent to reducing the set of innate features and referring directly to phonetic properties. However, mainstream distinctive feature theory has operated under the assumption that some phonetic properties are irrelevant and therefore a distinction needs to be maintained between properties which have features and properties which do not. But the abundance of counter-examples has shown that concluding that a phonetic property is irrelevant should be the result of careful study of that property, rather than the result of unawareness of or inattention to all but the classes which occur most frequently in the small fraction of human spoken languages which have been documented and discussed in the literature.

Relaxing the restrictions imposed by innate features, either by adding features or adding representational variants to retroactively predict different behavior, has the effect of reducing the ability of innate features to make predictions, without addressing the connections between phonetic ambiguity and phonological ambivalence, a retreat that does not introduce new insights or address additional relevant factors.

An alternative to a massive increase in the number of features is to posit only one [continuant] feature but to allow some segments flexibility in which side of the boundary they are on, or to allow different languages to interpret the feature differently. Features could be learned on the basis of experience.

Exposure to a language in which sound patterns motivate the grouping of laterals with fricatives but not stops would cause a learner to acquire a feature like [continuant$_{classic}$], and exposure to a language with sound patterns that motivate a grouping of laterals with stops but not fricatives would cause a learner to acquire a feature like [continuant$_{mid\text{-}sagittal}$]. In this case, though, innate features are not predicting sound patterns. They are simply not interfering with the representation of sound patterns. Innate features can be prevented from interfering with sound patterns involving ambivalent segments by allowing the specifications of some or all segments to be determined on the basis of patterning. Without evidence that any class is favored over another hypothetical class in a way that is not related to phonetic naturalness, language change, or such available sources of explanation, it is unclear what is gained, apart from continuity with previous theories of phonology, from having innate features which are *filled in* on the basis of experience as opposed to non-innate (emergent) features which are *learned* on the basis of experience. What would be useful in order to predict which features would be learned is not a theory of innate features but a theory of what causes certain sound patterns to be the ones that learners are likely to be confronted with, as argued, for example, by Bach and Harms (1972), Lass (1975), Anderson (1981), Dolbey and Hansson (1999), and Blevins (2004).

Innate feature theory makes the claim that some phonetic parameters (those with innate features associated with them) are privileged over others, and should be better represented among sound patterns. Phonetically defined innate features are (intentionally) an idealization of the many phonetic factors which are conceivably relevant to language; and on the basis of evidence from observed phonologically active classes, they appear also to be (unintentionally) an idealization of language data. While individual languages may discretize the phonetic space in different ways, evidence from ambivalent segments and elsewhere show that this discretization is not "determined absolutely, within general linguistic theory, and independently of the grammar of any particular language" (Chomsky and Halle 1968: 164). Innate feature theory equates "core" phonologically active classes with featurally natural classes, but while there is considerable overlap, there is not identity.

There is also considerable overlap between phonetic naturalness and phonological activity, so that featural and phonetic naturalness are quite confounded with one another, especially for the many familiar classes which are both phonetically and featurally natural, often involving a phonetic dimension with relatively clear phonetic correlates at both ends and a relatively clear boundary in between (such as voicing). The behavior of ambivalent segments appears to have more in common with the gradient nature of the phonetic dimension(s) in which features such as [continuant] are grounded than it does with the features themselves.

Nearly 25 percent of the classes from the survey are featurally unnatural in all three theories tested, and only a very small fraction of these pivot on the continuancy status of laterals and nasals. Making all of these featurally natural in innate feature theory (a point returned to below) would require a massive increase in the number of features in Universal Grammar, to the point where the theory no longer makes predictions about which classes are predicted and which are not (apart from predictions which can be made independently on the basis of phonetic naturalness, etc.).

The primary data for innate feature theory has been recurrent phonologically active classes. Innate features have been proposed to account for a wide range of the more commonly observed classes, and have done so most reliably for the segments with the most straightforward mapping between phonetic properties and phonological patterning. Where this mapping is relatively less categorical and more complicated (e.g. the patterning of laterals and nasals with continuants and non-continuants), innate feature theory has been relatively more stymied. While it appears that innate features are bypassed in cases such as those discussed in 4.1, there are other ways for phonetics to influence phonology and achieve many of the same effects attributed to innate features, and these are developed in the next chapter.

This first look at the survey results has provided evidence that the long-standing indecision over the continuancy of lateral liquids is well founded. Lateral liquids and nasals pattern with continuants as well as non-continuants, and also participate in numerous featurally and phonetically natural and unnatural classes. The recurrent classes often involve phonetically similar segments, even when they cannot be characterized with traditional distinctive features, and the segments that tend to be ambivalent are the ones that are not prototypical examples of the [+] or [−] value of a relevant feature. Universal distinctive features are most reliable for predicting the behavior of phonetically unambiguous segments, which suggest that the phonetic unambiguity is responsible for the phonological patterning. In the phonetic gray areas, where universal features would be expected to define clear boundaries between two values of a feature, the phonological patterning of sounds is as varied as the phonetic cues are ambiguous.

5

Emergent feature theory

Previous chapters have shown that many different phonetic properties can be relevant for defining sound patterns. Innate feature theories typically choose a set of features that is too small to handle all of these sound patterns. By positing no innate features which favor certain phonetic properties over others, emergent feature theory effectively says that any feature is possible, i.e. any feature can emerge. As in innate feature theory, some phonetic properties are expected to be involved in more sound patterns, but they are favored according to the robustness of their phonetic correlates and their propensity for involvement in sound changes that give rise to patterns referring to them.

Emergent feature theory is intended to account for crosslinguistic generalizations about phonological patterns without assuming innate features. Phonetically defined features are one way to describe classes of phonetically similar segments, but there are other ways to describe these classes and to predict common and rare ones. As will be shown, by exploiting factors such as phonetic similarity and the nature of sound change, emergent feature theory can account for the "unnatural" patterns that are beyond the reach of innate features as well as the "natural" patterns they account for more easily.

5.1 "Emergence"

Emergent models of language claim that linguistic structure emerges from the interaction of many smaller patterns. The term "emergent" carries a lot of baggage. While it is probably uncontroversial that distinctive features are emergent, the question is whether they emerge from language change or from genetic change. The use of the term "emergent" often evokes images of the former and often carries negative connotations. As used in linguistics, "emergent" has a narrow definition. One appropriate definition for "emergent" comes from the *Oxford English Dictionary* (Simpson 2004):

3. Science. An effect produced by a combination of several causes, but not capable of being regarded as the sum of their individual effects. Opposed to resultant.

A Google® search for "emergent definition" turns up the following nine-teenth-, twentieth-, and twenty-first-century definitions:

emergent: (a) an effect that is not the sum of the effects of each causal conjunct (Mill 1843).
  (b) the phenomenon wherein complex, interesting high-level function is produced as a result of combining simple low-level mechanisms in simple ways (Chalmers 1990).
  (c) a phenomenon for which the optimal means of prediction is simulation (Darley 1994).
  (d) behavior by something that is not a scaling up or adaptation of anything its parts do (Thornley 1997).
  (e) One set of variables, A, emerges from another, B if (1) A is a function of B, i.e., at a higher level of abstraction, and (2) the higher-level variables can be predicted more efficiently than the lower-level ones, where 'efficiency of prediction' is defined using information theory (Shalizi 2001).
  (f) Properties of a complex physical system are emergent just in case they are neither (i) properties had by any parts of the system taken in isolation nor (ii) resultant of a mere summation of properties of parts of the system (Terravecchia 2002).

If being interesting is treated as an optional feature of an emergent property, the definitions (a, b) and (d–f) can perhaps be reduced to the definition in (f). Given this definition, it may well be that the optimal means of prediction of an emergent phenomenon is simulation (c) (but that is beyond the scope of this question). Two more definitions are provided in the description of two emer-gentist models of language.

Emergentist and connectionist views of language take substance (or the perception and memory of experience with substance) to be directly represented, while structure is considered emergent from the way substance is categorized in storage, which in turn is based on patterns of actual language use. Under this view, phonological and morpho-syntactic regularities are emergent. This means that such patterns are not basic but a secondary result of aspects of speaking and thinking: they are not necessarily categorical, symmetrical or economical, but vary according to the nature of the substance involved, and the demands of communication. (Bybee 1998: 215, 'Usage-based Phonology')

According to this new view of language learning and processing, the behaviors that we tend to characterize in terms of rules and symbols are in fact emergent patterns that arise from the interactions of other less complex or more stable underlying systems. I will refer to this new viewpoint on language learning and processing as 'emergentism'. (MacWhinney 1998: 362, 'Emergent language')

These definitions are consistent with the definitions (a, b, d–f). An emergent property is not basic, but a secondary result of the interactions of other less complex or more stable underlying systems. In functional linguistics, such systems may be speaking and thinking. The definition used by MacWhinney is broader and can apply to the emergence of a wider variety of linguistic phenomena. For example, hypothesizing that the existence of phonological distinctive features is not a basic, inherent property of speech sounds or of Universal Grammar, but rather a property that results from the interaction of the speech production apparatus, the auditory system, the perceptual system, and the tendency of the human mind to form generalizations about data is to say that phonological distinctive features are emergent.

There is little argument over whether the structure of language is emergent. The controversy is over when linguistic structure emerged, or rather, when various elements of linguistic structure emerged. According to the Universal Grammar view, this structure is innate in the brain of every human, which means that it emerged in the course of human evolution. Any bit of linguistic competence that is not specified in the genome must either be emergent from functional factors related to the use of language or be learned when the child acquires her native language. The structure of the language, insofar as it is not accounted for by these other two sources of structure, is emergent from the evolution of the language itself, as an entity apart from (but dependent on) humans.

Contrary to a popular perception, emergent models can be more restrictive than innate models, because they only permit elements which have motivation in the ambient language. For example, Pulleyblank (2003) argues that a theory of emergent features is more restrictive than a theory of innate features in accounting for covert feature effects in Nuu-chah-nulth and Oowekyala, where a feature that is not active in an inventory plays a role in phonological patterning. Pulleyblank finds that covert feature effects appear only to involve features which are already evidenced in the language, and takes this as evidence that a theory of emergent features is more restrictive than a theory of innate features, because these effects seem to be limited to features which would be expected to have emerged in language acquisition, and fail to exploit features argued to be provided by Universal Grammar that are not phonetically recoverable in the language:

To the extent that cases of covert contrast involve phonetically recoverable properties . . . , the most restrictive hypothesis is that features are emergent. If cases can be found that are comparable to the cases presented here but involve features that are completely absent phonetically, then such cases would be compelling evidence for the UG theory [of phonological features]. (Pulleyblank 2003: 421)

5.2 Emergent features

In emergent feature theory, features emerge from phonological patterns rather than the other way around. This is illustrated in Fig. 5.1. Instead of being grounded directly in phonetics, the features reflect phonetics via the phonetically-grounded phonological patterns they are motivated by. This is consistent with exemplar models in which phonological categories emerge from the phonetics through experience (e.g. Pierrehumbert 2003). The phonological patterns result not from features, but from various external factors which influence language over time. Innate and emergent feature-based approaches both posit relationships among phonetic substance, abstract features, and the phonological patterns found in human languages. The difference lies in the nature of these relationships. For innate feature theories (Fig. 5.1a), abstract features are grounded directly in phonetics, and phonological patterns reflect both the features and the phonetic substance because features are the building blocks of phonological patterns. The relationship between phonological patterns and phonetics (bypassing features) is less direct, but still necessary in order to provide the phonetic or historical accounts for "idiosyncratic" phenomena which are difficult or impossible to analyze with features. For emergent features (Figure 5.1b), this loose relationship between phonetics and phonological patterns is the sole connection between phonological patterns and phonetic tendencies. Just as phonetics can be used to account for idiosyncratic phenomena in an approach which

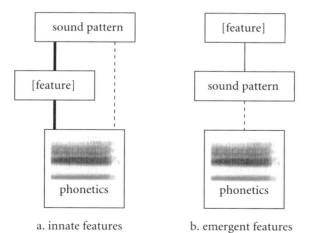

a. innate features   b. emergent features

FIGURE 5.1 Relationships between phonetics, features, and phonological patterns

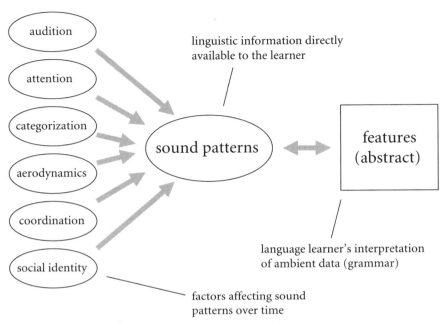

FIGURE 5.2 Abstract features from concrete external factors

otherwise depends on innate features, phonetics can account for these unusual phonological patterns, and *also* for more common ones, which also tend
to reflect more common phonetic tendencies. In this way, emergent feature
theory employs a single mechanism to account for common and rare phonological patterns, in contrast with innate feature theory, which requires two.

The phonological patterns which exist in a particular language may be
internalized by speakers in terms of features which are necessary to describe
them, rather than in terms of predetermined innate features. Using language
and abstracting from the available data necessarily involves all of the factors
pictured on the left side of Fig. 5.2, and the process of abstraction may cause
the output of the learner's grammar to differ from the ambient language,
which is why the arrow between abstract features and phonological patterns is
bidirectional. The influence of production, perception, and other factors is
not simply a matter of ease of articulation or ease of perception. These
external factors do not necessarily pressure phonology to be more optimal
or more natural, but nonetheless play a role in determining what kinds of
perception and production error may occur, as well as what kind of variability
occurs under the circumstances in which language is used. Thus, external

factors have an influence on what types of error and variability are most likely to become conventionalized. Consider the following typographical metaphor.

Due to the layout of the *qwerty* keyboard, some typographical errors are more likely than others. <d> is more likely to be mistyped as <e>, <r>, <s>, <f>, <x>, or <c> than as a letter it does not neighbor. Acknowledging the role of the layout of the keyboard (or vocal tract) in what types of deviations from a target are most likely does not amount to saying that the result of these errors is more natural or optimal than the intended target, <d>. It is not necessary for people who type to have a mental map of the keyboard in order to predict likely typos, although they likely do have such a map as a result of keyboard use. In speech production, [d] has a different set of neighbors, including [n], [t], and [ɾ]. [d] would naturally be expected to be accidentally realized as one of them more frequently than as an articulatorily more distant segment such as [ɣ]. Having already taken into account the articulatory similarity between [d] and its neighbors, featural similarity is an additional (possibly redundant) explanation.

While <d> has six equally distant neighbors on the keyboard, the six errors are not equally likely to be committed without being noticed. Of the six ways to mistype <noticed> shown in (25), (25c) has a distinct advantage in going unnoticed:

(25)   Some easy ways to mistype <noticed>
    a. noticee
    b. noticer
    c. notices
    d. noticef
    e. noticex
    f. noticec

This is because <notices> is the only error in (25) which can pass e.g. Microsoft® Word's spell check, and consequently it is more likely than the other errors to persist in a document, and possibly more likely to be typed in error in the first place, because it is a word in English. Similarly, a production error which results in an actual word may be more likely to go unnoticed and to become conventionalized.

Although it is hard to predict when a typing error will be committed, considering the layout of the keyboard and the content of the spell checker makes it possible to predict which deviations from the target are likely to occur, and which of those are likely to persist. Taking into account the reality in which typing (or language use) occurs does not require any sense of optimization or naturalness in order to be useful, although the issue of optimization is an interesting one. A different reality, which could involve a different keyboard layout or a different modality or language system, would make different predictions. Consider the following typographical error on page 475 of Martinet's (1968) article in *Manual of Phonetics* (Fig. 5.3).

This type of error (substitution of <y> for <s> and <s> for <y> on different lines) would appear to be a random coincidence if this were the output of modern word-processing software, where there is no single mechanism by which this transposition could occur. It would be surprising both for the coincidence of the complementarity of the errors and for the failure of a spell checker to catch these two nonwords. In the alternate reality of 1960s typesetting, this error is not surprising, given the opportunity for two letters at the edge of a page to get knocked out and then accidentally switched as they are replaced and the absence of automated spell checking.

If the goal is to understand why certain phonological patterns exist and why some are more common than others, it makes quite a lot of sense to consider the reality in which language is used. This makes it possible to determine which observations are explainable on the basis of external factors, before adding hypothetical new components to the reality (such as innate features) in order to explain the same observations. The following sections discuss some of the factors which lead to phonological patterns from which many familiar types of feature may emerge. The specific factors illustrated in Fig. 5.2 are revisited in Chapter 8.

There are many ways in which recurrent phonologically active classes may be predicted. As outlined below, members of phonologically active classes may be related by their participation together in regular sound change, or they may be related by generalization, by virtue of shared phonetic or non-phonetic properties. Social differences between societies may also play a role in determining what classes are likely, as may cognitive factors such as those

2.14. It is clear that the causes of unbalance of phonological systems must, in the last analysis, normally be found in pressures exerted by communicative needs if, under this fairly vague heading, we put not only those which characterize a homogeneous linguistic community — assuming that such communities do exist —, but also those which develop when people using different languages, dialects, or even different usages of the same language come in contact. The necessity, which then becomey apparent, of adapting one's speech or learning a new register certainls plays a considerable role in phonological evolution.

FIGURE 5.3 Typographical error from a different reality

claimed to be part of Universal Grammar. The extent to which innate features of sounds are necessary to predict phonologically active classes depends on what predictions can be made on the basis of other factors.

5.2.1 *Sound change*

Some recurrent phonologically active classes can be accounted for directly from sound change, as some types of recurrent sound change may affect multiple segments from the very beginning. These cases would occur when a phonetic effect is widespread before it becomes phonologized. For example, vowel nasalization can affect all vowels at once, if every vowel is phonetically nasalized and allophonic nasalization is reinterpreted as contrastive. A resulting alternation would affect all vowels by virtue of the fact that they were the segments which were phonetically nasalized before nasalization became phonologized. It would also likely involve all nasals consonants, if they were the only segments capable of inducing substantial phonetic nasalization in vowels. Thus, the phonological pattern that results would refer to the natural class of vowels and the natural class of nasals, in line with an observation made by Janda (2001: 05):

> It could thus be said that sound-change tends to be regular, not due to persistent influence from some kind of articulatory or auditory/acoustic phonetic naturalness, but instead because exaggerations and misperceptions of phonetic tendencies tend to involve stepwise generalizations based on the natural classes of phonology (i.e. . . . coronals, nasals, obstruents, and the like).

While the phonological patterns that result from phonetic tendencies (such as vowel nasalization) can certainly be described using features such as [vocalic], [consonantal], and [nasal], this only shows that they can be described this way, not that this is why they pattern together. Treating the features as the explanation obscures the chain of events which led to the creation of the phonological patterns.

Other types of frequent sound change which may affect multiple segments at once include final devoicing (results seen in Russian, German, Turkish, etc.) and postnasal voicing (results seen in Greek, many Bantu languages, etc.). In both cases, by the time phonetic voicing or devoicing is reinterpreted as a phonological distinction, several segments are already affected—voiced obstruents or voiced consonants generally are devoiced in the former case, and voiceless obstruents are voiced in the latter. The results of these changes could be described using features such as [voice] and [sonorant], but again, the features themselves do not solely account for the sound change. The sound change allows for the descriptive use of the features.

All these types of sound change are fairly common, and the classes of segments which participate in the resulting alternations are fairly common phonologically active classes. Not surprisingly, the features used to describe them are also fairly commonly used. Just by looking at a few common types of sound change, it is apparent that some common classes and features emerge readily as the result of sound change.

5.2.2 *Phonetically based generalization*

While there is reason to speculate that these types of sound change could involve multiple segments right from the start, there is no way to know for sure what happened at the inception of changes that occurred long ago. An alternative chain of events which produces the same result is one in which a phonetic tendency initially is phonologized for only a single segment, and then spread analogically to other segments. For example, when vowels are phonetically nasalized, lower vowels tend to be nasalized more profoundly than higher vowels, since tongue lowering facilitates velum lowering due to their connection via the palatoglossus muscle (Johnson 1997, Moll 1962, Lubker 1968). Phonemic vowel nasalization in Old French has been claimed (not uncontroversially) to have started with /a/ around the turn of the eleventh century and spread essentially one vowel at a time to ultimately affect /a e aj ej o oj i u/ in the fourteenth (Chen 1973; see Hajek 1997 for discussion). If it is true that all vowel nasalization starts with one segment rather than a wide range, it is not difficult to see how it could then spread very easily to include all vowels, if the other vowels share the phonetic property (nasalization) that has been phonologized, even if it is to a lesser degree.

Sound changes that appear to affect multiple phonetically similar segments constitute one source for emergent classes and features. It is also possible that they begin with one segment and spread to others. In each case, the phonetic property that is phonologized in one segment is present in other segments, making generalization to the larger class a straightforward process. Whether classes and features emerge from multi-segment sound change or from single-segment sound change followed by generalization, it is clear that common sound changes are a plentiful source for the features and classes of synchronic phonology, without reference to an innate feature set. Likewise, it is not a problem if multisegment sound change can account for observed phonologically active classes. Generalization may or may not be required to produce the phonologically active classes resulting from common sound changes such as vowel nasalization, postnasal voicing, and final devoicing. If generalization does play a role, then these are special cases of a more general situation in which the result of sound change is extended to similar segments. While the similarity is closely tied to the original change in cases like vowel nasalization, there are other cases where a change is generalized according to a completely independent phonetic property.

As it is used in this book, generalization is a process by which two or more entities which share certain properties are treated as equivalent in some way. One way for phonologically active classes to form is for a set of speech sounds which share a phonetic property to be treated as though they are phonologically similar, even if there is not direct phonological evidence in the ambient language, or if the sounds have other phonetic properties which differ.

A hypothetical illustration of the role of generalization in the development of a phonologically active class is shown in Fig. 5.4. Given evidence that [g] undergoes a phonological process (perhaps spirantization) and that voiceless stops do not, and a dearth of clear evidence either way about [b] or [d] (perhaps because they are infrequent segments), a language learner may learn or mislearn this pattern in various ways. She could treat all stops the same, and reverse the spirantization process (Fig. 5.4a), given that the majority of stops do not exhibit phonetic spirantization, or she could infer that spirantization applies only to segments produced with closure voicing and a constriction between the tongue and velum ([g]) (Fig. 5.4b), or that it applies to any stop produced with closure voicing (Fig. 5.4c). Closure voicing and velar constriction both involve sets of phonetic properties which are recognizable by speakers with or without cognitive entities [+voice] or [Dorsal]. The result of the latter case (generalization to other voiced stops) is the "natural" class of voiced stops. The outcomes illustrated in Fig. 5.4 may be expected to be the most likely, but if the generalization were to occur slightly differently, the result might be termed an "unnatural" class. The main point of emergent feature theory is that phonetically natural classes are the result of common sound changes or phonetically

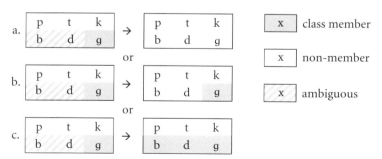

FIGURE 5.4 Generalization of a phonetic effect

based generalizations, while phonetically unnatural classes are the result of less common generalizations or sequences of events.

The process of linguistic generalization is also seen in cases such as the way different speech communities have generalized the use of the English verbal inflectional suffix -*s*, as shown in Fig. 5.5. It is a 3rd person present singular marker in most varieties of Indian, British, and North American English, a present singular marker in some varieties of Northern British English (Pyles and Algeo 1993), and absent from some varieties of African-American Vernacular English (Green 1998). In both of the innovative cases, the presence or absence of the suffix corresponds to semantically coherent sets of person–number combinations. The absence of the suffix in AAVE may be an undergeneralization or may also be attributed entirely or in part to phonological loss.

The three hypothetical outcomes above in Fig. 5.4 are analogous to the three English-*s* suffix examples here; only here it is semantically similar person–number combinations, rather than phonetically similar consonants, which are being treated similarly. Beyond its role in linguistics, generalization is a general cognitive process which is widely attested in other domains, discussed in the psychology literature (e.g. Spear and Riccio 1987). Generalization occurs when an individual infers a class from available positive evidence.

Phonetically based generalization (phonetic analogy) is an old and well-documented concept in linguistics, its modern exponents including Vennemann (1972), Andersen (1972, 1973), Anttila (1977, 2003), and Hock (2003). Analogical change (e.g. proportional analogy and paradigm leveling) depends on the cognitive process of generalization, and has been central to diachronic linguistics since the Neogrammarians (e.g. Whitney 1867, 1875, Scherer 1868). Whitney (1875) writes that "[t]he force of analogy is, in fact, one of the most potent in all language-history; as it makes whole classes of forms, so it has

I digitize.	*We digitize.*	*I digitize.*	*We digitize.*
You digitize.	*You digitize.*	*You digitize.*	*You digitize.*
She digitizes.	*They digitize.*	*She digitizes.*	*They digitize.*

Many English varieties   Some varieties of Northern
                                              British English

I digitize.	*We digitize.*
You digitize.	*Y'all digitize.*
She digitize.	*They digitize.*

Some varieties of AAVE

FIGURE 5.5 Generalization in English morphology

power to change their limits" (p. 75 of 1887 edn., cited in Anttila and Brewer 1977). In their bibliography of analogy, Anttila and Brewer trace the study of analogy to pre-Neogrammarian times, starting with Duponceau in 1816.

Analogy has had a complicated relationship with phonological theory, having been rejected, embraced, and ignored on different occasions by practitioners of Generative Grammar. Part of the reason why phonetic generalization has not played a role in Generative Phonology is that generalizations about sounds are intended to be provided by innate features, so that there is no role for analogical reasoning in accounting for patterns in synchronic and diachronic phonology. In recent times, analogy has been accepted back into the study of phonology, in Correspondence Theory (McCarthy and Prince 1995), Paradigm Uniformity (Steriade 1997), and other approaches.

Generalization is also invoked in the phonological learning algorithms of Clements (2001) and Dresher (e.g. 2003). Hume and Johnson (2001c) include it as one of four diachronic filters on phonological systems. According to Hume and Johnson, phonological systems are constantly filtered by external forces, and this can result in the filtering out or alteration of forms which are difficult to produce or perceive, which are not used by members of a speakers community, or which do not fit an existing or apparent generalization over the available phonological data.

Generalization is necessary for the ability of learners to acquire phonology at all, but it yields particularly interesting results when a language learner arrives at the "wrong" generalization, by forming an undergeneralization or overgeneralization of the prevailing pattern. In addition to an overwhelming number of correct generalizations, undergeneralizations and overgeneralizations are commonly observed in language-learning children (e.g. Vihman 1996, Pinker 1994, and references cited). The "wrong" generalization becomes *right* if it catches on and spreads.

Generalization to phonetically similar segments has been recorded in the laboratory. In a modified version of Goldinger's (1998) paradigm, Nielsen (2006) had subjects read a list of words including /p/ and /k/ before and after listening to a recording of a speaker reading a word list producing /p/ with extra aspiration. Subjects imitated the production of /p/ words, including words not heard with extra aspiration, and generalized the extra aspiration to words with the phonetically similar /k/, even though /k/ was never heard with extra aspiration. The voiceless stops behave as a phonologically active class even though only extra aspiration was originally motivated only for /p/.

A parallel case which appears to involve the same type of phonetic analogy is found in the development of Tigrinya spirantization. Leslau (1941) reports that velar stops spirantize intervocalically. A few decades later, Pam (1973: 16) reports that the class of spirantization targets appears to have expanded to include labials as well (i.e. the class of grave plain oral stops) (Fig. 5.6). Leslau's informants or their predecessors appear to have generalized the target class in a fashion similar to what Nielsen demonstrated experimentally. The phonetic similarity of a group of sounds appears to have caused them to pattern together even though only a proper subset were previously involved in the sound pattern.

(26)   Tigrinya spirantization
  a. Velar stops spirantize in both varieties.
       [kʌlbíː]   'dog (sg.)'   [ʔaxaːlɨbtíː]   'dog (pl.)'
       [gʌnʔíː]   'pitcher (sg.)'   [ʔaɣaːnìʔ]   'pitcher (pl.)'
  b. Labial stops spirantize in one variety.
       [ʔádːiːs ʔábʌbʌ]   'Addis Ababa' (Leslau 1941)
       [ʔádːiːs ʔáβʌβʌ]   'Addis Ababa' (Pam 1973)
  c. Coronal stops resist spirantization.
       [kʌfaːtíː]   'opener (masc. sg.)'

Phonetic analogy is just one way this change could have occurred. It is possible that labials possessed the phonetic motivation for spirantization and underwent a separate sound change. This would mean that phonetic similarity was relevant for the initiation of the parallel sound changes rather than in the extension of the result of one sound change to a larger class. In either case, the result is a group of sounds which pattern together as a result of their phonetic similarity. More detailed investigation of this and other phenomena is necessary in order to determine which pathway is correct, or if spirantization is present to varying degrees in all of the stops, leading to varying reports of which stops meet the threshold to be considered spirantized.

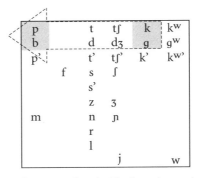

FIGURE 5.6 A phonologically active class in Tigrinya (*c.* 1973)

Another example of apparent generalization is /o/ lowering in northeastern varieties of Swiss German. As reconstructed, the original sound change only involved one conditioning segment, but as seen in variation among modern Swiss German varieties, different sets of consonants which do not cause phonetic lowering now condition lowering phonologically in different varieties. In northeastern Swiss German, /o/ is lowered to [ɔ] before certain consonants (Keel 1982). In and around the city of Schaffhausen, four different versions of /o/ lowering are observed, in which different classes of sounds condition lowering. Some of this variation is illustrated in (27). /o/ lowering originally occurred only before /r/, but it has been generalized differently in different communities (Keel 1982, Janda and Joseph 2001), as shown in Fig. 5.7.

(27)   Schaffhausen /o/ lowering
   a. /o/ is lowered before /r/ throughout Schaffhausen

[bɔrə]	'to bore'
[fɔrə]	'fir tree'
[hɔrn]	'horn'
[tɔrn]	'thorn'
[kwɔrffə]	'thrown. pp.'
[ʃpɔrə]	'spur'

   b. /o/ is lowered before coronal obstruents elsewhere in the canton, but not in the city of Schaffhausen itself.

Cantonal dialects	City of Schaffhausen	
[ʃtɔtsə]	[ʃtotsə]	'to push down'
[lɔsə]	[losə]	'to listen'
[rɔss]	[ross]	'horse'
[xrɔttə]	[xrottə]	'toad'
[gɔt]	[got]	'god'
[ʃnɔdərə]	[ʃnodərə]	'to stir, pp.'
[pɔttə]	[pottə]	'offered, pp.'
[ksɔttə]	[ksottə]	'boiled, pp.'
[tnɔssə]	[tnossə]	'enjoyed, pp.'
[kʃɔssə]	[kʃossə]	'shot, pp.'

In the city of Schaffhausen, the conditioning environment for lowering has been generalized to include nasals (i.e. other non-lateral sonorants) (Fig. 5.7b), while in seventeen nearby villages, the environments have been generalized to include other non-nasal, non-lateral coronal consonants (Fig. 5.7c). In thirteen other villages, the generalization includes nasals and coronal obstruents (i.e. segments which are similar to /r/ in one of two ways: sonorance

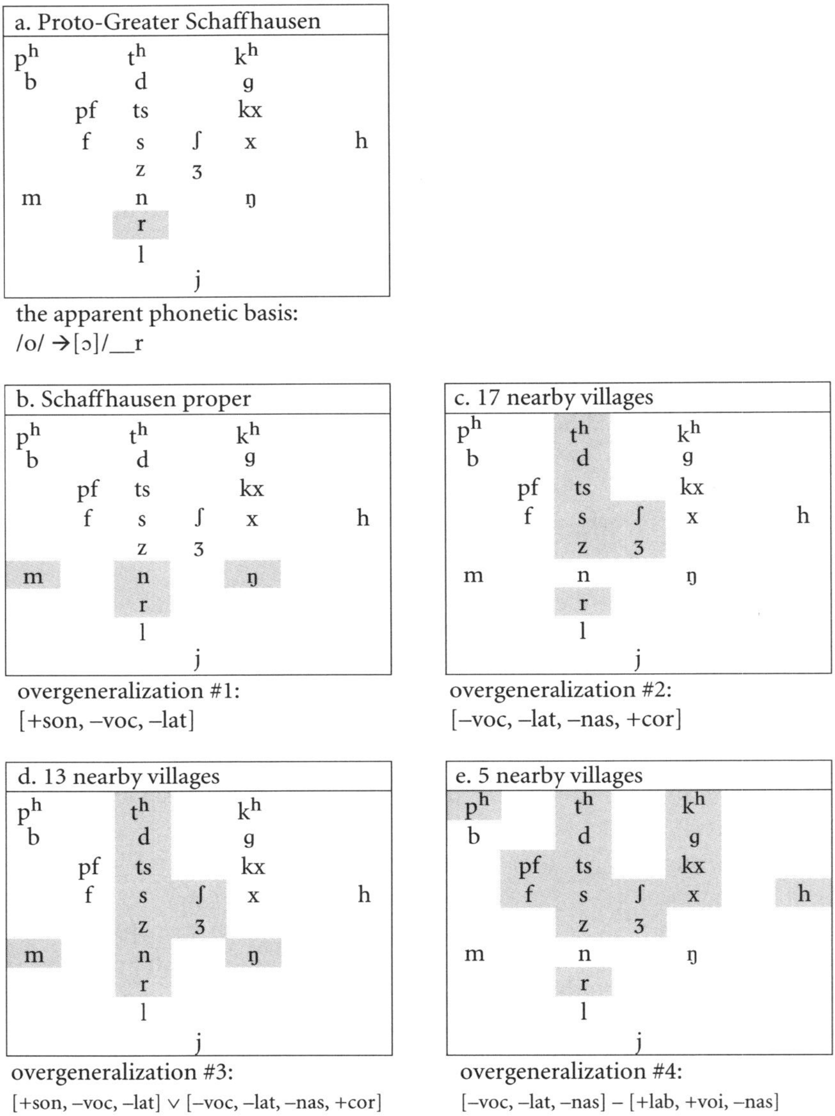

a. Proto-Greater Schaffhausen

p^h	t^h	k^h		
b	d	g		
	pf	ts	kx	
	f	s	ʃ	x	h
	z	ʒ		
m	n	ŋ		
	r			
	l			
		j		

the apparent phonetic basis:
/o/ → [ɔ]/__r

b. Schaffhausen proper

overgeneralization #1:
[+son, −voc, −lat]

c. 17 nearby villages

overgeneralization #2:
[−voc, −lat, −nas, +cor]

d. 13 nearby villages

overgeneralization #3:
[+son, −voc, −lat] ∨ [−voc, −lat, −nas, +cor]

e. 5 nearby villages

overgeneralization #4:
[−voc, −lat, −nas] − [+lab, +voi, −nas]

FIGURE 5.7 Generalization of the conditioning environment for a sound pattern in Schaffhausen

and coronality) (Fig. 5.7d). In five villages, the conditioning environment has apparently generalized to include all obstruents except /b/ (Fig. 5.7e) (see Janda and Joseph 2001, Janda 2003). /b/ is less similar to /r/ in some ways than most of the segments which *do* participate—for example, most of them are lingual consonants. On the other hand, /b/ is certainly more similar to /r/ than /pʰ/ is, but it is similarity to the segments already participating which is relevant, not just similarity to /r/. Because generalization from /r/ would likely have occurred in more than one step, similarity to /r/ would have been most critical only at the stage before other segments began participating. Perhaps the development of the class in Fig. 5.7e involved an intermediate stage at which the class was /r/ and lingual obstruents, and this was further extended to other fricatives and affricates, including /pf f/. Since there are no voiced labiodentals in the language, /pʰ/ is more similar to the participating segments than is /b/ at this hypothetical stage. /b/ is also rather similar to /m/, another segment which does not cause /o/ lowering.

The last two cases resulted in classes which are not characterizable with a conjunction of distinctive features. The class in Fig. 5.7d requires the union of featurally natural classes, while the class in Fig. 5.7e requires subtracting one featurally natural class from another, or else the union of a larger number of classes. The presence of featurally unnatural outcomes rather than a selection of featurally natural classes suggests that speakers simply learn the set of environments where /o/ lowering occurs in the speech of members of their community, regardless of whether or not the set of environments is expressible as a conjunction of distinctive features within any particular theory.

Cases like Schaffhausen /o/ lowering differ from the examples in the previous section in that phonologically active classes are produced by a generalization that is possibly unrelated to the initial motivation. Nonetheless, in both types of case, phonetically similar segments take on similar phonological behavior. In multisegment sound change (or sound change + related generalization), the segments are united by a phonetic property that is at the heart of the resulting phonological patterns. In sound change followed by generalization, a phonological pattern is analogically extended to segments which are similar in some way that may have nothing to do with the original phonetic motivation for the phonological pattern. While Schaffhausen /o/ lowering is conditioned by segments that do not necessarily share the property of /r/ which originally had the phonetic effect of lowering /o/, the extreme case is found in Zina Kotoko, where a class of depressor consonants appears to have been generalized to segments which have the *opposite* phonetic effect.

The classes of consonants involved in consonant–tone interactions in different languages tend to be similar. Typically, voiced consonants act as depressors,

Lowering ◄──────────────────────────────► *Raising*

breathy	voiced	sonorant	voiceless	voiceless	implosive
voice	obstruent		unaspirated	aspirated	

FIGURE 5.8 Hyman and Schuh's (1974) hierarchy of phonetic Fo lowering

lowering the tone of adjacent vowels, often from H to L (see e.g. Bradshaw 1999 for a survey of consonant–tone interaction and a formal account employing a single feature for voice and low tone). All known cases include at least voiced obstruents among the class of depressor consonants (Bradshaw 1999). This is consistent with the observation that voiced obstruents have a phonetic lowering effect on the Fo of a following vowel (Hyman and Schuh 1974), shown in Fig. 5.8.

Consonant–tone interactions arise when this phonetic lowering is reana-lyzed as phonological tone. Sometimes sonorants also function as depressor consonants (in Nupe, Ngizim, Ewe, and Kanazawa Japanese: Odden 2002a), and this is not surprising considering that sonorants do lower Fo, although not as much as voiced obstruents, and that voiced sonorants are phonetically similar (in voicing) to other voiced segments.

Zina Kotoko features a variety of tone-lowering processes, one of which occurs in the recent past verbal inflection. In this case, an underlying mid tone in the first syllable is realized as mid after [h] and voiceless obstruents (28), but lowered to low after voiced obstruents (29a), sonorants (29b), glottal stop (29c), and most interestingly, implosives (29d) (Odden 2002a, b).

(28)   An underlying mid tone surfaces in the first syllable.

a.	hēr-ə́m	'bite'	hērtʃ-ə́m	'slice'
	hwāt-ə́m	'inflate'	hɔ̄l-ə́m	'steal'

b.	skāl-ə́m	'pay back'	sāp-ə́m	'chase'
	pāj-ə́m	'bury'	kāh-ə́m	'take a handful'
	kāɗ-ə́m	'cross'	sɔ̄k-ə́m	'send'
	tām-ə́m	'touch'	tʃə̄nh-ə́m	'be sated'

(29)   An underlying mid tone surfaces as low after a depressor consonant.

a.	ɣàg-ə́m	'close'	gàh-ə́m	'pour'
	zə̀gl-ə́m	'carry'	bgwàr-ə́m	'jump pl.'
	gə̀ɓ-ə́m	'answer'	gə̀ɗ-ə́m	'open'
	gùlm-ə́m	'twist'	vàlf-ə́m	'give back'
	dùnk-ə́m	'throw'	zàk-ə́m	'beat'
	vìt-ə́m	'blow a fire'	dʒìk-ə́m	'begin'

b.	jèj-ə́m	'call'	wèh-ə́m	'be tired'
	làb-ə́m	'tell'	ràɗ-ə́m	'pull'
	màr-ə́m	'die'	làkf-ə́m	'bring'

c.	ʔəkf-ɔ́m	'approach'	ʔək-ɔ́m	'snatch'
d.	ɗəv-ɔ́m	'put'	ɗəh-ɔ́m	'write'
	ɓàl-ɔ́m	'dance'	ɗàm-ɔ́m	'eat'

It is of particular interest that implosives act as phonological depressors in Zina Kotoko, because implosives have the phonetic effect of *raising* Fo. Like many other consonant–tone interactions, the phonetic basis for this phonological patterns probably was the Fo lowering caused by voiced obstruents (see e.g. Hombert et al. 1979). However, speakers apparently generalized this category along the phonetic dimension of *voicing* to include segments such as sonorants and implosives, even though Fo lowering, not vocal fold vibration, is the phonetic effect likely responsible for the phonological pattern in the first place. As in Schaffhausen Swiss German, groups of phonetically similar segments participate together in phonological patterns, regardless of the original phonetic motivation. Discrete events can result in classes that may appear phonetically natural or unnatural, but children learn them regardless of their historical origins.

It should be clear at this point that shared phonetic properties may lead to shared phonological behavior, regardless of whether they are the phonetic properties fundamentally related to the original motivation for a phonological pattern. While it is not possible to predict when generalization will occur, when it does occur, there is a good chance that it will involve segments which are similar to segments already in the class. For example, if the class /bd/ is extended to include one more segment, the inclusion of /g/ is more likely than the inclusion of /i/. Two similar things are at play here: phonetics and phonetic similarity. Phonetics accounts for the grouping of (usually similar) segments in a phonetic effect (which may become phonologized), while phonetic similarity may account for the inclusion of additional sounds in an already-phonologized sound pattern. In both cases it is only possible to speculate about what changes would be likely.

5.2.3 *Frequency*

While all the examples given above involve generalization according to phonetic properties, other properties may also lead to a particular group of sounds patterning together as a class. Non-phonetic properties such as phoneme frequency may also be relevant. For example, Hume (2004b) argues that high frequency is responsible for /m/ and /ŋ/ patterning together as a class, to the exclusion of /n/, in Sri Lankan Portuguese Creole. SLPC has an assimilation pattern whereby the labial and velar nasals assimilate in place across morpheme (30a) and word boundaries (30c), while the coronal nasal does not (30b) (Smith 1978, Hume and Tserdanelis 2002).

(30)   Place assimilation in Sri Lankan Portuguese Creole

Nom. sg.	*Gen. sg.*	*Dative sg.*	*Verbal noun*	*gloss*
a. maːm	maːnsu	maːmpə	maːŋki-	'hand'

　　　 cf. [eli maːm ebeːrtu] 'he + hand open = He is a spendthrift'

vaːrzim	vaːrzinsu	vaːrzimpə	vaːrziŋki-	'harvest'
rezaːm	rezaːnsu	rezaːmpə	rezaːŋki-	'reason'
miːtiŋ	miːtinsu	miːtimpə	miːtiŋki-	'meeting'

b. siloːn	siloːn	siloːnpə	siloːnki-	'Sri Lanka'

　　　 cf. [siloːn avara taantu defreːnsa teem] /siloːn avara.../
　　　　　 'Sri Lanka is now very different'

bataan	bataansu	bataanpə	bataanki-	'button'
siːn	siːnsu	siːnpə	siːnki-	'bell'
tavn	tavnsu	tavnpə	tavnki-	'town'
kəlkun	kəlkuːnsu	kəlkuːnpə	kəlkuːnki-	'turkey'

　　　 c. perim + təsuwaː　 [pərin təsuwaː]　 'me + sweat = I am sweating'
　　　　 cf. [perim uŋ gaːrfu taːn triːja] /perim uŋ gaːrfu taːm triːja/
　　　　　 'me-DAT a fork also bring = Bring me a fork too'

pikiniːm + kaːzə	[pikiniŋ kaːzə]	'small + house = small house'
rezaːm + lej	[rezaːn lej]	'reason + like = reasonably'
uŋ + faːkə	[um faːkə]	'one knife' cf. [uŋ aːnu] 'one year'
uŋ + diːj	[un diːj]	'one day'

Place assimilation is often treated as a diagnostic of markedness, with unmarked places of articulation undergoing assimilation to more marked places. The pattern of assimilation in SLPC is surprising, because coronals are generally treated as unmarked relative to labials and dorsals. Hume (2004b) reinterprets markedness observations in terms of expectation, partly on the basis of frequency. Hume and Tserdanelis (2002) observe that the labial is the most common nasal in SLPC, occurring in twice as many words as the coronal nasal. The velar nasal occurs finally in only three words, but one of these is the definite article /uŋ/ (Hume 2004b), which is a very frequent word. Thus, Hume argues, it is the high token frequency of the labial and velar nasals which causes them to behave together as a phonologically active class. Further, the high frequency of coronal consonants can be invoked to account for cases where coronals act as though they are unmarked. For example, /t d/, which are frequently and famously flapped, deleted, and otherwise altered in American English, are by far the most frequent consonants as well, occurring in 40 percent of all words in the Buckeye corpus of conversational Central Ohio English (Pitt et al. 2004, Hume 2004b, Raymond et al. 2006).

It is an empirical question whether non-phonetic parameters such as phoneme frequency can account for a wide range of phonologically active classes, particularly the classes which have no apparent phonetic motivation, some of which are discussed in the next chapter. Invoking frequency is more complicated than invoking phonetic facts, because frequency is necessarily language-specific. While many phonetic facts are also language-specific, there are enough commonalities between languages (within a given modality) to allow phonetically based speculation to be made about a relatively unfamiliar language. Using phoneme frequency to account for a phonological pattern requires language-specific information like word frequency. Unfortunately, many of the languages with the most unexpected phonologically active classes have little or no readily available frequency data at this time.

5.2.4 *Social factors*

Social factors are probably relevant for the development of all sound patterns. For example Janda (1999, 2003) attributes phonemic split to socially motivated phonetic exaggeration perpetrated by successive generations. But social factors may also play a much more specific role, making certain patterns more likely in certain communities. Trudgill (2002) suggests that dense social networks can support complex alternations and unusual sound changes (see also Chambers 1995). For example, working-class speakers of Belfast English have a more complex system of vowel allophones than middle-class speakers, and they also have denser social networks (Milroy 1980). For middle-class speakers, the vowel phoneme in *trap* has only the allophone [a]. For working-class speakers, this vowel has allophones including [ɛ], [æ], [a], [ɑ], and [ɒ], with further complexity added by the fact that front [ɛ] occurs before back consonants and back [ɒ] occurs before alveolar nasals. Trudgill (2002: 723) argues that small, tight-knit communities are more able "to encourage continued adherence to norms from one generation to another, however complex they may be", and that complex and unusual phonological patterns may consequently be favored in small, close-knit and/or isolated communities.

If this correlation is correct, then emergent feature theory predicts that large communities with sparse social networks should display more phonologically active classes that are phonetically natural. These classes should be similar to the classes predicted by many feature theories. Smaller communities with denser social networks are more likely to support more unexpected "unnatural" classes that are less compatible with many feature theories. This is empirically testable, although the issue is complicated somewhat by the fact that for much of its history, linguistic theory has been focused mainly on standard languages spoken by large and diverse groups of speakers. These languages would already be expected to conform most willingly to the linguistic theories crafted by their speakers. Counterexamples are most likely to occur in languages spoken in isolated, small, and close-knit communities. These are precisely the communities in which Trudgill and others predict complex and unusual phonological patterns to be most prevalent anyway. So there are two very different factors at play. Not only are small, close-knit, and isolated communities potentially more able to sustain complex and seemingly unnatural phonological patterns, they are more likely to be more foreign to linguists. Therefore, the phonological patterns that they do have will be even more unexpected simply because of lack of exposure.

5.3 The abstractness of emergent features

Distinctive features of the innate variety have primary phonetic correlates which may be accompanied by additional phonetic properties which are redundant but enhance the main contrast. However, the decision to choose one phonetic property as primary is somewhat arbitrary. Similarly, it is sometimes the case that two innate features are equally able to define a natural class. For example, in languages with no voiced obstruents, [+sonorant] and [+voice] define the same group of sounds, and the linguist must choose which feature to use. In emergent feature theory, the feature that defines such a class is abstract and does not need to be related to the features which have been used to account for phenomena in other languages. If multiple phonetic properties are associated with a class, it is not necessary to choose one of them to define the abstract category. It is an (interesting) empirical question whether language users capitalize on certain phonetic properties over others, or if speakers differ from each other in terms of which phonetic properties define a class. Declaring that a particular innate feature is involved presupposes this.

In emergent feature theory, phonetic substance and language use are more fundamental to the explanation of recurrent phonological patterns than they are in innate feature theories. However, the features themselves are, if anything, more abstract than the phonetically defined innate features are argued to be. In emergent feature theory, phonologically active classes (which form the basis for features) are learned as the result of observations about the phonological patterns which exist in the adult language, and as a result of generalizations about the properties of the speech sounds. There is no direct connection between the features and the external factors which led to the phonological patterns. For the speaker, the phonological pattern is an abstract generalization over sounds, and the original basis for the phonological pattern is of little importance. The phonological pattern is related to the factors which caused it to emerge historically, as well as to each speaker's mental representation of it.

For example, vowel harmony is distinct from vowel-to-vowel coarticulation in that it is generally treated as a symbolic operation, although it bears a striking resemblance to coarticulation. The connection between the two phenomena, as well as the fundamental difference between the abstractness of a phonological process and the relative concreteness of a phonetic effect, is captured by emergent feature theory. A vowel harmony process can emerge over time via the external factors audition, attention, categorization, aerodynamics, coordination, and social identity (Fig. 5.2, above). Coarticulation between vowels occurs as a result of gesture mistiming (coordination), resulting in phonetically rounded vowels which are perceptually similar to contrastively rounded vowels (audition and attention). These phonetically rounded vowels are recategorized as rounded vowels by some speakers (categorization).[1] Then rounding harmony takes on social significance and spreads throughout a community (social identity). Learners of the language are exposed to a situation in which rounded vowels are only ever followed within a single word by another rounded vowel. They perceive that high-amplitude intervals produced with lip rounding and minimal obstruction in the oral cavity and featuring low $F2$ and $F3$ share some abstract property that they do not share with other segments (even segments which have some properties in common with them, such as labial consonants, or other vowels). For the speaker, all that is important is that these segments share an abstract property. Labeling the property is a task primarily for linguists. Since these segments share a clear phonetic property, linguists may refer to this abstract property as something like [flat], [+round] or [Labial] in order to reflect the phonetic similarity. However, since the phonetic similarity is secondary to the fact that the grouping is phonologically significant, the class could just as easily be thought of as "the segments that do X" and the abstract property that connects them could just as easily be called "z". This is the conclusion reached by Anderson (1981) and others.

Phonological features and phonologically active classes are potentially isomorphic. No feature needs to be learned that is not motivated by the presence of a phonologically active class. Treating phonological patterns as primary and features as secondary (see Fig. 5.2, above) may seem backwards because it is often thought that innate features facilitate the acquisition of phonological patterns by narrowing the search space and providing an alphabet with which to construct phonological patterns. This is a line of thinking

---

[1] If they are not recategorized, the result can be conventionalized coarticulation, which, like assimilation, is language-specific.

that has leaked over from syntactic theory. While syntax is recursive and generates infinitely many utterances, phonology is finite, and a comparatively easy problem for the language learner to tackle. See Blevins (2004) for more discussion on this topic.

Emergent features also raise questions about contrast. In innate feature theories, contrastive segments in inventories are built out of distinctive features. If only the features which are motivated by phonological patterns emerge, then there is no guarantee that all segments will be contrastive. Jakobson (1942) motivates features on the basis of the assumptions that unmotivated oppositions, such as those between phonemes, are taxing to memory and processing; reducing the number of oppositions by introducing features reduces the cognitive load. However, memory capacity is not as scarce as it was thought to be during most of the last century. For example, Wang et al. (2003) report that the memory capacity of the human brain is something along the lines of $10^{8,432}$ bits of information. Further, there is evidence that a wide array of details of spoken and written language are stored. Listeners remember details of voice quality which relate to information about age, sex, emotional state, region of origin, and social status, and readers remember fonts and the location of words on a page. Both these types of memory have been demonstrated in the laboratory (see Goldinger 1997 and references cited).

In accordance with these advancements in the study of memory and its relationship with language, most modern psychological models of phonology involve the storage of chunks larger than segments, such as whole words and even multiple exemplars of whole phonemes and words. It is an open question, then, whether speech sounds need to be contrastive in terms of features that are not relevant for phonological alternations, or whether they can simply contrast as whole segments or words. If the former turns out to be true (and this is suggested by Pulleyblank's 2003 study of covert feature effects), it is straightforward to include in emergent feature theory the emergence of features which are necessary to distinguish contrasting sounds but are not necessary to formulate any rules or constraints. This is empirically testable. If phonological features are important for phonological patterns but not for contrast, then speakers are expected to be more sensitive to abstract features that are involved in a phonological pattern than to those that are not.

5.4 Reinterpreting formal phonology

In most innate distinctive feature theories (e.g. Chomsky and Halle 1968), the features are universal cognitive entities specified in Universal Grammar which are directly related to their phonetic correlates, and which are the building blocks of phonological patterns. In emergent feature theory, features exist only as needed by a given language, but, as in innate feature theories, they correspond to phonological patterns. Phonetically grounded features are indirectly related to their phonetic correlates via the phonetically driven sound changes or analogical changes that produced the phonological patterns they refer to (Fig. 5.2, above). In innate feature theories, features are innately tied to their phonetic correlates, and phonological patterns are built directly out of features. The relationship between phonetics and phonological patterns is not direct, and is usually only invoked to account for things that cannot be accounted for with features as the sole intermediary. In emergent feature theory, phonological patterns emerge from sound change and analogical change, shaped by a range of external factors (Fig. 5.2 above) which are necessary anyway to account for exceptions to innate feature theories. The language user's internalization of the phonological pattern that arose this way uses features which are needed to describe the pattern. The phonetic content of the features is mediated by the phonological pattern, which may reflect its phonetic origins.

The discovery of distinctive features in the twentieth century was interpreted by many linguists as a discovery about Universal Grammar, about the nature of the innately determined building blocks of phonological patterns. This discovery is reinterpreted in emergent feature theory as a discovery about common and uncommon phonological patterns, which is in turn related to common and uncommon diachronic changes. Features which have often been thought to be innate and explanatory are created by learners in response to a phonological pattern. Innate feature theory's universal features are properties of sounds which are likely to be grouped in sound change or likely to be generalized to. The study of emergent features can continue from just where innate features stand. Arguments for innate features are directly translatable into arguments for why certain phonological patterns are likely to emerge.

Interpreting feature organization in emergent feature theory is similar. As discussed above, the organization of features in most versions of Feature Geometry mimics the organization of the vocal tract. As Clements (1985) argued in the original Feature Geometry proposal, the features which are grouped together are articulatorily dependent on one another, and the features which are under separate nodes (e.g. place features and laryngeal features) are articulatorily independent. By including this as part of Universal Grammar, these articulatory dependencies are given two opportunities to manifest themselves: first, by virtue of the fact that articulatorily independent parameters are far less likely to be involved in the same phonological patterns than articulatorily dependent ones, and second, because the same facts, in abstract form, are in Universal Grammar as the framework in which the resulting rules are stated.

Moving from innate features to emergent features eliminates the second opportunity but not the first. In this view, including the articulatory organization in Universal Grammar is redundant. The interdependency of articulatory parameters would be expected to influence which phonological patterns are most common regardless of whether it is repeated in UG. If an innate feature organization imposed structure on phonological patterns above and beyond what is explainable on the basis of physiology, we would expect two things to be true. First, spoken and sign language phonology would both show evidence of the same abstract feature organization, instead of only showing evidence of feature organization which is directly motivated by the modality of each language. Second, acoustic and auditory features would show evidence of feature organization. Since these are generally not observed, we can conclude that feature organization is limited to explaining facts which are already explained by modality-specific articulatory facts.[2] That being said, there is nothing wrong with describing assimilatory processes using articulatorily motivated feature hierarchies. Indeed, this is what Feature Geometry was designed for, and modeling the many naturally occurring phonological patterns which reflect human physiology is something it is well suited to doing. But the assumption that there is a single feature organization to handle all phonological phenomena is not supported. In fact, there is evidence for many of the models that have been proposed. There are many different ways to generalize across different segments, and different models capture different possible generalizations. The mistake is to treat these models as mutually exclusive. For example, competing approaches to place of articulation are compared in Chapter 6, and it is seen that the subgroupings predicted by different approaches are all observed; what is not seen is any evidence of a prohibition against subgroupings not predicted by a particular model.

The representations provided by innate feature theories often work because the articulatory facts they incorporate may have been involved in the diachronic changes which created the phonological pattern, not because the feature organization model represents language processing or is more explanatory than the articulatory basis for it, or because assimilatory phonological patterns are in any way limited to those which are expressible in this framework. Table 5.1 summarizes the main points of innate feature theory and emergent feature theory.

[2] One exception is the use of a Peripheral node in Feature Geometry (e.g. Rice 1999, and in the description of many Australian languages) for labial and dorsal segments. These are clearly not an articulatory natural class, but they do have acoustic similarities (the basis for the feature [grave]). However, Peripheral is used in Rice's theory not for phonetic reasons, or even necessarily in the interest of forming natural classes, but rather to facilitate the correlation of structure with markedness. Indeed, velars (the unmarked counterpart of marked dorsals), which share the acoustic properties represented by [grave], do not bear the Peripheral node, because they do not behave as marked. Consequently, Peripheral should not be interpreted as an instance of acoustic or auditory facts playing a role in feature organization.

TABLE 5.1 Summary of main points of innate feature theory and emergent feature theory

	Innate feature theory	Emergent feature theory
Features...	...are universal cognitive entities specified in Universal Grammar.	...are properties of sounds which are likely to be grouped in sound change or generalization.
	...are innate and explanatory.	...are created by learners in response to phonological patterns.
The discovery of features...	...is a discovery about Universal Grammar.	...is a discovery about common and uncommon phonological patterns, in turn related to common and uncommon diachronic changes.
Phonetic correlates...	...are directly and innately tied to features.	...are indirectly related to features via the phonetically driven changes.
Phonological patterns...	...are built directly out of features.	...are the basis for abstract generalizations (features).
Phonetics and phonological patterns...	...are related through features, but may also be related through diachronic changes (when necessary).	...are related through diachronic changes.
Interdependency of articulatory parameters...	...is stated in Universal Grammar (as feature organization).	...is part of the reality of speech production, directly affecting the development of phonological patterns.

Many issues that have been analyzed in innate features are directly translatable to an account involving emergent features. At the beginning of this chapter it was seen that certain features readily emerge as the result of common sound changes. While features such as [nasal] are frequently observed spreading in synchronic phonology, others, such as [consonantal], are seldom if ever seen spreading. This has caused some phonologists to argue that the latter is not a feature (see Hume and Odden 1996; cf. Kaisse 1992). While [consonantal] is not prone to spreading, it is often used to describe classes. Formal models of innate features do not account for why a feature might define classes but never spread, but this is straightforward in emergent feature theory. While the phonetic properties associated with [consonantal] may be salient enough to be involved in generalizations (and therefore define natural classes), there may be no sound changes which involve the phonologization of phonetic effects related just to the correlates of the feature [consonantal]. In emergent feature theory, there is no contradiction in saying that [consonantal] is useful for defining classes but seldom if ever spreads, because features involved in spreading and features involved mostly in defining natural classes emerge in different ways (coarticulation and generalization, respectively). The distribution of commonly emerging features in these two scenarios is an interesting question for future research.

5.5 Formalization

5.5.1 *Accounting for language data*

Emergent feature theory abandons some of the assumptions of recent mainstream phonological theory, but adopting it does not radically change the approach to phonological analysis. Decades of work have resulted in a list of common phonological features. It only makes sense for these features to be the starting point for a formal analysis of phonological phenomena. But there is no sense in forcing the features on data for which it is clearly ill suited.

Studying phonology is like studying birds. Years of research have produced an inventory of recognized bird species. There are common birds and there are rare birds, and there are species which have yet to be discovered. It would be absurd to approach ornithology with a list of the twenty-five most common species and force every bird encountered into one of these categories. It would be equally absurd to ignore the existing taxonomy and start afresh with each specimen encountered. The balanced approach is to expect birds to fall into one of the many categories already identified, but to allow for the possibility that new species will be discovered.

In phonology it is reasonable to suspect that new phonological patterns will resemble the ones we already know about, but it is important to be ready to describe phenomena in their own terms if they do not fit the existing taxonomy, which is of course based on incomplete data—the data did not include the new phenomenon being studied. While phonetic factors are expected to be applicable in many different languages, there are other factors which may be very relevant to a particular language's sound system, such as high frequency, which do not translate at all to universally preferred phonological patterns. Accounting for the phonological patterns within a language is primary, and can be informed by expectations gleaned from crosslinguistic studies, but these expectations should never override language-internal evidence. This marks a return to Jakobson's (1942: 241) view that "[t]he description of a system of values and the classification of its elements can be made only from that system's own perspective".

Naming phonological features is not necessary for creating an analysis of a particular language, and implicitly acknowledges features as independent entities. In the innate features approach, using named features has explanatory value. In emergent feature theory, names are a descriptive convention rather than a source of explanation. Understanding why a particular type of phonological pattern is common or rare or why it interacts with other phonological patterns in certain ways is still very important; but by removing explanation from the cognitive representation, the cognitive representation is left freer and better able to deal with things like variation. Below is an illustration of how a phonological pattern can be analyzed in emergent feature theory, compared with how it would be analyzed with innate features. The emergent features approach crucially does not say anything about how the sound patterns are processed, leaving this to be filled in on the basis of research about processing, instead of filling it in on the basis of typology.

In the Dravidian language Tulu (Bright 1972), the high unrounded central or back vowel [ɨ] is labialized if the preceding syllable contains either a labial consonant or a rounded vowel, as in (31).

(31) Labialization in Tulu

a.	naːɖɨ	'country'	b.	bolpu	'whiteness'
	kaʈʈɨ	'bond'		kappu	'blackness'
	pudarɨ	'name'		uccu	[kind of snake]
	ugarɨ	'brackish'		moroɖu	'empty'
	ari-n-ɨ	'rice' (acc.)		uːru-n-u	'country village' (acc.)

One of the breakthroughs enabled by Unified Feature Theory was the non-arbitrary representation of consonant–vowel interactions involving corresponding places of articulation. Intuitively, it does not seem coincidental that labial consonants and round (labial) vowels both condition rounding (labialization) of a vowel. In *SPE*, labiality in consonants is represented by [+anterior, −coronal], while labiality in vowels is represented by [+round]. Consequently, the *SPE* formalization of Tulu vowel rounding does not express the fact that round vowels and labial consonants both involve labiality, and there is no natural class of labial consonants and round vowels. The formulation of the class requires the disjunction of two feature bundles to achieve the union of two natural classes, as in the *SPE* formulation of the Tulu rule in Fig. 5.9.

In Unified Feature Theory, this sound pattern is treated as a single process conditioned by all labial segments (labial consonants and round vowels). This

$$i \rightarrow [+\text{round}] \; / \; \left\{ \begin{array}{c} \begin{bmatrix} -\text{voc} \\ +\text{ant} \\ -\text{cor} \end{bmatrix} \\ \begin{bmatrix} -\text{cons} \\ +\text{rnd} \end{bmatrix} \end{array} \right\} \; C_0 \, -\!\!-$$

FIGURE 5.9 Tulu rounding in *SPE*

is made possible by positing that consonants and vowels possess the same innate features for place of articulation. The formalization in Unified Feature Theory (based on Clements 1990: 84 and Clements and Hume 1995) is simple, and does not treat the involvement of labial consonants and round vowels as a coincidence (Fig. 5.10).

The Unified Feature Theory account leaves something to be desired, too. While it allows the more elegant representation of many assimilatory phonological patterns, captures insights overlooked by previous feature theories, and treats the rounding triggers in Tulu as a natural class (which *SPE* cannot do), it is able to represent fewer phonologically active classes than *SPE*, as shown in Chapter 6 (63.71 percent as opposed to 70.98 percent). While allowing elegant and explanatory formalizations of certain phenomena, theories which limit the features available to formulate rules render many other naturally occurring phonological patterns inexpressible. These theories require recourse to other mechanisms such as feature disjunction and direct historical explanation to account for these cases.

Stampe's (1979) *Natural Phonology* makes this a distinction between two formally recognized components of phonological systems: processes and rules. Processes are innate phonological patterns which are grounded in limitations on speech production, and rules are non-innate idiosyncratic processes. Processes are "constraints which the speaker brings to the language", and rules are "constraints which the language brings to the speaker" (Stampe 1979: 47). Despite the sharp distinction drawn in this and other

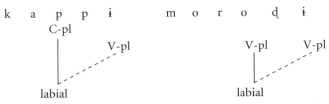

FIGURE 5.10 Tulu rounding in Unified Feature Theory

theories of phonology, there is little evidence beyond crosslinguistic frequency of occurrence (which does not support a sharp distinction anyway) to support a distinction. As will be seen in the next two chapters, some classes are indeed much more common than others, but there is no boundary at which to draw a distinction between core and marginal classes.

In emergent feature theory, the crosslinguistic preference for phonetically natural phonological patterns has a historical explanation, namely that the language has been spoken by humans with similar limitations, and has evolved to reflect that. In the terms of *Natural Phonology,* emergent feature theory asserts that *all* of the rules of the language are "brought to the speaker". It is just that some of the rules are particularly well suited to the speaker's physiology, because the language has been spoken for millennia by physiologically similar humans. The random changes which have been conventionalized tend to reflect that.

By incorporating the natural/unnatural distinction into the synchronic formalization/cognitive representation, innate feature theories prevent the representation of less common processes, or at the very least make the prediction that rarer phenomena should be dispreferred synchronically. So while the *SPE* account fails to express that the grouping of labial consonants and vowels is nonarbitrary, the Unified Feature Theory account does not express that the grouping of labial consonants and vowels *is* largely arbitrary synchronically (and is not intended to express this). The failure to recognize synchronic arbitrariness, and therefore the failure to represent less common sound patterns, is the basis of Vaux's (2002) critique of Optimality Theory (Prince and Smolensky 1993) and Articulatory Phonology (Browman and Goldstein 1992). If there truly is a distinction between classes that innate features are or are not accountable for, there should be a theory-external way to distinguish them.

One of the predictions of innate feature theory is that featurally natural sound patterns should be easier to acquire, because the features to represent them are already present in UG. Idiosyncratic diachronic residues would require a different kind of memorization. Experimental evidence suggests that phonetically unnatural sound patterns are readily learnable (Onishi et al. 2002, Peperkamp and Dupoux, 2007). Further, unnatural sound patterns are well attested, and have been shown to be stable (see e.g. Bach and Harms 1972, Buckley 2000). Survey evidence also does not support the natural/unnatural distinction among phonologically active classes (below). While studies such as Onishi et al. (2002) and Peperkamp and Dupoux (2007) have shown that phonetically unnatural sound patterns are learnable, others, such as Saffran and Thiessen (2003) and Wilson (2003), have shown that natural patterns may in fact be easier to learn. The finding that phonetically natural patterns are easier to learn is consistent with the *prevalence* of phonetically natural patterns in human languages (although learnability is not the only available explanation for their abundance), and the finding that phonetically unnatural classes are nonethless learnable is consistent with the *existence* of phonetically unnatural patterns in human languages. However, no study has shown a clear boundary between easily learned patterns or less easily learned patterns, or a sharp difference in learnability that is directly attributable to featural naturalness.

A goal of emergent feature theory is to permit the recognition of facts such as the crosslinguistic preference for phonetically natural classes (such as the class of labial segments) without letting this interfere with description of the synchronic grammar, for example by ruling out attested phonological patterns, making unsupported predictions about the processing of rare phenomena, or having difficulty dealing with variation.

Emergent feature theory makes use of the external factors listed in Fig. 5.2, and the model in which these factors participate is described in more detail in Chapter 8. Each of the external factors is viewed as a filter/prism, which filters and distorts language data in the production/perception cycle and presents the opportunity for a change driven by one or more filter to become conventionalized. This model is able to account for the fact that the class of rounding triggers in Tulu is phonetically natural in a way that is related to the phonological pattern. It is hypothesized that the sound change emerged in the following way, illustrated in Fig. 5.11. Prior to the diachronic changes that gave rise to the rounding pattern, the labial articulation of labial consonants and round vowels for the most part did not overlap with the unrounded high vowel (Stage 1). Later, gestural overlap, represented in the model by the COORDINATION Filter/Prism, causes some rounding on the vowel in some instances when it is near a segment with a labial gesture (Stage 2). It can spread past non-labial segments because the labial gesture does not interfere with their production. For unrelated social reasons, represented by the SOCIAL IDENTITY Filter/Prism, this pattern catches on. The social factors are crucial, although how they relate to phonology may be unpredictable. Gestural overlap is very common and usually does not result in a widespread change in linguistic norms (see e.g. Ohala 2003). Next, this slightly rounded $[\dot{\text{i}}^w]$ is reinterpreted as $[\text{u}]$ (Stage 3).

Coarticulatory rounding presumably affects other vowels as well, such as the high front vowel $[\text{i}]$. The fact that only the back vowel rounding was phonologized can be attributed to $[\dot{\text{i}}^w]$ vs. $[\text{u}]$ being less perceptually distinct than $[\text{i}^w]$ vs. $[\text{y}]$, or to the presence of a phoneme $/\text{u}/$ in the language and absence of $/\text{y}/$. In the latter case, $[\text{u}]$ is more *expected* than $[\text{y}]$, and so it is more likely that an

Stage 1: lip gesture generally does not overlap with [ɨ].

Stage 2: COORDINATION causes coarticulation, reinforced by SOCIAL IDENTITY.

Stage 3: AUDITION, ATTENTION, and/or CATEGORIZATION cause reinterpretation of [ɨʷ] as [u], reinforced by SOCIAL IDENTITY.

Stage 4: High back vowel is always [u] after when preceding syllable contains a labial segment.

FIGURE 5.11 Hypothetical developments in Tulu

ambiguous vowel will be categorized as /u/ than as /y/, since /u/ is an existing category and /y/ is not (see Hume 2004a for a much more complete discussion). The AUDITION/ATTENTION and CATEGORIZATION Filter/Prisms are all inclined to favor reinterpretation of [ɨʷ] as [u], subject to the approval of the SOCIAL IDENTITY Filter/Prism. Finally, the language has a phonological pattern in which /ɨ/ is [u] when preceded in the previous syllable by a labial segment (Stage 4). If rounding is also seen in new words or derivations, this is the result of analogy with existing forms, not coarticulation.

Alternatively, this type of phonological pattern could start on a more limited scale, either in terms of adjacency or in terms of the size of the trigger class, before being generalized to something like the modern Tulu pattern. An alternative in which only adjacent coarticulation is phonologized is shown in Fig. 5.12. This leads to a phonological pattern in which [u] occurs instead of [ɨ] only *immediately* after labial segments. The situations in which [u] occurs include some but not all situations in which the preceding syllable contains a labial segment, and may be generalized to include all cases where the preceding syllable contains a labial segment, formalized with the CATEGORIZATION and SOCIAL IDENTITY Filter/Prisms. The end result is the same as the end result in Fig. 5.11, although the non-adjacent vowel never went through a coarticulation

Stage 2: Conventionalized coarticulation only affects adjacent vowels.

Stage 4: High back vowel is always [u] after when preceding *segment* is labial.

Stage 5: Adjacent assimilation is reinterpreted to include nonadjacent preceding segments as triggers (a generalization represented by the CATEGORIZATION).

FIGURE 5.12 Hypothetical developments in Tulu: Alternate Reality A

stage, but was included by analogy with the already phonologized adjacent vowel.

Another possibility is for coarticulation only to be conventionalized in the case of preceding labial vowels but not labial consonants (Fig. 5.13), resulting in the corresponding phonological pattern. The situations in which [u] occurs includes some but not all situations in which the preceding syllable contains a labial segment (only the ones in which the segment is a vowel), and may be generalized to include all cases where the preceding syllable contains any labial segment, formalized with the CATEGORIZATION and SOCIAL IDENTITY

Stage 2: Coarticulation conventionalized only after vowels.

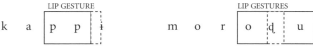

Stage 4: High back vowel is always [u] after when preceding syllable contains a labial *vowel*.

Stage 5: Assimilation triggered by labial vowels is reinterpreted to include labial consonants too (another generalization represented by CATEGORIZATION).

FIGURE 5.13 Hypothetical developments in Tulu: Alternate Reality B

Filter/Prisms. The end result is the same as the end results in Figs. 5.11 and 5.12, although the words containing a labial consonant but no labial vowel never went through a coarticulation stage, but were generalized directly.

All three of these scenarios result in the same synchronic pattern, and the language learner does not need to be concerned with the trajectory of the changes that led to the present language. Hypothesizing about the origins of phonological patterns as in Figs. 5.11–5.13 is no substitute for actual historical reconstruction, but neither is the use of synchronic formalisms that usurp historical explanation. The true scenario is unknown, and different languages may have similar patterns as a result of different historical developments. Synchronic formalisms which make phonetically natural phonological patterns simpler to represent are similar to those which recapitulate historical change.[3] These formalisms are not ideal as a model of cognitive representation (unless motivated by performance or other evidence), because they collapse information into the synchronic grammar that already exists elsewhere. The stages in between 1 and 4 are important for accounting for why such a pattern exists, but they are not relevant for describing the synchronic pattern or accounting for how a language user processes it. These are different questions which require different kinds of evidence. If the diachronic changes had been different, and coarticulation involving a different set of consonants (e.g. labial consonants and high round vowels but not mid round vowels) had been conventionalized, the synchronic phonological pattern would involve a different set of segments. Certainly the sequence of diachronic changes would be expected to be more complicated, but incorporating this into the synchronic grammar would require evidence that this situation is more complicated for the language user. In Tulu, the language user knows that high back vowels following syllables that contain /p b v m u uː o oː/ are round. From a synchronic perspective, it could just as easily be /p b v m u uː/ or /p b m u uː o oː/. As shown in the survey results, languages are able to handle rules which refer to very strange sets of segments. In emergent feature theory, this historical information is formalized as historical information, and the synchronic grammar reflects only synchronically available information. How the phonological patterns are represented in the mind of the language user is an interesting question, and one that is likely easier to address when historical explanations are removed from the synchronic grammar.

5.5.2 *Toward a cognitive representation of phonology*

In generative phonology, the explanation for recurrent phonological patterns and the cognitive representation of phonological patterns have generally been treated as one and the same. In emergent feature theory, as in some other

---

[3] See Anderson 1981, Blevins 2004, and Vaux 2002 for further arguments along these lines.

frameworks (see e.g. Hume and Johnson 2001c, Blevins 2004), much of the explanation resides elsewhere. While the language learner must construct a grammar based on language data, acquisition does not involve eliminating phonological patterns which are inexpressible in any innate feature framework. Instead, phonological patterns already exist in the language before the learner learns them, and at the extreme, phonological acquisition may be as trivial as learning all the words in the language. We know that some data compression does occur (i.e. every single utterance is not stored independently), evidenced by under- and over-generalizations seen frequently in language acquisition and occasionally in language change.

Since the typology of phonological patterns can be accounted for by factors that are largely external, typology is less relevant for understanding the cognitive representation of language. There is no shortage of competing models of cognitive representation of phonology, such as rule-based derivational phonology, Optimality Theory, and lexicon-based phonology. The first two, especially Optimality Theory, have relied heavily on typology for insight into the cognitive representation. If explanation for typology is removed from the cognitive representation, a move that is supported here (and also advocated for OT by e.g. Myers 2002), then this approach to understanding the cognitive representation broadly using typology can be viewed as wrong-headed.

History and typology are separate areas of study. If typology is to explained, then the mental representation of phonology is somewhat tangential, although it may hold some clues as to why phonological patterns are as they are. If the mental representation is to be explained, then there are better places to look than typology, because typology is the result of so many different factors. Phonological variation provides insight into how phonological patterns are stored and used. Experimental evidence can also tap into the mental representation of phonology. Both approaches should be pursued in order to understand the cognitive representation of phonology.

5.6 Summary

Emergent feature theory allows the separation of explanation from cognitive representation, and draws upon different sources of explanation for typological observations. Features and classes emerge from phonetically driven sound change and from generalization along different dimensions. As has been shown, description of phonological phenomena in emergent feature theory is very similar to description with innate features. While explanation is located outside the speaker in many cases (contrary to innate feature theory), many of the insights of innate feature theory exist independent of innate features, and are available to account for the emergence of features. By abandoning innate features as a source of explanation, emergent feature theory opens up new sources of explanation in formal phonology, without losing most of the insights of innate feature theory. Emergent feature theory is not a rejection of the work of Jakobson, Halle, Clements, and many others, but a continuation of it.

6

General survey results

Models with innate distinctive features assert that the phonological behavior of segments is predicted by their features, while in emergent feature theory, sound change and generalization provides the opportunity for segments to be grouped with sounds that are similar along some dimension, and therefore the behavior (and feature specification) of a segment can only be determined by observing the behavior. Quite a bit is known about what groupings are especially likely, as a result of innate feature theory work. Innate features and emergent features make very different predictions about the results of the survey of phonologically active classes, and it will be seen below that the results generally support emergent features over innate ones.

6.1 Predictions of different models

Innate and emergent feature models make different predictions about what types of phonological pattern are expected to occur and recur. The innate features approach predicts that certain classes of sounds (those which are expressible with the features of a given theory) may recur (Fig. 6.1, boxy shapes), and other classes occur only as historical accidents. Groupings inside the box are expected and groupings outside the box are not. In emergent feature theory, all classes are historical accidents, and some accidents are more likely than others. Emergent feature theory predicts that some classes are more likely than others to arise through language change, but none are explicitly ruled out (Fig. 6.1, curve). The shape of the distribution predicted by the innate features approach is not uncontroversial. The stepped box shape corresponds to Sagey's (1986) proposal that the simplicity of the representation predicts the frequency of the phono-logical pattern, i.e. that classes defined by few features should be more frequent than classes requiring many features. Other approaches which do not include Sagey's prediction simply assert that some classes are possible and some are not. In this case a rectangle is a more appropriate representation. This approach still requires a theory such as emergent feature theory to predict which of these classes are expected to be common, as it is clear that all expected classes

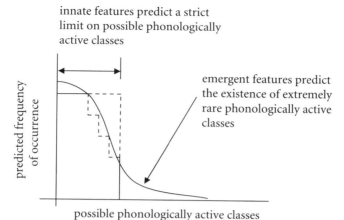

innate features predict a strict
limit on possible phonologically
active classes

emergent features predict
the existence of extremely
rare phonologically active
classes

predicted frequency
of occurrence

possible phonologically active classes

FIGURE 6.1 Predicted phonologically active classes

are not equally frequent. Emergent feature theory makes these predictions on the basis of phonetic facts and other information, but also holds that given these predictions, a separate innate feature theory is no longer needed. As will be seen below, the distribution of classes in the database, when analyzed in three different feature theories, matches the prediction of emergent feature theory each time.

Many approaches to innate features allow for the existence of unnatural classes as idiosyncrasies or historical oddities. If so, it is expected that there should be an identifiable boundary between the "natural" classes that are predicted by features and the idiosyncratic "unnatural" classes that are not. Innate feature theories also predict the occurrence of some apparent natural classes which are actually the union of two or more classes (formalized as a disjunction of feature bundles). In the event that two natural classes are affected by the same type of process, it would appear that the union of those two classes, perhaps an unnatural one, would be acting as a class. These cases are expected to be uncommon and, if they are recurrent, to involve the union of fairly common natural classes. The unnatural classes allowed by innate feature theory require and generally receive a historical explanation which is very similar to their explanation in emergent feature theory. Instead of two separate methods for accounting for common and rare classes, emergent feature theory accounts for both with the same mechanism.

Optimality Theory predicts unnatural-looking classes as a result of constraint interaction. Featurally unnatural classes would occur when a constraint referring to a natural class is dominated by an antagonistic constraint referring to a natural class which partially overlaps the first class. By preventing segments in the overlap region from participating in the phonological pattern mandated by the lower-ranked constraint, the higher-ranked constraint causes an L-shaped class to emerge, one which may not be specifiable with a conjunction of features, but which can be specified by subtracting one natural class from another. Similar to the case of unions, if these classes can be attributed to constraint interaction, it is expected that the component classes of recurring L-shaped unnatural classes will be very common ones. Flemming (2005) discusses differences between natural classes which result from features and apparent natural classes which result from constraint interaction.

    While innate feature theory predicts that the classes which can recur are those which are specifiable with a conjunction of innate features, emergent feature theory predicts that the most common classes will be those with identifiable phonetic similarities between the members. This may result from phonetically conditioned sound change or from generalization to phonetically similar segments. It also predicts that certain social factors and factors such as frequency could select which segments participate in a class. Because these factors depend on particular societies and language systems, it is not easy to make crosslinguistic predictions involving them. Similarly, it is expected that individual cases with complicated historical sources (which obscure phonetic similarity) will also be seen.

    Innate feature theories predict different possible subgroupings of segments, depending on what features or feature organizations are posited. For example, *Preliminaries to Speech Analysis* (Jakobson et al. 1952) predicts that labials and velars will pattern together as a result of the acoustic similarities represented by the feature [grave]. Unified Feature Theory (Clements 1990, Hume 1994, Clements and Hume 1995) does not make this prediction, because there is no node in the feature hierarchy which dominates [Labial] and [Dorsal] but not [Coronal]. But if a Lingual node is posited, coronals and velars are predicted to pattern together to the exclusion of labials. Likewise, *SPE* (Chomsky and Halle 1968) predicts that labials and anterior coronals will pattern together, due to the feature [+anterior], which covers labials as well as dentals and alveolars. All three of these subgroupings have clear phonetic correlates. Innate feature theories predict that only the subgroupings which have features or nodes associated with them will occur with greater than chance frequency.[1] Emergent feature theory predicts all three, because all three have clear phonetic correlates. Other subgroupings of places of articulation sharing acoustic or articulatory properties are also expected to occur more often than chance.

---

[1] In some approaches to features, segments which all lack a particular feature are expected to pattern together, but only in terms of failing to block the association of other features.

TABLE 6.1 Summary of predictions of innate feature theory and emergent feature theory

	Innate feature theory	Emergent feature theory
Common classes...	...can be specified by a conjunction of features in a particular theory.	....involve segments with clear phonetic similarities.
Uncommon classes...	...result from historical oddities, *or* from the union of more common classes, *or* from the subtraction of one more common class from another.	...involve segments with *less* clear similarities.
The common/ uncommon boundary...	...is clear, because common and uncommon classes have very different sources.	...does not exist, because common and uncommon classes have the same source.
Subgroupings (of place)...	...which correspond to features or nodes in a particular theory may recur. Others may not.	...involving segments with clear phonetic similarities are more common than others.
Ambivalent segments...	...are not predicted by phonetic ambiguity and should be equally common with all segments.	...are those which are not prototypical examples of either value of a feature.

As seen in Chapter 4, emergent feature theory correctly predicts that segments which are not prototypical examples of either value of a feature will be more prone to patterning ambivalently. Innate feature theories do not predict this type of behavior, because the explanation for the classes is the feature system itself, rather than the phonetic properties. The predictions made by the two approaches to features are summarized in Table 6.1. It will be seen below that the predictions of emergent feature theory are generally borne out in the survey results.

6.2 Overview

The survey involves several thousand sound patterns. Many of these are distributional patterns only, and these classes are substantially more idiosyncratic than the classes which are targets or triggers for phonological alternations. The results reported in this book are limited to classes of segments which participate in alternations as targets or triggers, and these classes are sufficient to address the questions asked here. If it turned out that the classes

TABLE 6.2 The ability of three feature systems to characterize 6,077 phonologically active classes with a conjunction of distinctive features

Feature system	Characterizable (Natural)		Non-characterizable (Unnatural)	
Preliminaries	3,640	59.90%	2,437	40.10%
SPE	4,313	70.97%	1,764	29.03%
Unified Feature Theory	3,872	63.72%	2,205	36.28%
ANY SYSTEM	4,579	75.35%	1,498	24.65%

involved in alternations are easily accounted for in the feature theories, a case could still be made that the classes involved in distributional patterns are not accounted for so easily. Since many of the classes involved in alternations are not easily accounted for in the feature theories, the classes involved only in distributional patterns are superfluous for the current study. The differences between classes involved in distributional patterns and classes involved in alternations are an interesting area for further study.

Often several sound patterns in a particular language involve the same set of segments. In the results reported here, these classes are each counted only once. Limiting the analysis to classes involved in alternations and counting each group of segments only once (even if it is involved in many different sound patterns) results in 6,077 distinct classes. Of these classes, more than one quarter cannot be described as a conjunction of features in any of the three feature theories, indicating that "unnatural" classes are not as marginal as they are often assumed to be. The success rates of the three theories are shown in Table 6.2. *Preliminaries* features are able to characterize slightly less than 60 percent of the classes in the survey as natural classes. *SPE* fares better, being able to characterize slightly more than 70 percent, and Unified Feature Theory characterizes almost 64 percent. For each feature theory, the remainder of the observed phonologically active classes are considered unnatural. Slighly less than 25 percent of the classes are unnatural in all three theories. The next section looks at the featurally unnatural classes in more detail.

6.3 Unnatural classes

The analysis of classes in the survey turns up a wide range of classes that cannot be accounted for by traditional distinctive features. From a phonetic standpoint, they range from the crazy to the sensible, with those on the sensible end being more prone to being found in multiple languages. This section showcases some of the crazier classes as well as some of the more frequent "unnatural" classes in the database. Where possible, these examples include alternations. When examples of alternations are not available, the underlying forms posited by the grammar authors are given, and the reader is referred to these sources for more motivation of the underlying forms.

6.3.1 *Crazy classes*

One crazy class is found in Kolami, where the suffix /-(u)l/ is a plural marker for a variety of nouns. The allomorphy is phonologically conditioned, with nouns ending in /ṭ ḍ ṇ r l i e a/ taking [-l] and nouns ending in /p ṯ k ḍ g s v z m ŋ j/ taking [-ul] (Emeneau 1961: 46–50), as shown in (32). The two classes are shown in the context of Kolami's segment inventory in Fig. 6.2. Other consonants and vowels in the language do not occur word-finally in this class of nouns.

(32)   Kolami plural allomorphy
    a. [-l] after /ṭ ḍ ṇ r l i e a/

singular	plural	
ḍuṭ	ḍuṭl	'hip'
eḍ	eḍl	'bullock'
toːreṇ	toːreṇl	'younger brother'
sir	siḍl	'female buffalo'
kaje	kayel	'fish'
biːam	biːl	'rice'
kala	kalal	'dream'

    b. [-ul] after /p ṯ k ḍ g s v z m ŋ j/

singular	plural	
roːp	roːpul	'plant'
keṯ	keṯul	'winnowing fan'
maːk	maːkul	'tree'
mooḍ	mooḍul	'man of particular exogamous division'
ḍeg	ḍegul	'heap, mass'
kis	kisul	'fire'
aːv	aːvul	'fathom'
gaːz	gaːzul	'bangle'
ḍem	ḍemul	'one draw on a pipe'
nenjeŋ	nenjeŋul	'meat'
poj	pojul	'hearth'

Even if one allomorph is treated as basic, the class of segments that needs to be referred to in order to derive the other allomorph is not specifiable with a

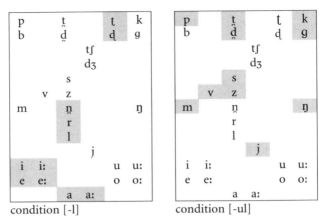

condition [-l]   condition [-ul]

FIGURE 6.2 A phonologically active classes in Kolami

conjunction of any traditional distinctive features. For example, the dental and alveolar nasal and liquids condition the [-l] allomorph, but cannot be excluded from the set of segments which condition [-ul] without also excluding the dental stops, which do condition [-ul].

Another very unnatural class occurs naturally in Evenki (Nedjalkov 1997: 320, 175). In this case, suffix-initial /v s g/ change to nasals when they follow nasal consonants, but other consonants do not nasalize in this position (33). This class, shown in Fig. 6.3, is far from being specifiable with traditional distinctive features. /g/ is distinguished from /d/ only by place of articulation, but ruling out /d/ on the basis of place would exclude other alveolars, such as /s/, which *is* included in the class.

(33)   Evenki consonant nasalization
    a. /v s g/ nasalize after nasals:

/oron-vA/[2]	→	oron-mo	'the reindeer (acc. def.)'
/oron-vi/	→	oron-mi	'one's own reindeer'
/ŋanakin-si/	→	ŋanakin-ni	'your dog'
/oron-gatʃin/	→	oron-ŋatʃin	'like a/the reindeer'

    cf. /girki-vi/ → girki-vi 'one's own friend'
        /lamu-gatʃin/ → lamu-gatʃin 'like a/the sea'

    b. Other consonants do not:
        /amkin-du/ → amkin-du 'bed (dative)'
        /ekun-da/ → ekun-da 'somebody/something/anything'

[2] /A/ is an archiphoneme whose phonetic realization is determined by the preceding harmonic vowel.

FIGURE 6.3 A phonologically active class in Evenki

In River West Tarangan (Nivens 1992: 219), /m/ assimilates in place to following /t̪ g s j/ when they are brought together by reduplication, as shown in (34). Assimilation to /t̪/ is obligatory while assimilation to /g s j/ is optional. Assimilated and unassimilated forms are in variation in some cases (e.g. "overcast", "rub", "female"), while assimilated and unassimilated forms are obligatory in others (e.g. "east" vs. "ant"). Place assimilation does not occur when /m/ precedes other consonants, although /n/ and /ŋ/ do undergo place assimilation in different, more restricted sets of environments. The class of segments which trigger place assimilation in /m/ is shown in the context of the consonant inventory in Fig. 6.4. The class is unnatural whether or not /t̪/ is included. Separate processes affect the reduplicant, altering vowel quality and deleting certain vowels and glides. The intermediate stage in (34) occurs after these changes and before the place assimilation. The place assimilation appears in the difference between the intermediate stage and the surface form.

(34) River West Tarangan nasal place assimilation
    a. /m/ may assimilate in place to /t̪ g s j/:
       /RED+bitem/   → bimtem   → [bintém] 'DUP small'
       /ɸaɸa+RED+   → ɸaɸamjɛmnə   → [ɸaɸanjemnə]'overcast 3s'
       jɛm+na/
                                        ∼ [ɸaɸamjemnə]
       /jɛr+RED+gum/ → jɛrgimgum   → [jɛrgiŋgum]'DUP NF rub'
                                        ∼ [jɛrgimgum]
       /RED+simar/   → simsimər   → [simsimər]'DUP east'
       /RED+sima/   → simsimə   → [sinsimə]'ant (sp)'
       /RED+kinir/   → kankinɪr   → [kaŋkinɪr]'DUP female'
                                        ∼ [kankinɪr]

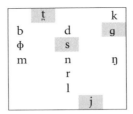

FIGURE 6.4 A phonologically active class in River West Tarangan

b. but not to other consonants:

/jɛr+RED+kɔm/ → jɛrkimkam → [jɛrkimkam]
'DUP NF dislike'

/RED+dum+di/ → dimdumdi → [dimdumdi]
'DUP six PL'

/RED+nam/ → nimnam → [nimnam]
'berry (sp)'

/RED+lema+in/ → limlemin → [limlémin]
'DUP five PL'

/RED+ruma+j/ → rimrumɛ → [rimrumɛ]
'sheath 3s'

In Thompson (Thompson and Thompson 1992), /t/ undergoes deletion in very specific circumstances. To delete, /t/ must be preceded by /n n' ʔ h/ and followed by /ʃ xʷ n/, and the entire cluster must be tautosyllabic, as shown in (35). The classes are shown in Fig. 6.5. Neither class is describable as a conjunction of traditional features, because the segments in them share very few features which have been claimed to be innate, and no combination of these is shared to the exclusion of all other segments.

(35) Thompson /t/ deletion
   a. /t/ deletes between /n n' ʔ h/ and /ʃ xʷ n/ when the cluster is tautosyllabic
      /ʔúqʷeʔː-t-es/ → ʔúqʷeʔts → [ʔúqʷeʔ-s] 'she drinks it'
      /kʼʷénmehː-t-es/ → kʼʷénmehts → [kʼʷén-me-s] 'she criticizes him'
      /kʷénː-t-es/ → kʷénts → [kʷén-s] 'he takes it'
      /ʔúʔèː-n-t-en/ → ʔúʔentn → ʔúʔenn 'I sing him a lullaby'
      → [ʔúʔe-ne]
      /ʔúʔèː-n-t-exʷ/ → ʔúʔentxʷ → [ʔúʔe-n-xʷ] 'you sing him a lullaby'
      /ɬúkʷʔː-n-t-es/ → ɬúkʷn'ts → [ɬúkʷ-n'-s] 'he bails it out'
   b. but not when the cluster is heterosyllabic
      /tʃékː-n-t-sem-es/ → tʃéknt.se.m-s → [tʃék-e-tʃm-s] 'she cools me'

c. and not between other consonants

/ʔúkʷeʔ:-t-p/   → [ʔúkʷeʔ-t-p]   'you people drink it'

/ɬúkʷʔ:-n-t-em/   → [ɬúkʷ-n'-t-m]   'we bail it out'

Each of these four cases involving unique phonologically active classes, along with hundreds of other unique classes in the database, must have an

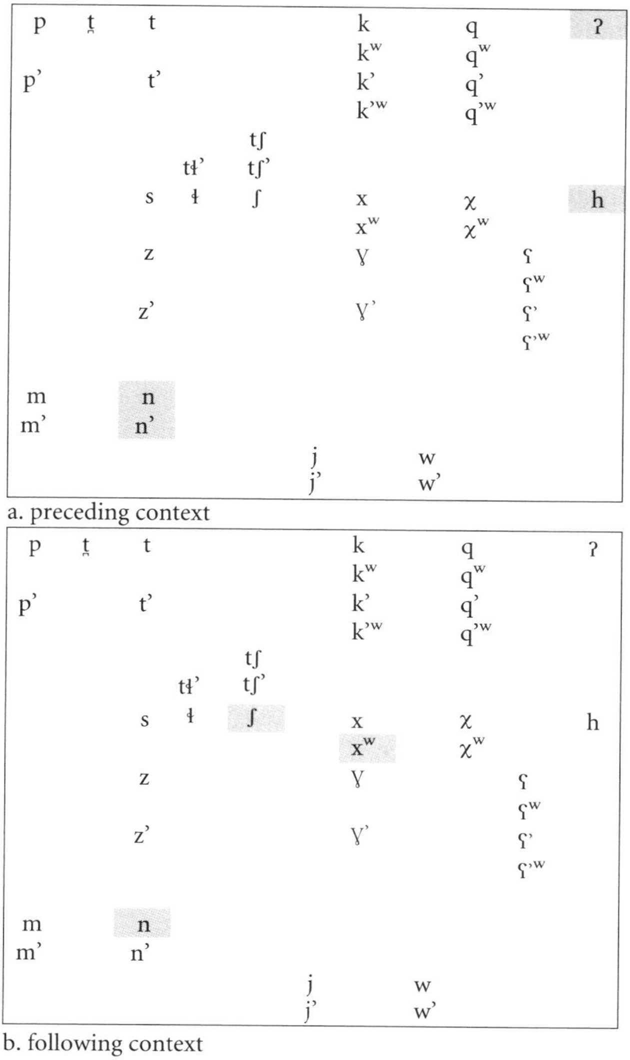

a. preceding context

b. following context

FIGURE 6.5 Phonologically active classes in Thompson

explanation in the history of the language, possibly a very complicated history. In addition to these unique unnatural classes, there are other, more common classes which can also be accounted for by drawing on the history of the languages in which they occur. Most of these classes, some of which are discussed in the next section, seem more natural in phonetic terms, even though many are challenging to traditional distinctive features. They presumably occur as the result of changes which are more common and less complicated than those which produced the classes in this section.

6.3.2 *Recurrent phonetically natural "unnatural" classes*

Among the frequent types of unexpected classes is one which occurs in languages with labiovelar consonants. Labiovelar consonants are generally treated as though they possess properties of bilabial consonants as well as velar consonants. As a result, they are predicted to pattern with labials and with velars. In *SPE*, labiovelars are anterior velars, sharing [+back, +high] with velars and [+anterior] with bilabials. In various Feature Geometry approaches, labiovelars possess both the features [Labial] and [Dorsal]. In Major Articulator Theory (Selkirk 1988, 1991, 1993), the two features are in a dependency relation so that if [Labial] dominates [Dorsal], labiovelars pattern as dorsals, and if [Dorsal] dominates [Labial], they pattern as labials, as in Fig. 6.6.

None of these approaches predicts that labials and velars could pattern together to the exclusion of labiovelars because the way to rule out labiovelars in a process involving place of articulation is to prohibit the labial features or the dorsal features. But labials and velars pattern together to the exclusion of

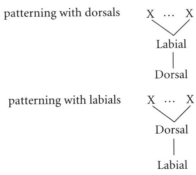

FIGURE 6.6 Labiovelars in Major Articulator Theory

labiovelars nineteen times in thirteen languages (in Bata (three times), Central Shona, Chakosi, Chori, Doyayo (twice), Dyirbal, Ejagham (four times), Gade, Gwari (Gbagyi), Jukun, Kporo, Lorma, and Urhobo). These examples suggest that languages capitalize on a distinction between consonants with complex places of articulation and singly articulated consonants that is not captured by reference to place itself. Some of these cases appear to be instances where labiovelars are limited in their distribution as well, and this fact alone may account for their failure to pattern with labials and velars. This does not appear to be the case in Gwari, however. In Gwari (Hyman and Magaji 1970), labial and velar consonants are optionally labialized before back rounded vowels, but labiovelars are not. The pattern is shown in (36) and the class is illustrated in Fig. 6.7.

(36) Gwari labialization: /p b k g/, but not /k͡p g͡b/, are optionally labialized before back rounded vowels.

[gò]	~	[g^{w}ò]	'to receive'
		[g^{w}ō]	'to grind'
		[zuk^{w}ô]	'hoe'
		[knūb^{w}à]	'ear'
		[gnīk^{w}ó]	'market'
		[túk^{w}ó]	'head'
		[àpwò]	'twin'
	cf.	[g͡bògnu]	'squirrel'

Another recurrent class not predicted by traditional distinctive features is the class of fricatives and sonorant consonants. These classes occur in fourteen languages (Abun, Amele, Aymara, Bukusu, Estonian, Faroese, Jacaltec, Libyan

p		t				k	k͡p
b		d				g	g͡b
ɓ							
			tʃ				
			dʒ				
	f	s	ʃ				
	v	z	ʒ				
m		n		ɲ			
						ŋʷ	
		l					
				j	ɥ		w

FIGURE 6.7 A phonologically active class in Gwari

Arabic, Lower Grand Valley Dani, Nigerian English Pidgin, Onti Koraga, Russian, Samish dialect of Straits Salish, and Tuvaluan). Fricatives and sonorant consonants are phonetically similar in some ways, but they are not featurally similar. All that distinguishes fricatives from stops and affricates in most feature theories is the feature [continuant], and the sonorant consonants that fricatives pattern with in these cases include many traditional noncontinuants such as nasals and some liquids. Thus, these innate feature theories do not predict that fricatives and sonorant consonants will pattern together, but emergent feature theory predicts that they will pattern together in some instances, because of their acoustic similarities, such as amplitude that is higher than oral stops but lower than vowels, and the absence of release burst or zeroes spanning the frequency spectrum (which are found in stops).

An example from Bukusu, in which nasals are deleted before fricatives and nasals, but not before other consonants (Austen 1974: 53–7), is shown in (15) in Chapter 4. The classes involved are shown in Fig. 6.8.

Further groupings of different manners of articulation provide more evidence that languages may exploit classes made up of segments sharing phonetic properties, regardless of whether property has had a feature proposed for it. Nasals and lateral liquids, which share formant structure as well as antiformants caused by side cavities, pattern together to the exclusion of all others in "unnatural" classes in Eastern Cheremis, Toba, and Warlpiri (twice), as well as in large numbers of classes which are natural in one or more theory due to other shared features. For example, in Eastern Cheremis (Sebeok 1961), /ḏ/ is reduced to a lenis [ḏ] before /l/ and nasals /m n ɲ ŋ/, as shown in (37a). It is produced as [ḏ] after nasals (37b), and reduced to [ð] everywhere else. The classes involved in this pattern are shown in Fig. 6.9.

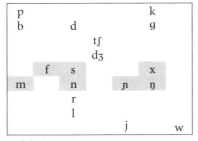

a. deletion triggers

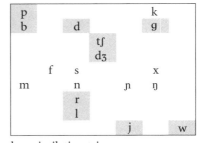

b. assimilation triggers

FIGURE 6.8 Phonologically active classes in Bukusu

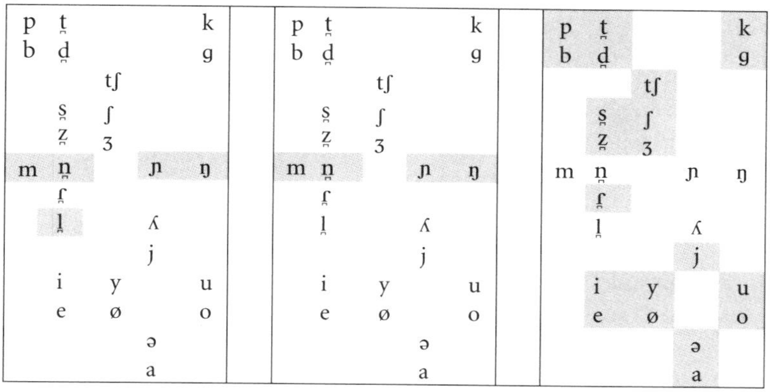

```
p  t̰          k        p  t̰          k        p  t̰                k
b  d̰          g        b  d̰          g        b  d̰                g
      tʃ                      tʃ                        tʃ
   s̰  ʃ                    s̰  ʃ                      s̰  ʃ
   z̰  ʒ                    z̰  ʒ                      z̰  ʒ
m  n̰      ɲ  ŋ          m  n̰      ɲ  ŋ          m  n̰      ɲ  ŋ
   ɾ̰                       ɾ̰                        ɾ̰
   l̰      ʎ                l̰      ʎ                 l̰      ʎ
          j                        j                          j
   i  y   u                i  y   u                i   y      u
   e  ø   o                e  ø   o                e   ø      o
          ə                        ə                        ə
          a                        a                          a
```

a. /d̰/→[d̰]/ __ X   b. /d̰/→[d̰]/X __   c. /d̰/→[ð]/__X

FIGURE 6.9 Phonologically active classes in Eastern Cheremis

(37) Eastern Cheremis /d̰/ lenition
     a. /tud̰lan/   →   [tud̰lan]   'to him'
       /mod̰maʃ/   →   [mod̰maʃ]   'game'
     b. /ʃənd̰as/   →   [ʃənd̰as]   'to set, put, plant'
     c. /tʃod̰ra/   →   [tʃoðra]   'forest'
       /lud̰o/   →   [luðo]   'duck'

/d̰/ may or may not occur before /ʎ/. While the class of nasals and laterals may be described as [+sonorant, −continuant] in some cases (in theories where laterals are [−continuant]), this approach does not allow nasals and laterals to pattern together to the exclusion of a flap or other non-continuant sonorant, as in Eastern Cheremis.

Nasals and sibilants pattern together in four unnatural classes in Navajo, Tswana (twice; see Fig. 6.10), and Uneme. Cole (1955) reports that the raising of the lower mid vowels /ɛ ɔ/ in Tswana is conditioned by a combination of vowels and consonants. The raised allophones [e o] occur when the following vowel is /i u e o/, and usually when followed by strident and nasal consonants (38b). One example in (38b) also shows a raised allophone occurring between /f/s, which are strident in some theories and nonstrident in others.

(38) Tswana vowel raising
     a. /sèlépè/   →   [sèlépè]   'axe'
       /tsὲbé/   →   [tsὲbέ]   'ear'
       /gòrékà/   →   [gòrékà]   'to buy'
       /r̀ré/   →   [r̀ré]   'my father'

/dìjɔ́/	→	[dìjɔ́]	'food'
/gòbɔ́nà/	→	[gòbɔ́nà]	'to see'
/kòbɔ̀/	→	[kòbɔ̀]	'blanket'
/lèrúmɔ̀/	→	[lèrúmɔ̀]	'spear'

b.
/mòèŋ̀/	→	[mòɛ̀ŋ̀]	'stranger'
/gòbèsà/	→	[gòbɛsà]	'to roast'
/mètsé/	→	[mɛtsé]	'water'
/m̀mɔ́nì/	→	[m̀mɔ́nì]	'seer'
/kgɔ̀mó/	→	[kgɔ̀mó]	'cow'
/mòlɔ̀mò/	→	[mòlɔ̀mò]	'mouth'
/sèfɔfù/	→	[sèfɔfù]	'blind person'
/mòrɛ́kì/	→	[mòrɛ́ kì]	'buyer'

Flemming (2002) proposes auditory features to account for various phonological phenomena which involve segments with acoustic/auditory similarities that cannot be described using articulatory features, including cases where laterals and nasals pattern together (and see also Ohala 1993b for discussion of the sibilant–nasal connection in sound change). In emergent feature theory, the phonetic similarity between nasals and laterals (part of Flemming's motivation for positing a feature for them) is the reason why

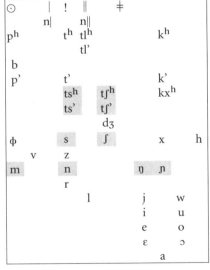

a. consistently trigger mid vowel raising   b. often trigger mid vowel raising

FIGURE 6.10 Phonologically active classes in Tswana

these classes are recurrent. In innate feature theory, nasals and laterals may pattern together only when they share features that are not shared by other segments—a claim which is falsified by cases such as Eastern Cheremis above, where nasals and laterals pattern together to the exclusion of a flap.

This section has featured phonetically natural classes which are recurrent crosslinguistically but have no features assigned to them in traditional innate feature theories. Because these classes are not describable as a conjunction of features, innate feature theories predict them to be no more common than the "crazy" classes of the previous section. Emergent feature theory correctly predicts that because of their phonetic similarity, they are more common.

6.3.3 *Recurrent classes appearing to involve generalization in two directions*

Several types of recurrent class in the database are cases which appear to involve generalization in more than one direction, resulting in a concave distribution of segments. In the Swiss German example in Chapter 5, a class which originally contained only /r/ was generalized in different directions in different dialects. In one case the class was generalized in two different directions, to include segments which are similar to /r/ in manner (nasals) alongside segments which are similar to /r/ in place (coronals). Many classes in the database also appear to involve generalization in two different directions. For example, it is reasonable to attribute a class involving labials and nasals, but not non-labial non-nasals, to generalizations in two directions from a class which originally contained only /m/, as in Fig. 6.11a. All of the segments are similar to /m/, but they are not necessarily more similar to other members of the class than to other segments which do not participate.

In addition to classes involving two generalizations from a "kernel", emergent feature theory predicts that languages could exploit differences in the similarity of members of one traditional class to the members of another. For example, if /g/ is less fully voiced than the other voiced stops in an inventory, it is conceivable that /g/ but not other voiced stops would be grouped with voiceless stops in some sound pattern.

The innate feature theories predict that generalization should only occur by means of feature conjunction, resulting only in convex classes (Fig. 6.11b), and that the concave classes produced by generalization in two directions should arise only by chance, as the accidental union of two classes which happen to participate in identical sound patterns, and be no more frequent than non-overlapping classes participating in identical sound patterns—something which turns out in the next chapter to be comparatively rare.

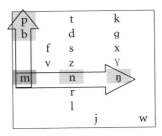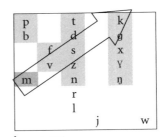

a. concave:
  segments which match
  /m/ in place or manner

b. convex:
  segments which share
  features with /m/

FIGURE 6.11 Convex and concave classes

L-shaped classes are also predicted by constraint interaction in Optimality Theory (see e.g. Flemming 2005 and Yip 2005). This potential explanation for concave classes is also explored further in the next chapter. This situation is predicted to occur as a result of generalization in two directions but not predicted to occur as a result of the interaction of two constraints, because the "bite" taken out of the class of obstruents and nasals (lingual and labiodental obstruents) does not consititute a natural class.

One of the most common types of classes appearing to involve generalization in two directions is the class of back and high vowels, with seventeen instances (in Agarabi, Amharic, Ciyao, Dagur, Eastern Cheremis, Efik, Greek, Itzaj Maya, Kinyamwezi (twice), Koiari, Mohawk, Mongolian, Pero, Sacapultec, So, and Tukang Besi). For example, in Kinyamwezi (Maganga and Schadeberg 1992: 32), /i u ʊ/ are desyllabified before other vowels (39a–c). Other vowels (/ɪ e o a/) merge with following vowels into a single long vowel (39d, e). The phonologically active class is illustrated in Fig. 6.12.

(39)   Kinyamwezi desyllabification

a.	/mi-íko/	→ [miikó]	'taboos'
	/mi-ɪ́ga/	→ [mjɪ́ɪga]	'speeds'
	/mi-énda/	→ [mjeenda]	'clothes'
	/mi-áka/	→ [mjaáka]	'years'
	/mi-ojo/	→ [mjoojo]	'hearts'
	/mi-úje/	→ [mjoojé]	'breaths'
b.	/mu-íβa/	→ [ŋwiiβá]	'thief'
		[ŋwɪɪlú]	'light-colored person'
		[ŋweezí]	'moon'
		[ŋwaaná]	'child'

			[ŋwooβa]	'coward'
			[ŋwʋʋβí]	'someone who takes shelter'
c.	/kʋ-íβa/	→	[kwiiβá]	'to steal'
	/kʋ-íta/	→	[kwɪɪtá]	'to do'
	/kʋ-eŋha/	→	[kweeŋha]	'to bring'
	/kʋ-anʋkʋla/	→	[kwaanʋkʋla]	'to receive'
	/kʋ-ókaja/	→	[kookája]	'to fill'
	/kʋ-úmɪka/	→	[kʋʋmíka]	'to dry'
d.	/a-lɪ-íβa/	→	[aliiβá]	'he is stealing'
	/a-lɪ-íta/	→	[alɪɪtá]	'he is doing'
	/a-lɪ-eŋha/	→	[aleeŋha]	'he is bringing'
	/a-lɪ-anʋkʋla/	→	[alaanʋkʋla]	'he is receiving'
	/a-lɪ-ókaja/	→	[alookája]	'he is filling'
	/a-lɪ-úmɪka/	→	[alʋʋmíka]	'he is drying'
e.	/a-ka-íβa/	→	[akiiβá]	'she stole'
	/a-ka-íta/	→	[akɪɪtá]	'she did'
	/a-ka-eŋha/	→	[akeeŋha]	'she brought'
	/a-ka-anʋkʋla/	→	[akaanʋkʋla]	'she received'
	/a-ka-ókaja/	→	[akookája]	'she filled'
	/a-ka-úmɪka/	→	[akʋmíka]	'she dried'

These cases may have started with /u/ (the high back vowel) and spread both to other high and to other back vowels. Parallel to cases such as this one in Kinyamwezi, there are eight classes of front and high vowels which may have started with /i/ (in Abujmaria Agn Armenian, Chamorro, Greek, Michigan German, Mwera, Gwandum dialect of Pero, and Sekani).

Among the consonants, there are twenty-two classes appearing to involve generalizations in both place and manner (Breton, Catalan, Coast Tsimshian, Comanche, Desano, Diola-Fogny, Gujarati, Inor dialect of West Gurage, Izi, Kolami, Manipuri, Michoacán Nahuatl, Muruwari, Navajo, Northern Tepehuan, Oklahoma Cherokee, Orma, Pengo, Tepuxtepec Mixe, Welsh, Western Shoshoni, Xakas), ten appearing to involve generalizations in place and voice (in Batibo

FIGURE 6.12 A phonologically active class in Kinyamwezi

Moghamo, Boraana Oromo, Faranah-Maninka, Hungarian, Irish, Kapampan-gan, Nangikurrunggurr, Nkore-Kiga, Orma, and Waata Oromo), and six appearing to involve generalizations in voice and manner (in Argobba, Bulgarian (twice), Greek, Kombai, Slovene, and Tiv). In Navajo (Reichard 1974: 19), /t k γ x k'/ are labialized before /o/ (and /t k/ are aspirated), as shown in (40a) and Fig. 6.13. This pattern may have gotten its start with just /k/ and spread to another voiceless stop (/t/) and other velars (/γ x k'/).

(40) Navajo aspiration and labialization

  a. /tó/   →   [t^{hw}ó]   'water'
      /t'á-ʔákó-d-ígí/   →   [t'á-ʔák^{hw}ó-d-ígí]   'that very one'
      /bi-γoʃ/   →   [boγ^{w}oʃ]   'its thorn'
      /bi-xo-γan/   →   [box^{w}o-γan]   'where his house/home is'
      /dik'ṓːdʒ/   →   [dok'^{w}ṓːdʒ]   'it is sour, salty, acidulous'

  b. /-zṍːs/   →   [zṍːs]   'tear fabric'
      /bé-so/   →   [bé-so]   'money, dollar'
      /ʔálá-c-t'óːdʒ/   →   [ʔálá-c-t'óːdʒ]   'bark of tree'
      /ʔá-dóː/   →   [ʔá-dóː]   'from a remote point off'
      /ʔát'é-go/   →   [ʔát'ê-go]   'that way, just as that is'

As with any of these classes which appear to involve generalization in two directions, it could be claimed that there are two classes (plain voiceless stops and voiceless velars) which coincidentally do the same thing. Investigation into the history of these sound patterns is necessary before reaching the conclusion

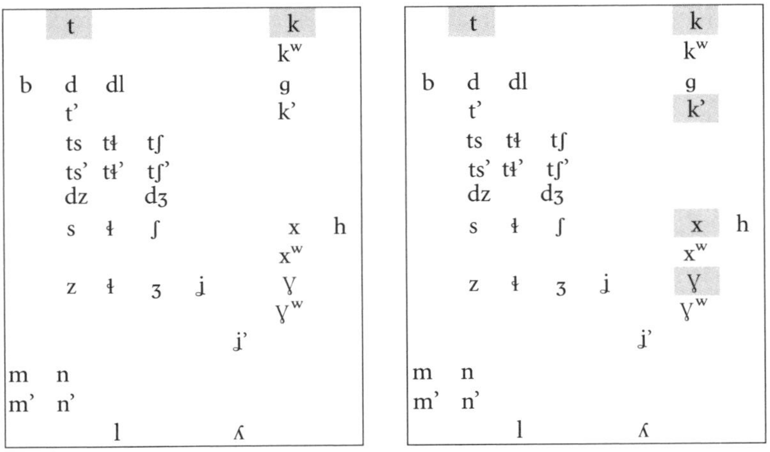

t				k	
				k^{w}	
b	d	dl		g	
	t'			k'	
	ts	tɬ	tʃ		
	ts'	tɬ'	tʃ'		
	dz		dʒ		
	s	ɬ	ʃ	x	h
				x^{w}	
	z	ɮ	ʒ	ʝ	γ
					γ^{w}
			ʝ'		
m	n				
m'	n'				
		l		ʎ	

a. aspirated before /o/

t				k	
				k^{w}	
b	d	dl		g	
	t'			k'	
	ts	tɬ	tʃ		
	ts'	tɬ'	tʃ'		
	dz		dʒ		
	s	ɬ	ʃ	x	h
				x^{w}	
	z	ɮ	ʒ	ʝ	γ
					γ^{w}
			ʝ'		
m	n				
m'	n'				
		l		ʎ	

b. labialized before /o/

FIGURE 6.13 Phonologically active classes in Navajo

that they did indeed arise from overgeneralization in two directions from a "kernel" that now appears as the overlap between the two generalizations.

6.4 Related patterns in related languages

Groups of related languages often possess what appear to be different versions of the same sound pattern. This can be the result of parallel sound changes, multiple sound changes, contact, or generalization. Although innate feature theory would predict that sound pattern variants would be chosen from among featurally natural classes, the classes often do not correspond to proposed distinctive features, even when they are clearly related to phonologically active classes in related languages. Data on the following pages illustrate processes which affect slightly different segments in related languages: pre-stopping in Pama-Nyungan, consonant nasalization in Edoid, and postnasal strengthening in Bantu. The point of this section is not to argue definitively for a particular set of diachronic changes, but to argue for a hypothetical explanation that does not require hypothetical innate features and that is capable of accounting for observations that innate features are unable to address.

The first case involves a process affecting a group of laterals and/or nasals which appears to have been generalized differently in different languages. In many Pama-Nyungan languages spoken in and south of the Lake Eyre Basin, nasals and/or liquids are pre-stopped (e.g. /l/ → [dl]) either syllable-finally or after a stressed syllable (Austin 1981, Breen 2001, Dench 1995, Dixon 2002, Hercus 1994). Butcher (2006) relates pre-stopping to the large number of places of articulation found in Australian languages. Anticipatory vowel nasalization interferes with place cues found in the vowel–consonant transitions, and Butcher argues that speakers delay the onset of nasalization to preserve cues to place. When nasalization does not begin until after the start of the oral closure, the result is a stop-like interval, and this has been reinterpreted in some languages as a stop consonant.

An example from Diyari is shown in (41). Apico-dental and lamino-alveolar nasals and laterals are optionally pre-stopped when following the main stress and preceding a vowel, Nasals do not undergo pre-stopping in nasal-initial words (because laterals do not occur word-initially, it is unknown whether laterals would behave similarly).

(41) Pre-stopping in Diyari (Austin 1981: 18–19).
    a. /jula/ → [júdlʌ] ∼ [júlʌ]   'you too'
       /n̪ulu/ → [n̪údlu] ∼ [n̪úlu]   'he'
       /kal̪u/ → [kʌ́d̪l̪u] ∼ [kʌ́l̪u]   'liver'
       /mul̪a/ → [múd̪l̪ʌ] ∼ [múl̪ʌ]   'nose'

    b. /kani/ → [kʌ́dni] ~ [kʌ́ni]   'frill-necked lizard'
        /wana/ → [wʌ́dnʌ] ~ [wʌ́nʌ]   'yamstick'
        /jiṇa/ → [jíḏṇʌ] ~ [jíṇʌ]   'mother's mother'
    c. /ŋana/ → [ŋʌ́nʌ]   'to be'
        /ṇaṇa/ → [ṇʌ́ṇʌ]   'her'

The identity of the class of sounds targeted by this process appears to have been interpreted differently in each language, as the result either of separate parallel sound changes or of under- or over-generalizations in some languages. Bowern (1998: 42) attributes the the different versions of the pattern found in the Karnic branch of the Pama-Nyungan family to diffusion. Koch (2004: 134) suggests that the phonemicization of pre-stopped nasals (the reinterpretation of the stop-like interval as a stop) probably took place independently in the Centralian languages. Simpson and Hercus (2004: 188) suggest that pre-stopping patterns found in modern Thura-Yura languages represent innovations. They do not reconstruct pre-stopping for Proto-Thura-Yura, and report an increase in the recording of pre-stopping in twentieth-century sources compared to sources from the nineteenth century.

The classes of consonants involved in various instantiations of pre-stopping are shown in Fig. 6.14. /l/ and other lateral liquids pattern with nasals in five of the languages (Fig. 6.14a–d), while pre-stopping is limited just to nasals or laterals in one language each (Fig. 6.14e, f). The class of pre-stopping consonants is further limited by place in four different ways (Fig. 6.14a–d), only two of which are readily expressible as a conjunction of traditional features (Wangkangurru and Diyari), assuming that laterals are [–continuant], flap is [+continuant], and labials are [+anterior]. Kuyani, Adnyamathanha, and Arabana require feature disjunction. The segments active in Kuyani and Adnyamathanha are described as the union of the classes defined by [+son, –cont, +lab] and [+son, –cont, +cor] (unless [–velar] is proposed). The segments active in Arabana are [+son, –cont, +ant] [+son, –cont, –ant, –distr], assuming that [+ant] includes labials.

While these processes in related languages are obviously connected to one another, there is no way to unify the classes in terms of a single set of the distinctive features that have been proposed so far. It is clear that various segments were added or removed from the class of pre-stopped sonorants in the different languages. New generalizations were formed concerning what consonants are involved, but these generalizations are not consistent with a universal feature set. A look at the genetic relationships between these seven languages (*Ethnologue*, Grimes et al. 2000) reveals that the languages which limit

a. Kuyani and Adnyamathanha					
p	t̪	t	ʈ	c	k
m	n̪	n	ɳ	ɲ	ŋ
	l̪	l	ɭ	ʎ	
		ɾ	ʈ		
w				j	

[+son, −cont, +lab]∨[+son, −cont, +cor]

b. Arabana					
p	t̪	t	ʈ	c	k
m	n̪	n	ɳ	ɲ	ŋ
	l̪	l	ɭ	ʎ	
		r			
w		ɻ	j		

[+son, −cont, +ant]∨[+son, −cont, −ant, −distr] ([+ant] includes labials)

c. Wangkangurru					
p	t̪	t	ʈ	c	k
m	n̪	n	ɳ	ɲ	ŋ
	l̪	l	ɭ	ʎ	
		ɾ			
		r			
w		ɻ	j		

[+son, −cont, +ant] (only if [+ant] refers to labials; otherwise requires disjunction)

d. Diyari (Dieri)					
p	t̪	t	ʈ	c	k
		d	ɖ		
m	n̪	n	ɳ	ɲ	ŋ
	l̪	l	ɭ	ʎ	
		ɾ			
w		ɻ	j		

[+son, −cont, +cor +ant]

e. Lower Southern Aranda					
p	t̪	t	ʈ	c	k
m	n̪	n	ɳ	ɲ	ŋ
	l̪	l	ɭ	ʎ	
		ɾ			
w		ɻ	j	h	

[+nas]

f. Martuthunira					
p	t̪	t	ʈ	c	k
m	n̪	n	ɳ	ɲ	ŋ
	l̪	l	ɭ	ʎ	
		r			
w		ɻ	j		

[+lat]

FIGURE 6.14 Pre-stopping consonants in some Pama-Nyungan languages, generally requiring [−continuant] laterals

pre-stopping to a proper subset of the labial and coronal places of articulation are all in the Karnic branch of the Pama-Nyungan Family (Fig. 6.15), and the differences may have developed in the course of the diffusion of the pattern suggested by Bowern. The exclusion of laterals in Lower Southern Aranda and of nasals in Martuthunira appears to be innovative (undergeneralizations or separate developments), while the inclusion of the velar nasal in Lower Southern Aranda appears also to be innovative (probably a separate development).

A similar type of example comes from Edoid languages (Elugbe 1989), where certain consonants are generally nasalized when they precede nasal vowels. Consonant nasalization in Edo is illustrated in (24).

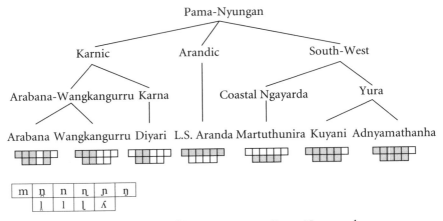

FIGURE 6.15 The genetic relationships among seven Pama-Nyungan languages

(42)   Edo consonant nasalization (Elugbe 1989: 77, 133–81)
    a.   /lɔ̃/ → [nɔ̃]   'ask'
         /lɛ̃/ → [r̃ɛ̃]   'know'   ([ɹɛ̃] → /ɹ̃ɛ̃/ for most younger speakers)
         /ʋɛ̃/ → [ṽɛ̃]   'have'
         /jã/ → [ɲɛ̃]   'tear apart
         /wɔ̃/ → [ŋwɔ̃]   'drink'

    b.   /lo/ → [lo]   'use'
         /a-ɭo/ → [a-ɭo]   'eye'   (/a-ɹo/ → [a-ɹo] for younger speakers)
         /ʋɛ/ → [ʋɛ]   'be wide'
         /o-ji/ → [o-ji]   'thief'
         /wa/ → [wa]   'you (pl.)'

Several Edoid languages with this sound pattern are shown in Fig. 6.16. While
the process is similar in all of the languages, the set of consonants involved varies
from language to language. These classes include the lateral liquid, the tap, and
the glides in Okpe, Urhobo, and Uvbie (Fig. 6.16a–c), the lateral liquid, the
glides, and the voiced bilabial fricative in Ehueun (Fig. 6.16d), the lateral liquid
and the voiced bilabial fricative in Ukue (Fig. 6.16e), non-nasal sonorants and
the voiced bilabial stop in Eruwa³ (Fig. 6.16f), the lateral liquid, the glides, and
the velar fricative in Epie (Fig. 6.16g), the lateral liquid, the glides, and the glottal

³ Elugbe (1989: 61) reports that [b] and [m] appear to be in complementary distribution in Eruwa,
with [b] never occurring before nasal vowels, and he hypothesizes that [m] is the allophone of /b/
which occurs there.

fricative in Aoma, and the lateral liquid, the tap, the glides, and the oral stops (which acquire nasal release before nasal vowels) in Edo (Fig. 6.16h).

Elugbe (1989) reconstructs Proto-Edoid with phonemically nasalized consonants and allophonically nasalized vowels, as in several modern Edoid languages such as Auchi, Egene, Emhalhe, Ghotuo, Ibilo, Isoko, Oloma, Uhami, and Uneme. The nasalization patterns in the languages in Fig. 6.16 must then have resulted from restructuring. This restructuring appears to have occurred differently in different languages and without the guidance of an innate feature set. Speakers of some of these languages have passed up numerous classes which are characterizable with a conjunction of distinctive features (e.g. [+voice], [+sonorant], [+voice, +sonorant]), in favor of classes which are not.

The segments which participate in this sound pattern vary between languages. In addition to /l/, (traditionally continuant) glides nasalize in all but one language (Fig. 6.16e), and a non-lateral flap nasalizes in three languages (Fig. 6.16a–c). A single bilabial fricative or stop nasalizes in three languages (Fig. 6.16d–f), while a velar fricative nasalizes in one (Fig. 6.16g). /h/, a lateral flap, or the set of all oral stops are each affected in one language each (Fig. 6.16h, i). The segments involved in these processes cannot be formally related within or between languages if their feature specifications are universally determined. This is because universal feature set predicts that, for example, fricatives such as /h/, /β/, and /ɣ/ should be systematically included or excluded depending on whether or not features such as [sonorant] are targeted by the nasalization process. What appears actually to be the case is that the restructuring process in each language caused the pattern to be generalized to a set of phonetically similar segments which is different in different languages. Alternatively, the relevant sound changes are less likely to affect these "ambivalent" segments because the relevant phonetic properties are present to a lesser exent.

If the consonant nasalization is innovative, as Elugbe (1989) argues, then the innovation appears to have occurred multiple times, because all four major branches of the Edoid family contain languages with consonant nasalization, as shown in Fig. 6.17. This would also be true if vowel nasalization turned out to be innovative, because languages with vowel nasalization also occur in all four major branches of the Edoid family. This state of affairs suggests that the innovation and accompanying generalization to a class of consonants either spread through contact or occurred at least four separate times after Proto-Edoid split into four branches. Further, languages which include at least one obstruent in the class of nasalizing consonants

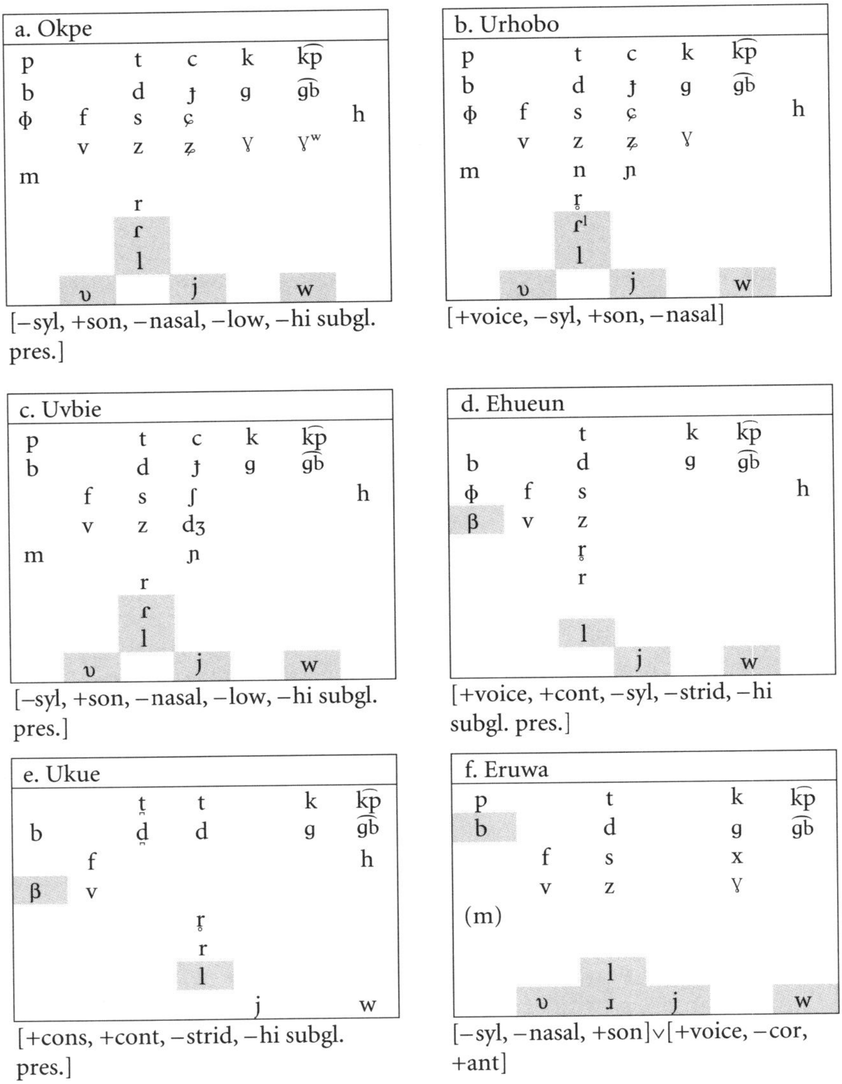

a. Okpe

p		t	c	k	k͡p	
b		d	ɟ	g	g͡b	
ɸ	f	s	ç			h
	v	z	ʐ	ɣ	ɣʷ	
m						
		r				
		ɾ				
		l				
	ʋ		j		w	

[−syl, +son, −nasal, −low, −hi subgl. pres.]

b. Urhobo

p		t	c	k	k͡p	
b		d	ɟ	g	g͡b	
ɸ	f	s	ç			h
	v	z	ʐ	ɣ		
m		n	ɲ			
		ɽ				
		ɾˡ				
		l				
	ʋ		j		w	

[+voice, −syl, +son, −nasal]

c. Uvbie

p		t	c	k	k͡p	
b		d	ɟ	g	g͡b	
	f	s	ʃ			h
	v	z	dʒ			
m			ɲ			
		r				
		ɾ				
		l				
	ʋ		j		w	

[−syl, +son, −nasal, −low, −hi subgl. pres.]

d. Ehueun

		t		k	k͡p	
b		d		g	g͡b	
ɸ	f	s				h
β	v	z				
		ɽ				
		r				
		l				
			j		w	

[+voice, +cont, −syl, −strid, −hi subgl. pres.]

e. Ukue

		ṭ	t		k	k͡p
b		d̥	d		g	g͡b
	f					h
β	v					
		ɽ̥				
		r				
		l				
			j			w

[+cons, +cont, −strid, −hi subgl. pres.]

f. Eruwa

p		t		k	k͡p
b		d		g	g͡b
	f	s		x	
	v	z		ɣ	
(m)					
		l			
	ʋ	ɹ	j		w

[−syl, −nasal, +son]∨[+voice, −cor, +ant]

FIGURE 6.16 Nasalizing consonants in Edoid languages, generally requiring [+continuant] laterals

```
g. Epie
 p        t        k    k͡p
 b        d        g    g͡b
 ɓ        ɗ
      f   s
      v   z             ɣ
 m
          (r)
          l
              j        w
```
[+cont, −syl, −strid, (−hi subgl. pres.)]

```
h. Aoma
 p        t        k    k͡p
 b        d        g    g͡b

      f   s        x         h
      v   z        ɣ
 m
              r
          l
          ɹ    j        w
```
[+son, −syl, −hi subgl. pres.]

```
i. Edo
 p        t        k    k͡p
 b        d        g    g͡b
      f   s        x         h
      v   z        ɣ
 m

          r̥
          r
          l
          ɹ
      ʋ       j        w
```
[+son, +voice, −hi subgl. pres.,
+cont, −syl] ∨ [−nasal, −cont]

FIGURE 6.16 (Continued)

also occur in all four major branches, and for the most part, the consonant or consonants which are included are different in each subfamily (/β/ in Northwestern, stops (or /h/) in North-Central, (/b/ in Southwestern, and /ɣ/ in Delta), also supporting the notion that four or more separate changes occurred.

There is a very similar case in some Bantu languages, where a similar array of consonants is involved in a different process. In this case, various consonants are strengthened to stops after nasals (Austen 1974, Besha 1989, Brown 1972, Cole 1967, Fivaz 1986, Madan 1906, Mutonyi 2000, Ngunga 2000, Odden 1996, Poulos 1990, Rubongoya 1999, Takizala 1974, van Sambeek 1966). For example, in Runyoro-Rutooro (shown in 43), /l/ and /r/ strengthen to [d] after a nasal, and /h/ strengthens to [p].

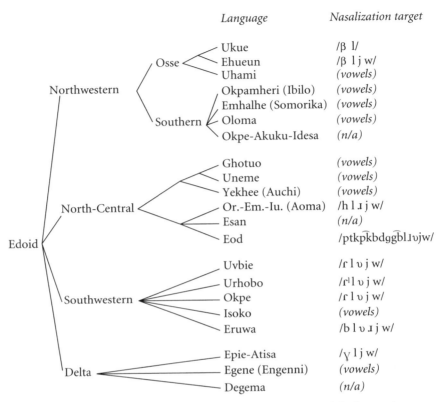

FIGURE 6.17 The genetic relationships among Edoid languages (Elugbe 1989)

(43)   Postnasal strengthening of /h l r/ in Runyoro-Rutooro
        /nleka/ → [ndeka]   'leave me alone'
        /nragiira/ → [ndagiira]   'show me'
        /oranha/ → [orampa]   'I am hearing'

As in the Edoid example, /β/, /ɣ/, /h/, and other fricatives exhibit ambivalent behavior; in the languages where these sounds occur, they participate in the sound pattern in some cases and not in others. In both cases, these segments share some but not all properties, with the sonorant consonants which consistently participate, more so than the segments which never participate. The patterning of glides and /r/ is not completely consistent from language to language, either. The Bantu classes can be described in various ways: e.g. non-nasal sonorant consonants in Ganda, Wisa (Lala-Bisa), and Ciyao (Yao)[4] (Fig. 6.18a–c), non-nasal sonorants and fricative in Kimatuumbi (Fig. 6.18d), lateral

---

[4] /l/ and /j/ become nasal stops in Ciyao and /w/ only strengthens after prefix /n/ in Wisa.

and voiced fricative in Bemba (non-labial oral stops also turn into voiced stops after nasals) (Fig. 6.18e), non-nasal sonorants and bilabial fricative in Lumasaaba (Masaba) and Bukusu[5] (Fig. 6.18f, g), non-nasal sonorants and voiced velar fricative in Oshindonga (Fig. 6.18h), palatal glide, velar, and glottal fricatives in Shambala (Fig. 6.18i), liquids and voiceless fricatives in Kihungan[6] (Fig. 6.18j), liquids and glottal fricative in Runyooro-Rutooro (Fig. 6.18k), and liquids, labiovelar glide, and assorted fricatives in Venda (Fig. 6.18l). /h/ strengthens to [p] in Shambala, Runyoro-Rutooro, and Venda.

As in Edoid, the class of segments which undergo postnasal strengthening appears to have been generalized differently in the different languages. The voiceless fricatives which participate in Kihungan, Runyoro-Rutooro, and Venda are the result of a separate historical process (Odden, p.c.). The participation of voiced fricatives is interesting, in that they are less consistent participants than the liquids, and that only the non-coronal voiced fricatives participate, i.e. those which are most similar to sonorants. The genetic relationships between these languages (*Ethnologue*, Grimes et al. 2000) suggest either that similar changes occurred many times in different branches of the Bantu family or that contact is responsible for some of the shared features. Voiceless fricatives strengthen in H, P, and S branches of Central Bantu (Kihungan, Kimatuumbi, and Venda, respectively), but not in Ciyao, which also belongs to the P branch. /h/ strengthens in G, H, J, and S (Shambala, Kihungan, Runyoro-Rutooro, and Venda), but not in e.g. Ganda, which like Runyoro-Rutooro is in the Nyoro-Ganda branch of the J classification. /β/ strengthens in Lumasaaba and Bukusu (both of the Masaba-Luyia branch of J), Bemba (M), and Venda (S), but not in the aforementioned Nyoro-Ganda branch, or in Wisa (M). /ɣ/ strengthens in Shambala (G) and Oshindonga (R), which are no more closely related to each other than to the other branches represented here. While it is difficult to speculate without knowing more about the contact situation, it appears that the similar events may have occurred in different families multiple times, with the result of including segments which are similar phonetically, but not featurally, to the common members of the classes.

This case in Bantu, along with sonorant pre-stopping in Pama-Nyungan and consonant nasalization in Edoid, supports the idea that classes of segments arise as a result of sound changes or generalizations involving segments which are phonetically similar to each other. Both similarities and differences

---

[5] Austen (1974) treats [β] in Bukusu as an intervocalic allophone of /b/, whereas Mutonyi (2000) treats [b] as a postnasal allophone of /β/ (and posits no voiced stop phonemes). In either case, the distributional pattern for /β/~/b/ matches /w/~/b/, /j/~/dʒ/, /l/~/d/, and /r/~/d/).

[6] /f/, /s/, and /h/ become voiceless affricates, and /t/ and /k/ become aspirated after nasals in Kihungan.

a. Ganda

p			t	c	k
b			d	ɟ	g
		f	s		
		v	z		
m			n	ɲ	ŋ
			l		
w					j

[−syl, −nasal, +son]

b. Wisa (Lala-Bisa)

p		t	tʃ	k
b		d		g
	f	s		
	v	z		
m		n	ɲ	ŋ
		l		
w			j	

[−syl, −nasal, +son]

c. Ciyao (Yao)

p		t	tʃ	k
b		d	dʒ	g
		s		
m		n	ɲ	ŋ
		l		
w	ʋ		j	

[−syl, −nasal, +son]

d. Kimatuumbi

p	t	tʃ		k
	s			
m	n		ɲ	ŋ
	l			
w			j	

[−syl, −nasal, +cont]

e. Bemba

p		t	tʃ	k
	f	s	ʃ	
β				
m		n	ɲ	ŋ
		l		
w			j	

[+voice, +cons, +cont]

f. Lumasaaba (Masaba)

p		t	k
b		d	g
	f	s	
β		z	
m		n	ɲ
		l	
		j	

[−syl, −strid, +cont]

g. Bukusu

p			tʃ	k	
b		d	dʒ	g	
	f	s		x	
β					
m		n	ɲ	ŋ	N
		l			
		r			
w			j		

[−syl, −strid, +cont]
(assuming /r/ is [+cont])

h. Oshindonga

p		t		k	ʔ
		ts			
	f	θ	s	ʃ	x	h
	v	ð	z		ɣ	
m		n		ŋ		
		l				
w			j			

[+high,+voice,−nasal,−voc] (/j w ɣ /)
∨ [+ant, −nasal, +son] (/l w/)

FIGURE 6.18 Consonants that undergo postnasal strengthening in some Bantu languages

i. Shambala

p		t	tʃ	k	
b		d	dʒ	ɣ	
	f	s	ʃ		h
	v	z		ɣ̞	
m		n	ɲ	ŋ	
		l			
w			j		

[−high, +son, +cont, −syl] (/h l/)
∨ [−strid, +cons, +cont] (/l ɣ/)

j. Kihungan

pʰ		tʰ	kʰ	
		t	k	
b		d	g	
	f	s		h
	v	z		
m		n	ŋ	
		l		
		r		
w		j		

[−voice, +cont] ∨ [+lat]

k. Runyoro-Rutooro

p	t̞		k	
b		d	g	
		tʃ		
		dʒ		
	f	s		h
β	v	z		
m		n	ŋ	
		l		
		r		
w		j		

[−high, +son, +cont, −syl]

l. Venda

pʰ	t̪ʰ	tʰ		kʰ	kʰʷ
p'	t̪'	t'		k'	pʷ'
b	d̪	d	dʲ	g	bʷ
	pfʰ	tsʰ	tʃʰ	tsʷʰ	
	bv	dz	dʒ	dzʷ	
ɸ	f	s	ʃ	sʷ	x	h
β	v	z	ʒ	zʷ	
m	n̪	n	ɲ	ŋ	ŋʷ
	l̪	l			
		r			
		j		w	

[−voice, +cont, −round] (/f h s x ɸʃ/)
∨ [+ant, −strid, +cont] (/l̪ l r w ɸβ/)

FIGURE 6.18 (Continued)

between the phonologically active classes in related languages, and the nature of the particular classes which are active in each language, support the idea that these classes were formed by historical events which occurred under similar linguistic and environmental circumstances, and neither supports the idea that they are attributable to innate features.

6.5 Recurrent phonetically unnatural classes

A few recurrent classes are not predicted by any innate feature theories and also do not have obvious shared phonetic properties. Labial, velar, and glottal consonants pattern together in seven languages (Cabécar, Chontal Maya,

Dhivehi, Inor (dialect of West Gurage), Midland Mixe, North Highland Mixe, and Sie), and sonorant consonants and voiceless obstruents pattern together to the exclusion of voiced obstruents in twelve cases in eight languages (Catalan (twice), Faroese, Khmu[?] (twice), Kiowa, Lithuanian, O'odham, Pero (twice), and Vietnamese (twice)). In Pero (Frajzinger 1989: 23, 33), morpheme-final stops undergo total assimilation to a following nasal or voiceless stop (44a), while a following voiced stop triggers not assimilation but epenthesis (44b). This grouping (shown in Fig. 6.19) is not predicted, since sonorants and voiceless obstruents share no features or obvious phonetic properties that they do not also share with voiced obstruents.

(44)   Pero stop assimilation

a. /káp/ + /kò/   → [kákkò]   'he told'
   /pét/ + /nà/   → [pénnà]   'he went out'
   /tʃúp/ + /kò/   → [tʃókkò]   'he has shown'
   /tʃìrép/ + /mù/   → [tʃírémmù]   'our women'

b. /káp/ + /dʒí/   → [kávídʒì]   'eat (habitual)'
   /tʃúg/ + /dʒí/   → [tʃúgídʒí]   'talk (habitual)'

Finally, corner vowels (usually /a i u/) pattern together to the exclusion of mid vowels (tense, lax, or both) and in some cases, other high and low vowels, in twenty-three languages (Assiniboine, Ciyao, Ejagham, Ekigusii, Ikalanga, Kilivila, Kimatuumbi, Kiowa, Kuvi, Mundari, Nkore-Kiga, Pa'anci, Runyoro-Rutooro, Sayula Popoluca, Shambala, Swazi, Telugu, Tsishaath Nootka (Nuuchahnulth), Tswana, Wiyot, Xhosa, Yapese, and Zezuru Shona).

What these three vowels share in most of these inventories is that they are the most peripheral vowels in the vowel space. A natural phonological pattern for these peripheral segments to participate in, to the exclusion of vowel closer to the center of the vowel space, is neutralization. In Kiowa (Watkins 1984), /i ī u ū a ā/ are lowered, lowered, and raised, respectively, when they

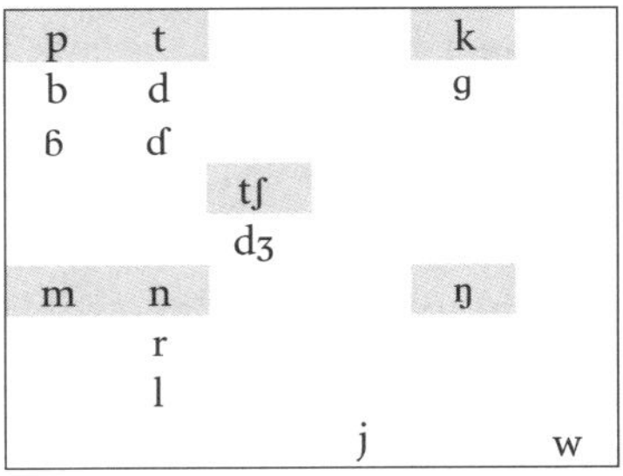

FIGURE 6.19 A phonologically active class in Pero

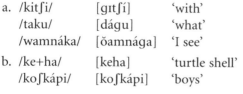

FIGURE 6.20 A phonologically active class in Kiowa

occur before nasals (45a), but not elsewhere (45b). Mid vowels /e ē o ō ɔ ɔ̃/ are unaffected (45c). The phonologically active class is illustrated in Fig. 6.20.

(45) Kiowa vowel lowering and raising
    a. Corner vowels are raised or lowered when a nasal follows,

/min/	[mĩn]	'about to'
/bimkʰɔj/	[bĩmkʰɔj]	'bag'
/gun/	[gũn]	'dance/pf'
/jan/	[jẽn]	'2sg/pat:pl/obj'

    b. but not before other consonants.

/kil/	[kid̦l]	'dwell, be camped'
/gul/	[gud̦l]	'write/imp'
/sal/	[sad̦l]	'be hot'

    c. Mid vowels are unaffected.

/ton/	[tõn]	'be fat'
/dɔm/	[dɔ̃m]	'earth, ground'

A different pattern involving corner vowels occurs in Pa'anci (Skinner 1979). /k/ is voiced before unaccented /i u a/ (46a), and voiceless elsewhere (46b). The class of triggers is shown in Fig. 6.21.

(46) Pa'anci /k/ voicing
    a.

/kitʃi/	[gɪtʃí]	'with'
/taku/	[dágu]	'what'
/wamnáka/	[ŏamnága]	'I see'

    b.

/ke+ha/	[keha]	'turtle shell'
/koʃkápi/	[koʃkápi]	'boys'

FIGURE 6.21 A phonologically active class in Pa'anci

The effort to categorize "unnatural" classes is compromised somewhat by the fact that they are harder to describe consistently than classes which are accounted for using traditional distinctive features. Often one or more shared phonetic properties are identifiable, but the less common classes lack common terms to describe them. Further, in the same way that many classes can be described in several different ways using distinctive features, many classes can also be described in several different ways using phonetic descriptions. This makes categorizing them difficult. Nevertheless, the existence of recurrent phonologically active classes involving a wide variety of shared phonetic properties suggests that innate feature theories merely highlight some of the most common phonetic properties which can form the basis for phonological patterns. Innate feature theories claim that there are phonetic properties (those which are not associated with any innate feature) which cannot form the basis for phonological patterns, but it is not clear what those properties are, given that there are many unpredicted properties which actually are relevant for many phonological patterns. In short, innate feature theories appear to be unnecessarily restrictive. Emergent feature theory, on the other hand, predicts that any phonetic property can form the basis for a phonological pattern, and that phonological patterns based on the most salient phonetic properties will be most prevalent. This prediction is investigated in the next chapter. Further, the fact that many classes which are unnatural in featural terms have phonetic properties in common, much like their "natural" counterparts, suggests that they should indeed be accounted for by the same mechanism, as they are in emergent feature theory. The next chapter provides a more detailed analysis of the survey results in terms of the innate feature theories.

7

Survey results in terms of feature theories

This chapter reports an analysis of the 6,077 phonologically active classes in the database in terms of three well-known feature theories. Additional feature theories are brought in as appropriate when they are able to account for recurrent classes that the other theories cannot account for. As theories of universal features, these theories have been proposed ostensibly in order to describe all phonological phenomena in all (spoken) languages. As seen in Chapter 5, there are many classes they cannot account for. Some of these are crazy and some are phonetically sensible. The ranges of frequent/infrequent and phonetically natural/unnatural classes suggest a more gradient method for predicting the likelihood of a group of sounds patterning together; at the end of this chapter a model based on phonetic similarity is sketched, and it is seen that this has some promise.

7.1 *Preliminaries, SPE,* and Unified Feature Theory

The ability of innate feature theories to account for the observed phonologically active classes is measured in different ways in this chapter. The first, discussed in this section, is a simple success/failure rate. Given a set of segments within a given inventory with a feature matrix specified by a particular feature theory, it is either the case that the segments can be described to the exclusion of all others using a conjunction of features, or that they cannot. Therefore, each of the feature theories can be assigned a success rate based on the portion of phonologically active classes it can characterize. The success rate of all three approaches combined can also be computed, according to whether or not *any* of the three approaches can characterize a particular class.

SPE features are able to account for 70.97 percent of the phonologically active classes, the most of the three theories. More than one quarter of the classes cannot be described with a conjunction of *SPE* features. Unified

Feature Theory features are able to account for 63.72 percent of the phonologically active classes, and *Preliminaries* features are able to account for 59.90
percent of the observed classes. The similarity between UFT's and *Preliminaries'* success rates is a somewhat surprising considering that UFT effectively
has more than three times as many features (in part because natural classes
can be defined by place features in three different ways (V-place, C-place, or
either). While Unified Feature Theory has substantially more features than
the other two theories, the fact that many of them are unary limits the possible
natural classes it predicts. Further, Unified Feature Theory was designed with
considerations other than natural class coverage, such as simplicity in formulating phonological rules. The fact that more than a third of the classes these
rules need to refer to are inexpressible as conjunctions of features is nonetheless troubling.

Fig. 7.1 shows the overlap between the coverage of the three feature systems.
There is substantial overlap between the three systems, and *Preliminaries'*
coverage is almost entirely within the coverage of *SPE*, which is not surprising
given that *SPE* is a more or less direct descendant of *Preliminaries*. *SPE* has
substantial overlap with each of the other two systems individually. Each of
the different regions of partial coverage in Fig. 7.1 is dominated by particular
types of class that are problematic for each theory.

Of the 30 classes describable in *Preliminaries* and UFT but not *SPE*, 22
involve the class of dental/alveolar and palatal consonants, inexpressible in
SPE where palatals are [–coronal]. Of the 571 classes accounted for by *SPE* and
UFT but not *Preliminaries*, 192 involve the class of consonants (vs. vowels),
which require the disjunction [consonantal] ∨ [non-vocalic] in *Preliminaries*,
79 involve the class of sonorants, inexpressible in *Preliminaries*, and 45 involve
vowels as opposed to rhotic approximants, which are vocalic in *Preliminaries*.
Of the 474 classes describable in *Preliminaries* and *SPE* but not UFT, the
majority require the minus value of a place feature, which is not available in
UFT, such as non-front vowels (84), non-back/non-round vowels (67), labial
and coronal ("anterior") consonants but not velars (59), labial and velar
("grave") but not coronal (44), non-labialized consonants (36), and unrounded vowels (36).

Of the 185 classes describable only in UFT, 26 are dental/alveolar/postal-
veolar/retroflex and velar ("lingual") consonants, as opposed to labial, and 15
are dental/alveolar/postalveolar/retroflex and palatal consonants. Parallel to
the first case are front and back (but not central) vowels (12 cases), statable
only in UFT, although the class of central vowels (16 cases) is not statable in
UFT. Central vowels are not statable in UFT because they lack place features
and place features are privative. While the classes of round, front, and back

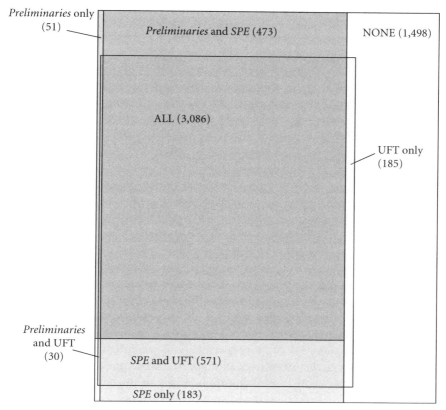

FIGURE 7.1 Coverage overlap of primary feature systems (number of classes in parentheses)

vowels can be stated as the vowels possessing [Labial], [Coronal], and [Dorsal] features respectively, central vowels share no features that are not shared by all other vowels. Of the 183 classes describable only in *SPE*, 13 involve various labial, dental/alveolar/postalveolar/retroflex, and palatal consonants as opposed to velars, and 7 involve velar and glottal consonants. Of the 51 classes describable only in *Preliminaries*, 25 involve labial and velar consonants as opposed to dental/alveolar/postalveolar/retroflex and palatal consonants, and seven involve non-retroflex consonants.

Table 7.1 shows the success of various alternative approaches to representing the classes in the feature theories. When classes were not representable with a conjunction of features, a disjunction of multiple feature bundles was attempted. Disjunction of feature bundles amounts to unions of natural

TABLE 7.1 The ability of three feature systems to characterize 6,077 phonologically active classes with a conjunction, subtraction, or disjunction of distinctive features

Best analysis	*Preliminaries*		SPE		Unified Feature Theory	
Natural (feature conjunction)	3,640	59.9%	4,313	71.0%	3,872	63.7%
Disjunction (2 classes)	1,443	23.8%	1,248	20.5%	1,266	20.8%
Subtraction (2 classes)	59	1.0%	71	1.2%	94	1.6%
Disjunction (3 classes)	233	3.8%	201	3.3%	205	3.4%
Disjunction (4 classes)	64	1.1%	56	0.9%	67	1.1%
Disjunction (5 classes)	17	0.3%	21	0.4%	17	0.3%
Disjunction (6 classes)	0	0.0%	4	0.1%	5	0.1%
Disjunction (7 classes)	1	0.0%	0	0.0%	0	0.0%
Disjunction (8 classes)	0	0.0%	0	0.0%	1	0.0%
Disjunction (9 classes)	0	0.0%	1	0.0%	0	0.0%
Unnatural (even w/disjunction)	620	10.2%	162	2.7%	550	9.1%

classes. For example, the grave class is not representable as a conjunction of features in UFT, but it is representable as the disjunction [Labial] ∨ [Dorsal]. If a disjunction of two specifications was not successful, a subtraction of one class from another was tried. If neither approach involving two classes was successful, the disjunction of more specifications was attempted. In the event that each segment in an inventory has a unique feature specification, *any* class is specifiable as a disjunction of feature bundles. In the worst-case scenario, this amounts to one class per segment. As seen in Table 7.1, as many as nine classes were necessary in order to represent a class with disjunction.

The classes which are unnatural even with disjunction are cases where segments do not have unique feature specifications and therefore cannot be distinguished from each other with a theory (e.g. prenasalized stops vs. nasals in *Preliminaries*) or in cases where there is no way to identify a particular

TABLE 7.2 Phonologically active classes and randomly generated classes in Japanese

Phonologically active classes	*Prelims.*	SPE	UFT	Randomly generated classes	*Prelims.*	SPE	UFT
/i ɯ/	👍	👍	👍	/b ʃ/	👎	👎	👎
/h k p s t ʃ/	👍	👍	👍	/aː d eː k z ɥ/	👎	👎	👎
/a aː e eː i iː o oː ɯ ɯː/	👍	👍	👍	/b e iː j m o t ɥ ɾ ʃ/	👎	👎	👎
/h k s t ʃ/	👎	👎	👎	/aː eː i oː p/	👎	👎	👎
/b d z g/	👍	👍	👍	/d m z ɾ/	👎	👎	👎

segment to the exclusion of others (e.g. central vowels vs. other vowels in UFT).

For comparison, the three feature theories were tested with randomly generated classes. Ideally, the theories would reject a large number of these classes. If they can describe randomly generated classes easily, then their ability to distinguish natural from unnatural classes is undermined. For each of the 6,077 classes in the database, a class of equal size was created by randomly selecting segments from the inventory of the language in which the class occurs. Table 7.2 shows an example from Japanese, where all three theories reject one of five observed phonologically active classes, but reject all five classes created by randomly selecting segments from the segment inventory of Japanese.

As seen in Table 7.3, very few of the randomly generated classes are natural in any of the theories, but a fairly large number of classes can be described using disjunction. All three theories succeed in being able to describe far more phonologically active classes than randomly generated classes with a conjunction of features. However, about half (or more) of the randomly generated classes can be described with the union of no more than three classes in each of the three theories (49.9 percent in *Preliminaries*, 60.3 percent in *SPE*, 49.2 percent in UFT). This suggests that the ability of the theories to describe a substantial number of "unnatural" phonologically active classes

TABLE 7.3 The ability of three feature systems to characterize 6,077 randomly generated classes with a conjunction, subtraction, or disjunction of distinctive features

Best analysis	*Preliminaries.*		*SPE*		Unified Feature Theory	
Natural (feature conjunction)	347	5.7%	480	7.9%	280	4.6%
Disjunction (2 classes)	1,727	28.4%	2,011	33.1%	1,756	28.9%
Subtraction (2 classes)	9	0.1%	11	0.2%	17	0.3%
Disjunction (3 classes)	947	15.6%	1,160	19.1%	939	15.5%
Disjunction (4 classes)	624	10.3%	774	12.7%	630	10.4%
Disjunction (5 classes)	339	5.6%	456	7.5%	352	5.8%
Disjunction (6 classes)	247	4.1%	292	4.8%	246	4.0%
Disjunction (7 classes)	107	1.8%	126	2.1%	121	2.0%
Disjunction (8 classes)	29	0.5%	29	0.5%	48	0.8%
Disjunction (9 classes)	8	0.1%	3	0.0%	16	0.3%
Unnatural (even with disjunction)	1,693	27.9%	735	12.1%	1,672	27.5%

with feature disjunction is not a point in their favor. Rather, this simply reflects the fact that half of all possible classes can be represented with the union of three or fewer classes, and the naturally occurring classes which are unnatural in these theories are no exception. One interesting fact is that very few random classes can be accounted for using subtraction of natural classes. The ability to handle unnatural classes using subtraction seems to be a better means of discriminating real from random classes than the ability to handle natural classes with a conjunction of features.

The most common classes in each theory are familiar classes which are easily defined in phonetic terms. The most common classes in *Preliminaries* features are [non-consonantal, vocalic] (vowels) occurring 306 times, [nasal], occurring 164 times, [diffuse, tense] (tense high vowels), occurring 88 times, [unvoiced], occurring 85 times, and [acute, tense] (tense front vowels), occurring 65 times. The most common classes in *SPE* features are [+syllabic] (vowels and any syllabic consonants), occurring 433 times, [–syllabic] (everything else), occurring 180 times, [+nasal], occurring 164 times, [+high, +tense] (tense high vowels), occurring 86 times, and [+tense, –back] (tense front vowels), occurring 80 times. Excluding [+/–SYLLABIC] (involving only a feature which is used to capture a distinction intended to be beyond the scope of the feature system), the most common classes in UFT features are [+nasal], occurring 163 times, [+SYLLABIC, Coronal] (front vowels), occurring 124 times, [+SYLLABIC, Labial] (rounded vowels), occurring 91 times, [+vocoid, –SYLLABIC] (glides), occurring 70 times, and [+SYLLABIC, –open2] (typically non-low vowels), occurring 61 times. Tables B.1–3 in Appendix B show many more of the most common natural classes within each of the three feature theories.

Sagey (1986) predicts that the frequency of natural classes should be negatively correlated with the number of features used to describe them. Other versions of innate feature theory do not make these predictions. Natural classes found in the database involve between one and six features. Many of the most common natural classes in each theory require two or more features. Figs. 7.2–7.4 show the 25 most common classes for each number of features (ranked by frequency), within each theory.

Classes with few features are favored by the algorithm which minimizes the number of features used to specify a class. On the other hand, classes with more features are favored by the fact that there are simply more possible combinations of larger numbers of features, and thus they constitute a larger percentage of the possible classes, including the frequent ones. In all three cases, two-feature classes seem to get the best of both worlds. Even so, of the 195 possible two-feature classes in *Preliminaries*, only 145 occur at least once in the database, and only 271 of the 575 possible *SPE* two-feature classes occur

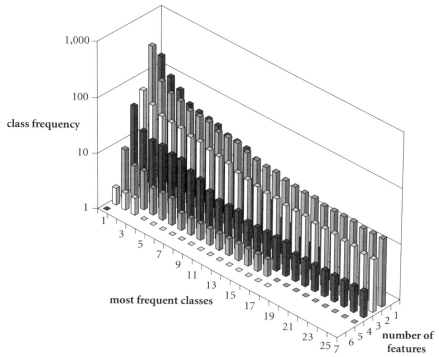

FIGURE 7.2 The most common natural classes by number of features (*Preliminaries*)

one or more times. 267 of the 1,392 possible UFT two-feature classes are
attested at least once. If features were truly the building blocks of phonological patterns, we would expect to see more of these classes appearing. Their
absence indicates that other factors (such as those which emergent feature
theory attributes natural class behavior to) are at play.

Figs. 7.5–7.7 show the distribution of frequent and infrequent classes
according to the three theories. Natural classes are shown as light bars and
unnatural classes as dark bars. The x and y axes both use log scales so that all
of the classes for each theory can be shown on the same chart. The unnatural
classes are stated as disjunctions or subtractions, and since all the unnatural
classes are (by definition) ones that the theories are not intended to represent,
the frequency of many unnatural classes is probably under-represented here,
with various disjunctions and subtractions actually referring to the same type
of unnatural class. While innate feature theories predict that natural classes
definable in their features will be more frequent than any idiosyncratic

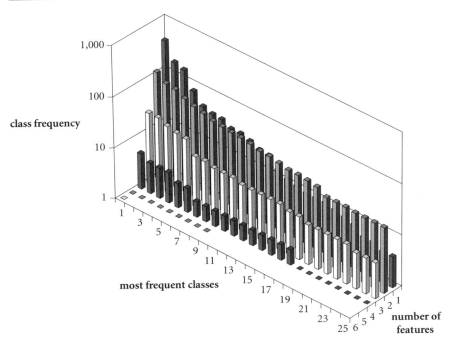

FIGURE 7.3 The most common natural classes by number of features (*SPE*)

unnatural classes which may occur, there is no evidence of this in the data. In *Preliminaries* and Unified Feature Theory, unnatural classes rank among the most common recurrent classes. Even in *SPE*, there is no objective way to partition classes into natural and idiosyncratic categories. Many apparently unnatural classes recur in multiple languages, and ranking classes according to frequency results in a distribution which slopes gently from the common classes, which are easily described in phonetic terms and easily characterized in traditional phonetically defined features, all the way down to the rare classes which occur only once in the survey. Not only is there no visible boundary between the natural and the unnatural, but the two are interleaved, with some of the most common unnatural classes being more frequent than most natural classes, and with the vast majority of the natural classes which are predicted by combining distinctive features completely unattested.

In *Preliminaries* (Fig. 7.5), seven unnatural classes rank among the most common classes, even in a theory that is not well suited to counting them. These are [consonantal, oral] ∨ [non-vocalic] (consonants), occurring 40 times, [consonantal] ∨ [non-vocalic] (also consonants), occurring 31 times,

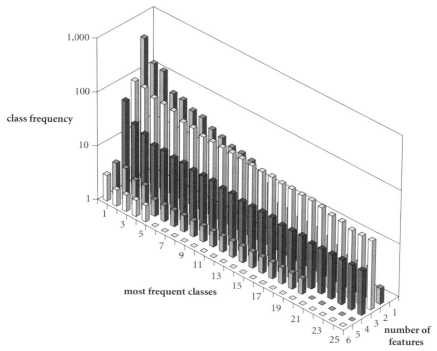

FIGURE 7.4 The most common natural classes by number of features (UFT)

[cons, mellow] ∨ [non-vocalic] (non-strident consonants), occurring 17 times, [non-consonantal, plain (not flat), vocalic] ∨ [tense] (essentially vowels), occurring 10 times, [consonantal] ∨ [non-vocalic, oral] (consonants again), occurring 9 times, and [consonantal, vocalic] ∨ [nasal] (nasals and liquids), occurring 9 times.

In *SPE* (Fig. 7.6), the most common unnatural class is [+high, +tense] ∨ [+vocalic, −tense] (/i u a/ or /i u ɛ ɔ a/), occurring 6 times. This chart looks much better than the other two. In fact, the 113 most common classes are statable as a conjunction of *SPE* features. The situation is actually worse than it appears, for a couple of reasons. First, the unnatural classes are more recurrent than they appear when they are counted in terms of the very theory that has difficulty representing them. As mentioned above, there are recurrent classes which *Preliminaries* and UFT can handle but *SPE* cannot, such as the 22 classes involving dental/alveolar and palatal consonants. When forced into *SPE* features, common classes such as this one are fragmented, and register instead as several less common classes, because they are represented with different disjunctions in different inventories. One of the reasons for this is that there are often several

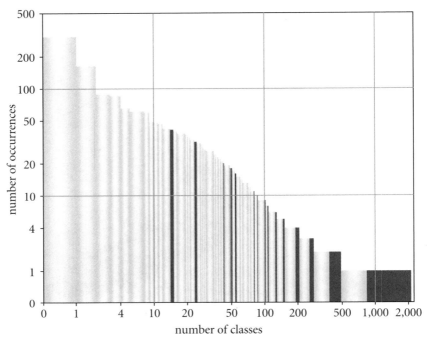

FIGURE 7.5 The distribution of frequent and infrequent natural (light) and unnatural (dark) classes (*Preliminaries*)

different ways to represent classes, particularly classes which require feature disjunction, and so classes which are common do not appear to be common, because each possible feature analysis is counted separately. A more theory-neutral method of counting recurrent classes would reduce this problem.

In UFT (Fig. 7.7), several unnatural classes are shown in the top part of the chart, ranking among the most common classes. These are [+SYLLABIC, Labial] ∨ [+open1] (round back vowels and /a/), occurring 31 times, [+SYLLABIC, Coronal] ∨ [+open1] (unrounded front vowels and /a/), occurring 27 times, [+open1] ∨ [+open2, Labial] (round non-high back vowels and /a/), occurring 20 times, [+open1] ∨ [+open2, Coronal] (unrounded non-high front vowels and /a/), occurring 17 times, [−sonorant, Dorsal] ∨ [−sonorant, Labial] (grave obstruents), occurring 12 times, [+SYLLABIC, −open2] ∨ [+open1] (high and low vowels), occurring 12 times, [+distributed, −open6] ∨ [−open6, Labial] (non-low front vowels and non-low round vowels), occurring 10 times, and [+SYLLABIC, Dorsal] ∨ [+open1] (back vowels and /a/), occurring 10 times.

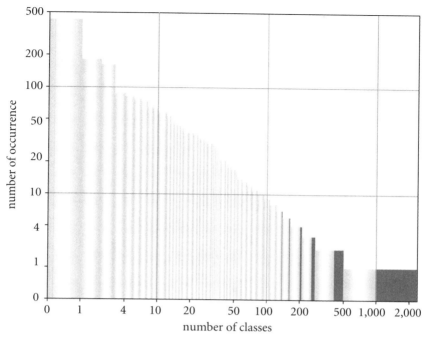

FIGURE 7.6 The distribution of frequent and infrequent natural and unnatural classes (*SPE*)

Just as there is a wide range of frequencies among the classes occurring in the database, there is a wide range of frequencies of the specific features used to define them. Tables B.4–6 in Appendix B show the frequency of occurrence of each feature in the natural classes descriptions in each of the three feature theories. It is clear that all features are not equal. Some are more commonly used than others. In *Preliminaries*, [vocalic] and [non-consonantal] are the most frequently used feature values. In *SPE*, [+syllabic] and [–sonorant] are most frequent, and [–sonorant] and [–continuant] are the most frequent of the UFT features (after +/–SYLLABIC).

The features which are most common in natural class specifications are those which occur in the most inventories. For example [sharp] in *Preliminaries* is rare in large part because few languages have contrastive palatalization. Emergent feature theory predicts that the number of occurrences of a particular feature is directly associated with how clear the phonetic correlates are (and how likely the features are to be involved in a phonetically based generalization) This prediction is examined later in this section.

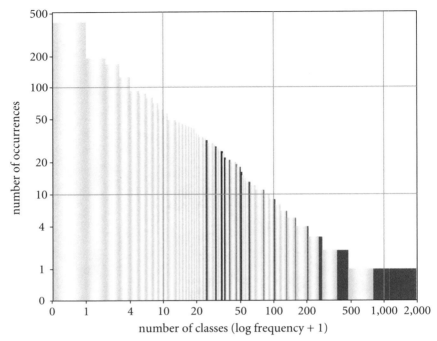

FIGURE 7.7 The distribution of frequent and infrequent natural and unnatural classes (UFT)

Each of the three theories has features which are used to define a large number of natural classes as well as features which are used very little. The theories are right to posit the commonly used features, which do indeed allow the specification of many of the classes which occur. The seldom-used features do not seem to share the same status as the commonly used ones, in terms of being part of the set of innate features. In general, these theories do not have anything to say about why some features are more useful than others (nor were they intended to), and some possible factors are explored below. None of the theories comes close to accounting for all the phonologically active classes or even all the recurrent ones, indicating that more ways of defining classes are needed. The wide variety of recurrent "unnatural" classes indicates that simply adding more seldom-used features is not a very good solution.

7.1.1 *Place of articulation*

The above show that in general, these feature theories exclude from natural-ness many naturally occurring classes, including many which are quite common. A specific example of this is in predicted subgroupings of place.

Different feature theories predict different possible subgroupings of major places of articulation (Labial, Coronal, and Dorsal) among consonants.

Preliminaries and *SPE* both use place features which crosscut segments produced with different articulators. For example, in *SPE*, [+anterior] applies to labial consonants as well as dentals and alveolars. *Preliminaries* does the same with the feature [diffuse]. These labials and coronals would be expected to pattern together in sound patterns referring to [+anterior] or [diffuse] (47a), and labials would be expected to pattern with velars and palatals in sound patterns involving [grave] or [−coronal] (which also applies to uvulars). In more recent approaches to place of articulation, each of the three major places has its own unary feature, and these three features are dominated by a place node, as in (47b). This organization does not predict that subsets of places of articulation should pattern together on the basis of shared features, because there is no node that dominates any proper subset of place features. If an intermediate [Lingual] node is introduced, as in some versions of Unified Feature Theory, then coronal and dorsal segments are expected to pattern together on the basis of this shared feature.

The conventions of Feature Geometry do not allow nodes to be immediately dominated by more than one node, so it is not possible to add, for example, a node such as Grave, which would dominate Labial and Dorsal, without eliminating Lingual. Consequently, different feature theories make very different predictions about subgroupings of places of articulation that are expected to be frequent. Each theory makes predictions about what should be common on the basis of observed patterning, and each predicted natural class has a phonetic basis. [diffuse] and [grave] are defined acoustically, while [−coronal] and Lingual are defined articulatorily.

(47)   Organization of place features

(a) [+anterior] / [diffuse]: labials and many coronals
[−coronal] / [grave]:   labials, velars, and palatals (and uvulars)

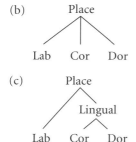

To test these predictions, the survey database was searched for all of the classes which involve segments from two or more places of articulation to the exclusion of at least one other place, provided that the distinction cannot be made in some other dimension such as manner. For example, /m n/ does not count as an example of labials and coronals patterning together if these are the only nasals in the language. The three most common classes are the three possible combinations of two places from among labial, coronal, and velar. Each of the three feature theories predicts at least one of these classes, but none predicts all three. Table 7.4 shows the predictions and results for these three pairs of places. Table B.7 in Appendix B shows the complete results for subgroupings of different places of articulation found in the database. While feature theories disagree over which places of articulation should pattern together, each pair is robustly attested, and approximately equally frequent. Most of the labial/coronal classes do only involve anteriors (as predicted by two of the feature theories), but 48 of them involve posterior coronal consonants as well.

Each theory is right about the subgroupings of places it predicts, but wrong about the ones it excludes. The only reason not to expect these subgroupings is that some theories prohibit them, but this is clearly not right. Indeed, the fact that various groupings are observed is part of the reason why there are many feature theories. Each theory predicts an internally consistent set of possible generalizations, and this is part of a larger picture. This picture includes a wide range of phonetic dimensions which are variably exploited by different feature theories. All three subgroupings involve places of articulation with clear acoustic and/or articulatory properties in common, and each theory predicts that some should be rare or unattested because they have no feature specification in the theory.

UFT predicts no classes involving labials and coronals but not velars, because its place features have no negative values and the lowest node that dominates [Labial] and [Coronal] also dominates [Dorsal]. With a Lingual node, UFT explicitly predicts the class of coronals and velars, which *SPE* does not predict under most circumstances. But UFT does not predict the grave class, which *Preliminaries* predicts explicitly. Each theory is a different set of snapshots showing some common classes while neglecting others. None of them shows the entire range of classes which can arise from sound change and generalization.

SPE makes the claim that phonological patterns can be described using only articulatory features, so the presence of classes that can only be defined acoustically are problematic. *SPE* predicts the grave class indirectly, in articulatory terms, with the negative value of the feature [coronal]. In addition to many

TABLE 7.4 Patterning of subgroupings of major places of articulation

Feature theory	Labials and coronals	Coronals and dorsals	Labials and dorsals
Preliminaries	PREDICTED: [diffuse] (acoustic similarity)	(not predicted)	PREDICTED: [grave] (acoustic similarity)
SPE	PREDICTED: [−coronal] (articulatory similarity)	(not predicted)	PREDICTED: [+anterior] (articulatory similarity)
Unified Feature Theory (with Lingual)	(not predicted)	PREDICTED: (articulatory similarity)	(not predicted)
Survey says	ATTESTED: n = 127	ATTESTED: n = 132	ATTESTED: n = 101

unnatural grave classes (unnatural in ways unrelated to place), there are 25 phonologically active classes of labial and velar segments in languages with palatals and/or uvulars which are handled easily by *Preliminaries* and UFT, but not by *SPE*, whose articulatory features are only capable of defining grave classes in languages whose inventories of places of articulation are limited enough that [grave] equals [−coronal].

The fact that all three pairs of [Labial], [Coronal], and [Dorsal] are robustly attested indicates that each theory is right about the subgroupings of places it does predict, but wrong about the ones that it excludes. There are many examples of all kinds of subgrouping involving these three places and many less common classes. The findings suggest that any class is possible, but that certain ones involving common places of articulation which share clear articulatory or perceptual properties are most common. The fact that so many different groupings are observed is part of the reason why there are different feature theories. Examining a lot of data at the same time demonstrates that the theories are correct in positing many of the generalizations that they do, but that none of them is universal.

7.1.2 *Phonetic correlates*

Emergent feature theory predicts that the features with the clearest phonetic correlates will be the most useful for describing natural classes, because these phonetic correlates, rather than the features themselves, are the basis for the generalizations which gave rise to many of the classes. In this section, the phonetic groundedness of the features is compared to the frequency of the features. How frequent a feature can be within natural classes is dependent upon how frequent the feature is in inventories, i.e. how "available" it is to define classes. To control for this, the frequencies of the features are adjusted for their relative availability.

Availability is based on the number of segments in an inventory which bear each value of a feature. If no segments in the inventory are specified for a particular feature value, then the feature is not available for describing natural classes, no matter how phonetically robust it is. Similarly, if only a small portion of the segments are defined for one of the values, the feature is relatively unavailable. A feature is maximally available for natural class formation/description when half of the segments are specified for one value of the feature and half are specified for the other. The numerical representation of availability is defined as the percentage of segments in the language which bear the least common value of the feature. Thus, availability can never be more than 50 percent. For example, if two out of 25 segments in an inventory are [+spread glottis], then the availability of [spread glottis] is 8 percent. If 30 out of 50 segments in an inventory are [+sonorant] and 20 are [−sonorant], then the availability of [sonorant] in that language is 40 percent. The cross-linguistic availability of a feature, as shown in the following tables, is the average of the availability values for all the languages in the survey. The adjusted frequency of occurrence of a feature is the sum of the occurrence of each value (if the feature has more than one value) divided by the availability, i.e. the projected number of occurrences of the feature in a database of the same size in which all features have an availability of 50 percent. Alternatively, availability could be estimated on the basis of the random classes in Table 7.3.

Several perception studies have examined the usefulness of phonetic features for discrimination of segments under various listening conditions. Table 7.5 shows the relative rankings of features in terms of sequential information analyses from confusion matrices from various studies. Shown here are results from Miller and Nicely (1955), Singh and Black (1966), Graham and House (1971), and Wang and Bilger (1973); see Wang and Bilger for discussion of these results. The results also show a correlation with the adjusted frequencies of the distinctive features.

Emergent feature theory claims that the phonetic properties of speech sounds, rather than distinctive features, are primarily responsible for their groupings into phonologically active classes. The fact that there is a correlation between the frequency of phonetically grounded features and experimental measurements of their perceptual distinctiveness, even with all the complications presented by the feature theory itself, is promising.

TABLE 7.5 Sequential information analysis results (rankings) for various features compared with *SPE* survey results (Wang and Bilger 1973)

Feature	Sequential information rank				Adj. freq.	Avail.	Frequency	
	M&N	S&B	G&H	W&B			+	−
round	−	−	6	−	2,697.0	6.5%	173	175
nasal	1	1	8	1	2,113.2	9.7%	245	164
back	−	4	−	5	1,209.0	29.0%	307	395
voice	2	5	4	2	1,059.6	35.5%	373	379
low	−	7	9	4	893.8	9.7%	20	153
vocalic	−	2	−	−	814.6	29.0%	333	140
high	−	−	−	6	757.3	45.2%	402	282
consonantal	−	−	7	−	487.5	35.5%	180	166
anterior	−	−	5	6	467.6	38.7%	251	111
continuant	4	−	−	4	409.2	48.4%	185	211
strident	3	−	1	7	342.9	25.8%	80	97
[place]	5	8	10	8	n/a	n/a	n/a	n/a
[frication]	−	−	3	−	n/a	n/a	n/a	n/a
[duration]	−	−	2	−	n/a	n/a	n/a	n/a

7.1.3 *Defining unnatural classes*

It was expected that innate feature theories would be forced to use feature disjunction in order to account for many of the classes in the database as the unions of smaller classes which they are capable of describing. As seen above, this is true. Feature theories predict that this will happen on occasion, as there is nothing which prevents multiple classes from being affected by the same process. The result would be the union of two natural classes appearing to behave as a single phonologically active class.

Emergent feature theory predicts that the most common of the classes which require recourse to disjunction or subtraction will be those which are phonetically natural but inexpressible in the theory with a conjunction of features. The innate feature theories predict that the most common complex classes will be composed of classes which are very common natural classes on their own. The results show that while many unnatural classes are describable as the union of two natural classes, the most common of the classes which can be analyzed in this way are composed of phonetically similar segments, but analyzable only as the union of classes which are very rare on their own.

A good example is the most common unnatural classes in *Preliminaries* features. Four of the five most frequent unnatural classes define the class of consonants (as opposed to vowels) using the disjunction of different feature bundles: [consonantal, oral] ∨ [non-vocalic], occurring 40 times, [consonantal] ∨ [non-vocalic], occurring 31 times, [consonantal, mellow] ∨ [non-vocalic], occurring 17 times, and [consonantal] ∨ [non-vocalic, oral], occurring 9 times. The natural classes which are combined to make these classes are not so frequent that they would be expected to co-occur by accident. The most frequent component is [consonantal], which occurs 34 times, slightly less than the most frequent unnatural class, and only slightly more than the most frequent unnatural class it is used to define.

While the class of consonants is a phonetically natural class, the natural classes which are patched together to represent them are even less common than the class being constructed by this ad hoc means. Clearly, this is an indication that *Preliminaries* leaves a hole in its coverage. It is unable to characterize the set of consonants (including glides and liquids), even though this is a common class. The fact that this class can be constructed from smaller, rarer classes that *Preliminaries* can describe is a coincidence.

Tables B.11–B.13 in Appendix B list the number of occurrences of the most common classes requiring disjunction or subtraction, along with their rank among common unnatural classes. The number of occurrences of the natural classes on which they are based are also listed, along with their ranks among the most common natural classes. It is clear that the most common unnatural classes do not result from combinations of the most common natural classes.

Many of the unnatural classes listed for UFT are classes involving front or back vowels and a single low vowel. These classes are inevitably unnatural for UFT because the low vowels are not specified for the place features which define the other members of the classes. The components of complex classes that provide the low vowel are more numerous than they appear for two reasons. First, in UFT, as in Particle Phonology, the features used to define the lowest vowel height depends on the number of vowel heights in the language. This means that the class /a/ in a language like Japanese, which has three heights, is featurally different from the class /a/ in a language like Yoruba which has four heights ([+open2] and [+open3] respectively). Second, the phonologically active classes counted in the survey were those involving more than one but fewer than all the sounds in a language's inventory. This means that classes such as [+open3], which typically define only one sound, are typically not counted. Since these feature specifications are used when necessary to define unnatural classes, but most commonly only apply to natural classes that were not counted in the survey (because they usually contain only one member), they do not provide a very good test case.

However, most of the classes which are far more common as components of unnatural classes than as natural classes are not of this type.

The innate feature theories predict that the classes occurring most frequently in the feature description of unnatural classes should also be the most common natural classes, if these classes arise as a result of the co-occurrence of different natural classes that happen to be involved in similar phonological patterns. The results are far from this prediction.

The feature [non-vocalic] is the most frequent component of unnatural classes in *Preliminaries* features, helping define 150 unnatural classes, but it only defines 23 natural classes. The feature bundle [consonantal, vocalic] helps to define 123 unnatural classes, but only defines 36 natural classes by itself. Among *SPE* feature bundles, [+coronal, −tense] helps define the most unnatural classes (51), but only defines two natural classes. The feature [+open1] is the most frequent component of unnatural classes in UFT features, although, as mentioned above, it is artificially under-represented. Appendix B shows the most common components of complex unnatural classes. The classes are simply the ones necessary in order to piece together the actually occurring classes that these feature theories cannot represent as conjunctions of features.

While most theories of innate features do predict that unions of natural classes can participate in phonological patterns by chance, they do not predict the types of disjunction shown here to be necessary to characterize many of the phonologically active classes in the database. Further, it was seen above in Table 7.3 that the theories are quite effective at describing even randomly generated classes using the disjunction of two or more feature bundles. These findings weaken one of the remaining caveats available to innate feature theory.

7.2 Other feature theories

While the analysis in this chapter has focused on three feature theories, it is helpful to consider other features that have been proposed, in order to account for some of the classes these three theories do not account for.

One feature not included in any of the above theories is [guttural] (McCarthy 1991), which applies to uvulars, pharyngeals, and laryngeals. This feature accounts for classes which were accounted for in *SPE* using [−high]. Since [−high] was no longer in use to refer to consonants in this way at the time, [guttural] was a useful addition to Feature Geometry. McCarthy (and Chomsky and Halle) are correct to propose that sound patterns may make use of a distinction between sounds produced at the uvula or farther back, and sounds produced in front of the uvula. But there are also classes which utilize a similar but slightly different distinction, in which velar fricatives pattern with gutturals. These classes (e.g. in Libyan Arabic) are natural in a theory in which [pharyngeal] refers to laryngeal consonants as well as velar fricatives, which has been proposed by Paradis and LaCharité (2001). However, similar classes which also include velar stops (e.g. in North Israel Bedouin Arabic) require still another definition of the relevant feature.

Avery and Idsardi (2001) propose an account of laryngeal features in which the features form constituents below the laryngeal node. The features [spread] and [constricted] form the constituent Glottal Width, [stiff] and [slack] form the constituent Glottal Tension, and [raised] and [lowered] form the constituent Larynx Height. This and some other Feature Geometry proposals are intended to serve purposes other than to refine the set of predicted natural classes, but such a refinement is nevertheless a consequence. If this arrangement of laryngeal features is assumed, then in addition to the predictions about laryngeal contrast within inventories, a wider range of possible classes defined by laryngeal configuration is expected, possibly including an account for classes in which implosives, but not ejectives, pattern together with both voiced and voiceless stops, or vice versa (e.g. in Adilabad Gondi, Boraana Oromo, Dahalo, Orma, and Waata Oromo).

The feature [sonorant voice] has been proposed as a feature that voiced sonorants possess in lieu of the traditional feature [voice] (Rice and Avery 1989, Rice 1992). This feature allows for straightforward analyses of voicing-sensitive phonological patterns which ignore voiced sonorants. The proposal for this feature recognizes phonetic differences between sonorant voicing and obstruent voicing, namely that the former involve spontaneous voicing and the latter do not, and therefore predicts (correctly) that phonological patterns may exploit this distinction.

Supplementing a set of articulatory features with auditory features (Flemming 2002) allows for the representation of some phonologically active classes which are unnatural if only articulatory features are available, such as the full range of classes including just laterals and nasals, and the classes containing sibilants and nasals.

Finally, as shown by Flemming (2005) and Yip (2004, 2005), constraint interaction in Optimality Theory predicts a potentially unlimited array of phonologically active classes. It was seen above that Optimality Theory represents class subtraction directly, with antagonistic constraints referring to overlapping classes of segments. If factorial typology is taken seriously, then classes which are defined by fewer interacting constraints are expected to be more common, and this in turn depends on the feature set which is used to formulate the constraints. It is expected that the classes describable by subtraction of classes would involve the subtraction of common classes. The only highly ranked subtraction class in the three theories is [+back, −low, −round]−[+vocalic, −tense] in *SPE*. This class is defined in terms of the class of tense vowels, which is quite common, and the class of non-low non-round back vowels, which does not occur as a class in the database, casting doubt on the idea that this subtraction class results from the interaction of constraints referring to more common classes. In order to evaluate the predictions of Optimality Theory approaches to natural classes, it will be necessary to see how many of the classes formed by the union of natural classes can be described as the subtraction of one class from another, and if the component classes are indeed common.

Many of the approaches discussed in this subsection have the effect of adding to the range of possible classes predicted by innate distinctive features. Some of them also withdraw predicted classes from other areas, either by abandoning certain features, which is easily remedied by reintroducing them, or by redefining features, which is less easily remedied. None of these approaches is able to characterize as many phonologically active classes as one would expect if it truly involved a feature set that is specified in Universal Grammar and is the alphabet from which phonological patterns are constructed.

7.3 Summary

Every proposal for a new feature or a new feature definition recognizes the connection between a particular set of phonetic properties and the existence of phonological patterns which exploit them. This aspect of innate feature theory is in complete agreement with emergent feature theory: various recognizable phonetic properties are associated with phonological patterns. But none of these feature proposals has accompanied evidence for the existence of certain predicted phenomena with evidence *against* the existence of other non-predicted phenomena, and none of the approaches examined is able to account for more than three quarters of the phonologically active classes in the survey. In short, while there is a consensus that there is a connection between phonetic similarity (signified by distinctive features) and phonological activity, there is disagreement over which phonetic properties are appropriate for defining phonologically active classes, and there is no theory of what phonetic properties are *prohibited* from defining phonologically active classes. Feature theories disagree on what is not predicted, and for each theory, there is a wide range of naturally occurring phonologically active classes that they do not predict.

The many instantiations of innate feature theory have provided strong evidence that certain, usually robust, phonetic properties are involved in phonologically active classes. The decades spent on this enterprise have provided quite a bit of insight into what phonetic properties are most likely to define classes. Indeed, phonological theory is greatly indebted to innate distinctive feature theory for this information. But there is also a wide range of less common classes with less robust phonetic correlates, and no evidence that any classes are ruled out. It must be concluded that the positive proposal of innate distinctive feature theory is correct, and the negative proposal incorrect. To progress further in the pursuit of explanation for phonologically active classes, it is necessary to abandon the hypothesis that features are innate, and to focus on the phonetic properties which actually underlie the phonological groupings and on how abstract features are learned.

The idea behind emergent feature theories is that the connections between sounds which may tend to pattern together are a result of similarities between these sounds. Sounds have articulatory and acoustic properties, and therefore similarities, because they are produced by a vocal tract and propagated as acoustic signals. The physical properties of speech sounds, as well as their existing roles in sound systems, afford them the opportunity to group together in sound patterns. When this happens, this grouping, a cognitive category if speakers recognize it, can be interpreted as a feature that can be said to have emerged and which learners of a language may acquire. In innate distinctive feature theory, these features have been interpreted as pre-existing cognitive entities. In emergent feature theory, recurrent classes are not the result of innate features, but the result of properties possessed by sounds simply as a result of the fact that they exist.

After being together for years, sound patterns, phonetic naturalness, and distinctive features may all benefit from decoupling, in order to learn the ways in which the three are related. The innate features approach has revealed many correlations between phonetic naturalness and phonological patterning, and it would be worthwhile at this point to investigate larger forces which contribute to these correlations, giving rise to the well-behaved cases that provide primary evidence for innate features, as well as ambivalent segments and unnatural classes.

7.4 Towards a phonetic similarity model

All the feature theories discussed above make use of phonetically defined features. If the features they propose are not actually innate, then the classes they correctly predict must be attributed to the phonetic dimensions the features are grounded in. In emergent feature theory, phonologically active classes are accounted for in part as the result of generalizations to groups of phonetically similar segments. This predicts that a model of phonetic similarity should be able to predict likely phonologically active classes at least as well as any phonetically based feature theory. The point here is not necessarily to do better than an innate feature-based model (although this should be possible), but to show that roughly the same level of accuracy can be achieved without assuming innate features.

In order to capture all the factors which are expected to contribute to phonologically active class formation, an adequate model of phonetic similarity would need to draw upon perceptual and articulatory information, and to include information on a wide range of segments. Constructing a model which would be sufficient to address all the questions a phonetic similarity model is intended to answer is beyond the scope of this book, but it is possible to construct a pilot model to at least demonstrate the promise of this pursuit.

The pilot model draws on the confusion matrices from Wang and Bilger's (1973) perception study. This study was selected because it involves a greater number of segments than other studies such as Miller and Nicely (1955), who test only 16 consonants. Wang and Bilger's study examines confusions among 25 English consonants (/p t k b d g tʃ dʒ f θ s ʃ h v ð z ʒ m n ŋ l ɹ j ʌ w/) in CV and VC syllables. Wang and Bilger's four confusion matrices (different overlapping subsets of consonants were tested separately) were combined into one large 25 × 25 matrix. This confusion matrix was converted into a distance matrix, and a multidimensional scaling analysis was performed in SPSS, to give a five-dimensional model. A second model was constructed based on a four-dimensional multidimensional scaling analysis and an artificial fifth dimension representing place of articulation, a dimension which is under-represented by the perception data.

The pairwise single-linkage hierarchical clustering algorithm in the C Clustering Library (de Hoon 2002) was used to locate clusters of segments which are similar with respect to up to five dimensions. A sample dendrogram (Fig. 7.8) shows the clusters found in the consonant inventory of Jamaican Creole, based on all five dimensions in the model. Both these models can then be compared with the innate feature models in terms of their ability to predict the phonologically active classes that occur.

The phonetic similarity and innate feature models each assign a score to any set of segments within an inventory, reflecting the likelihood of that set of segments participating being a phonology active class. The innate feature models assign scores according to how many classes are required to represent the set of segments. Classes describable as a conjunction of features receive a

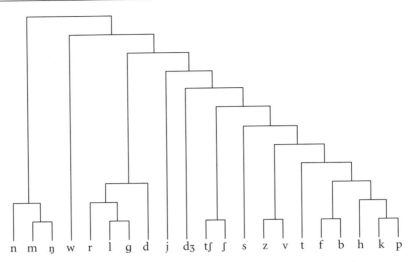

F IGURE 7.8 A dendrogram based on overall similarity of Jamaican Creole consonants

score of zero, and one point is added for every additional feature-defined natural class needed to describe the observed class. Because it was the most successful of the innate feature models, *SPE* is used for comparison to the phonetic similarity models. Many different scoring schemes are possible, but these were chosen in order to be in the spirit of the way unnatural classes are handled in each approach, i.e. by combining natural classes in innate feature theory, and by extending a generalization in emergent feature theory.

The phonetic similarity models assign scores according to how well the segments cluster with respect to the model. A set of segments which is a cluster according to the hierarchical clustering algorithm gets a score of zero. Classes which are not clusters are examined starting with the largest cluster which is a subset of the set of segments in question. The score assigned to the class is the sum of the distances from each segment not in the cluster to the nearest segment which is in the cluster.

The data against which the models are tested was limited to the 16 varieties of 15 languages in the database whose consonant inventories employ a subset of the 25 consonants from the Want and Bilger study: Agta (Casiguran Dumagat), Berbice Dutch, Daga, Desano, Jamaican Creole, Kickapoo, Lingala, Meriam, Mishmi, Montagnais, Ndyuka, Nyanja, Sawai, Sentani (including Central dialect), and Xakas. Classes were limited to those which involve no vowels, a total of 59 classes.

The purpose of each of these models is not simply to give good ratings to likely classes, but to distinguish likely classes from unlikely ones. Randomly created classes were used as a control. For each class in each language, a class of the same size was generated randomly. The control for each language was created from ten iterations of this process. The same control was used for all three approaches. Because the purpose is to distinguish likely classes from unlikely ones, each model ideally should give high scores to the randomly selected classes and low scores to the actual classes. The average scores provided for each language by each model were scaled, and all of these are listed in Appendix C.

The ability of all three approaches to distinguish real from random classes is significant, based on univariate analyses of variance (ANOVA) [5 dimensions: $F(1,15) = 32.663$, $p < 0.001$; 4 dimensions + place: $F(1,15) = 18.990$, $p < 0.001$; SPE: $F(1,15) = 89.006$, $p < 0.001$]. A single ANOVA with model and real vs. random as factors did not show a significant interaction between these two factors [$F(1,2) = .538$, $p = 0.586$], but means and 95 percent confidence intervals are shown in Fig. 7.9.

The ANOVAs and Fig. 7.9 show that SPE and the two phonetic similarity models are basically equal in their ability to distinguish real from random classes. The fact that a phonetic similarity model based only on confusion matrices from a single perception study can come so close to a thoughtfully constructed innate feature model is cause for optimism about the prospect of making a less rudimentary model using more comprehensive perceptual and articulatory data.

The ability of this pilot phonetic similarity metric to be on an equal footing with an innate features model shows that the success of innate feature models is not due to the features, but the phonetic facts they are grounded in. Further, it is completely reasonable to attribute the occurrence of phonologically active classes to sound change and generalization based on phonetic similarity. A more advanced model would be expected to make better predictions about likely generalizations. The collection of phonetic parameters used to predict classes is not intended to be part of linguistic competence, but simply a picture of the phonetic factors that are relevant for generalization, which is one of the sources of phonologically active classes in emergent feature theory.

7.5 Conclusions

This chapter has presented the results of the survey of phonologically active classes in terms of various theories of distinctive features. The predictions made by feature theories have been shown to be correct in the sense that many of the classes they predict truly are common. Nevertheless, many classes which occur and recur in the database are not predicted by these theories at all, and innate feature theories require something like emergent feature theory to

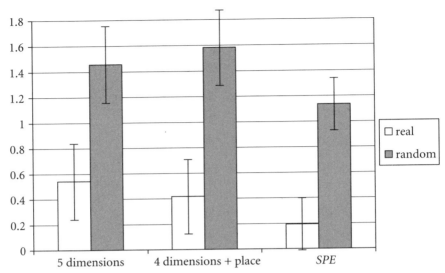

FIGURE 7.9 Means and 95 percent confidence intervals for three models

account for the actual frequency of occurrence of predicted natural classes. A rudimentary model based on phonetic similarity is able to predict likely classes just as well as *SPE*, indicating that the phonetic facts features are grounded in, not the features themselves, are responsible for the theories' success.

8

The emergence of linguistic structure

There are no recorded cases of human rabies in the United States caused by gerbils, chipmunks, guinea pigs, squirrels, mice, rats, rabbits, or hares.[1] A plausible explanation for this would be that these animals are unfit hosts for the virus, perhaps because their body temperature is too high. However, Louis Pasteur created the first rabies vaccine by manually infecting rabbits with the virus. If rabbits can carry rabies, then why is it never transmitted to humans by wild rabbits afflicted with the disease? The answer is that a small animal such as the aforementioned rodents and lagomorphs usually cannot survive an attack by a rabid animal. Larger rodents such as beavers and groundhogs (which are large enough to survive an attack) have been reported to carry rabies. So there is a diachronic story for a typological generalization about small animals: there is no naturally occurring event which results in a rabid chipmunk. It has to do with interactions between chipmunks and external factors such as large animals who attack chipmunks, rather than an inherent property of chipmunks. The interaction, over time, with animal-external factors does not tell the whole story. Opossums in North America typically do not carry rabies either, even though they grow larger than groundhogs, who are large enough to get the disease. In this case the answer may indeed be an inherent property of opossums: their body temperature is too low for rabies. A complete understanding of who can get rabies and why requires paying attention both to inherent properties resulting from the evolution of animals and to interactions over time between animals and external factors. Relying too much on just one of these types of information could make it difficult to see the other.

Understanding language also requires attention to these two types of explanation, and this chapter outlines a general model for the emergence of linguistic structure that takes them into account. The design of the model has overlap with Hume and Johnson's (2001c) model of the interplay of external factors and

---

[1] Pasteur (1885), Hankins and Rosekrans (2004), Bowers et al. (2004).

phonology, Blevins' (2004) *Evolutionary Phonology*, and various innatist approaches, combined with several new elements. Many aspects of this model are also largely compatible with and inspired by work in historical linguistics (see e.g. Labov 1994, 2001, Hale 2003, Janda 2003, Janda and Joseph 2003, Kiparsky 2003, and references in Joseph and Janda 2003). The purpose of the general model is to provide a formal means of accounting for linguistic patterns and generalizations whose explanation can be found in language change and factors which are external to the language faculty. The role of Universal Grammar in accounting for linguistic structure is not rejected, but included alongside many other potential factors. Consequently, these competing mechanisms can be compared in the same terms in an effort to see which components of the model are best able to account for observed linguistic patterns.

This general model is then used to address specific questions about phonologically active classes and phonological features. While the general model is capable of attributing the emergence of natural class behavior to biological evolution (i.e. the evolution of Universal Grammar) or to language change (via external factors included in the model), it will be seen that much of the evidence points to external factors and language change. This is the basis of emergent feature theory, which takes external factors as the starting point, and leaves open the possibility that Universal Grammar could be invoked in response to unambiguous evidence. By taking this approach, nothing is assumed to be accounted for by innate features if it has an explanation elsewhere. The innate features approach proceeds in the opposite direction, using language change to account for facts which find no explanation in innate features. This may not be the best direction in which to approach these different factors, because language change and external factors are independently motivated, and innate features are motivated only by the need to account for phonological patterns. If language change and external factors are explored adequately, then these motivations may disappear.

Emergentist approaches focus on the emergence of structure through the use of language and exposure to environmental factors, but this is not the only way in which structure could have emerged. All of the theories which assume Universal Grammar components such as an innate set of distinctive features posit the existence of structure which emerged in a different way, i.e. through the development of the human "language organ" through natural selection or divine intervention. The use of "emergence" in this chapter refers to emergence of structure in both language use/change and biological evolution, and the existence of linguistic structure should make it uncontroversial that this structure did indeed emerge in some way. The question of emergence is not Yes or no?, but When and how?

In generative grammar, the formalism used to represent synchronic linguistic patterns has been intimately tied to a model of cognitive language processing. An example of this is the notion of innate distinctive features. The features are not simply the formal means of representing speech sounds and sound patterns; they are claimed to be what speech sounds and sound patterns are *made of* in the human mind. Constraining the set of formally statable phonological patterns to the set of common phonological patterns amounts to a hypothesis about what phonological patterns the human language faculty is capable of dealing with. When the only way to account for typological observations about phonological patterns is to manipulate the model of the phonological component of Universal Grammar, incorporating other means of accounting for typology is difficult. In this chapter, synchronic language processing will be dealt with separately from accounting for typological observations. This is not to rule out the possibility that the two are tied to one another, but to allow for the possibility that there can be instances where they are not, to allow the connection between synchronic processing and typology to be a conclusion.

8.1 Formalization

Considering explanation to be independent of the cognitive representation of language allows for a wide range of methods for formalizing synchronic phonological patterns. These formalisms may be capable of representing languages which are unattested, but this is not problematic as long as independent explanation exists for accounting for the non-occurrence of unattested phonological patterns. More importantly, the formalism must be able to represent all *possible* phonological patterns. Formalisms which have variants that are capable of representing a very wide range of phonological patterns include rule-, constraint-, and lexicon-based approaches, which are summarized briefly in the next few paragraphs. The issue of choosing between these formalisms has been clouded by efforts to make the synchronic formalisms responsible for typological predictions. The model proposed in this chapter is intended to remove this responsibility from the synchronic grammar, and this should have the effect of making the choice between formalisms a clearer one, as discussed at the end of the section.

Powerful rule-based formalisms in the style of *SPE* may be desirable if unattested or rare patterns are ruled out or disfavored elsewhere. Vaux (2002) argues that by trying to incorporate explanation for phonological patterns directly into the grammar, Optimality Theory is unable to deal with many arbitrary phonological patterns which have clear historical origins but do not fall out easily from synchronic interaction between faithfulness and markedness constraints. Reiss (2003) argues that Feature Geometry is not powerful enough to handle all phonological patterns, and suggests that it should be abandoned in favor of incorporating existential and universal quantifiers into the synchronic grammar, something he argues is necessary anyway. Both of these rule-based approaches to synchronic phonology are intended to allow the representation of a wide variety of attested and unattested phonological patterns, with the understanding that explanations for general typological facts and specific synchronically arbitrary phonological patterns may be found outside the synchronic grammar.

A powerful constraint-based formalism could work as well as a powerful rule-based approach. Again, the most important criterion for choosing a synchronic formalism is the ability of the formalism to represent all possible phonological patterns. As Vaux (2002) points out, representing all of a language's phonological patterns with a single constraint ranking is difficult when there are synchronically arbitrary processes, and separating explanation from synchronic formalization may be more difficult or pointless in OT than in a rule-based approach, because the interaction of general (explanatory) constraints is more fundamentally integrated into the workings of the synchronic grammar. Nevertheless, OT is able to account for observed patterns with liberal use of indexed constraints (e.g. Pater 2004). Lexicon-based approaches to synchronic phonology (e.g. Bybee 1998, Pierrehumbert 2001) are also compatible with a model of phonology in which synchronic representations are not the only source of explanation. In lexicon-based models, rich lexical representations of words allow more redundancy to be stored, and phonological patterns are essentially generalizations over the lexicon, rather than formally distinct constructs. Similar words exhibit similar phonological behavior as a result of analogy, but do not necessarily behave identically, due to differences in factors such as frequency.

When synchronic formalisms are no longer assumed to be responsible for making typological predictions, the issue of choosing between competing models of synchronic grammar is changed. If typological observations are readily explained by diachronic facts, the choice of synchronic formalisms should be informed more by synchronic facts about variation and performance.

8.2 Explanation

As argued in previous chapters, the typological facts which have been used to motivate universal distinctive features may also be approached diachronically. Common phonological patterns are those which result from common diachronic changes. This section examines some approaches to diachronic accounts of common synchronic patterns. The importance of language change as an explanation for synchronic typological facts has been argued for by Ohala (e.g. 1981, 2003), Hyman (2001), and many others. Two recent approaches by Hume and Johnson (2001c) and Blevins (2004) are superficially different from each other but, as will be argued in this section, the models are quite compatible and both are integral and largely separate parts of a more general model of diachronic phonology.

Hume and Johnson (2001c) argue that external filters (e.g. perception, production, generalization, conformity) impact language change. The filters are not part of the language user's linguistic competence, but simply a way of formalizing the idea that, for example, a perceptually indistinct contrast may tend to be misheard.

Blevins (2004) argues that sound patterns that are common are the result of recurrent sound changes, or the result of more than one type of sound change. Sound patterns that are rare simply do not have as many common diachronic changes that result in them, or they result only from a sequence of common changes. No synchronic markedness theory is necessary, because in both cases history is used to account for what is common and what is rare.

A useful formal device for illustrating these models is to conceptualize language change as a Markov chain, introduced as a way to represent hypotheses about language change by Greenberg (1966, 1978). The states represent possible languages or possible types of language, and transitions between states represent the probability that a particular language or type of language will change into something else. Fig. 8.1 shows an example in which possible languages are divided into three categories according to their morphological properties. After some arbitrary period of time, one of three things may have happened to any of the languages represented by these states: it may have remained at the same state, or it may have passed to one of the other two states.

There is a probability associated with each of these three events, and the sum of the probabilities (the arrows leading out of a given state) is equal to 1. The arbitrary interval of time chosen will have an effect on the weights of the transitions. The shorter the amount of time, the higher the weight on the transition leading back into the same state (i.e. the greater the likelihood that a language remains in the same state). The nine weights relevant to this three-state Markov chain may be determined by examining historical changes or by examining what is known about the factors which contribute to the likelihood of certain morphological changes. One of the interesting pieces of information that can be represented in this model is the observation that the counterclockwise circuit is more likely than the clockwise one (Vennemann 1974).

The illustration in Fig. 8.1 is able to show an observation about diachronic change, and this is not the same as accounting for *why* the counterclockwise circuit is more common than the clockwise one.

Another set of observations which can be illustrated with a Markov chain concerns the status of click consonants in the segment inventories of the world's languages. Clicks are found only in Khoisan and (to a limited extent) in Bantu languages spoken in southern Africa. Clicks are crosslinguistically rare, but they do not seem to be particularly disfavored in the languages where they occur, and there does not seem to be a tendency for them to be eliminated from languages which have them. Indeed, they are perceptually robust and articulatorily non-challenging for native speakers. But there are few if any known sound changes which result in clicks where there were none before (see e.g. Engstrand 1997), and known instances of clicks being intro-duced into an inventory involve language contact. Since most languages with no clicks are not in contact situations with languages that do have clicks, the

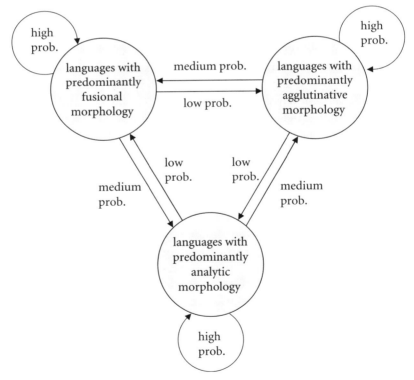

FIGURE 8.1 Language change as a Markov chain: morphological properties

probability of a given language without clicks developing them is very small. The probability of a language with clicks losing them also appears very small. These observations are illustrated with the Markov chain in Fig. 8.2. If it is true that the earliest human languages did not have clicks or were predominantly clickless, then it is completely expected, on the basis of the observations represented in Fig. 8.2, that clicks would be very rare, because languages rarely travel between the two states, without ever invoking markedness or attributing anything to the formalization of the synchronic grammar. In this case the initial state is very important. If clicks were common in the initial state, the situation depicted in Fig. 8.2 would lead to a modern-day scenario where clicks are also common, leading to different claims about markedness, even if they are treated in exactly the same way in languages that have them.

Stating an observation such as the one represented in Fig. 8.2 is not the same as accounting for it, and this representation allows a clear distinction. The presence of weights on the transitions in the network and their implications of typology do not explain themselves. Accounting for why the weights are as they are is a matter for a theory of language change, one which involves many external factors that are often invoked directly in phonetically grounded phonological models.

It is conceivable, if not implementable, to create a Markov chain with a state for every logically possible language. For every language, there is a probability that it will change into each of the other languages. Knowing all the probabilities would amount to knowing all there is to know about language change. Knowing all the probabilities as well as the original proto-language(s) (an initial state) would amount to knowing all there is to know about typology. The Markov chain model is intended to represent complete (and unattainable) knowledge about language change. Various theoretical approaches to attaining this knowledge (both innatist and emergentist) can be illustrated in this model.

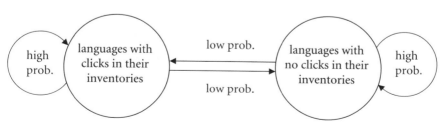

FIGURE 8.2 A small number of (stable) languages with clicks

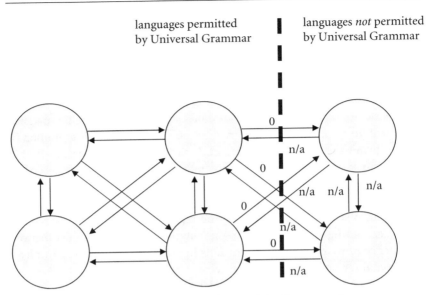

languages permitted
by Universal Grammar

languages *not* permitted
by Universal Grammar

FIGURE 8.3 Universal Grammar in a Markov model of language change

The probability of a language changing into an impossible language is zero. While it is difficult to find positive evidence that a particular language is impossible, it is straightforward to illustrate this type of prediction in this model; Universal Grammar and theories of what logically possible aspects of language are physically or cognitively impossible amount to assertions as to which languages have zero possibility of being the result of change from any of the other states (Fig. 8.3).

Realistically, an investigation into the role of language change in predicting typology would involve a much smaller number of states corresponding to more broadly defined collections of properties, like the ones in Figs. 8.1 and 8.2. The goal of constructing this type of model is to account for observations about language by filling in the probabilities of as many transitions as possible, and to figure out why the probabilities are as they are. There is more than one way to fill in and account for the probabilities, and they correspond to different research programs currently under way.

8.2.1 *The Macro Model*

The first of these, which is called the Macro Model, is to investigate historical changes which are believed to have occurred, and to fill in the probabilities based on actual rates of change from languages with certain properties to languages with other properties. This is exemplified by Blevins' (2004) approach (which also contains micro elements), which is to explain typological observations about phonology in terms of the record of historical sound changes.

Blevins' (2004) CCC model of sound change takes into account the ways in which sound change actually occurs. Blevins divides sound change into three types: CHANGE, CHANCE, and CHOICE. CHANGE occurs when one form is misperceived and the misperceived form gradually becomes the norm. CHANCE occurs when the underlying representation of a form is misanalyzed and the new analysis becomes the norm. CHOICE occurs when a new form along the hypoarticulated–hyperarticulated continuum (Lindblom 1990b) is taken as the norm.

This approach tackles the Markov weights directly, by examining attested diachronic changes. As a result, Blevins is able to account for typological facts on the bases of common and uncommon changes, obviating the need for some synchronic constraints on phonological patterns. For example, Blevins (to appear) argues that consonant epenthesis is not a response to any universal constraints favoring syllables with onsets. This is because synchronic epenthesis sound patterns can be accounted for in terms of the diachronic changes which produce them. The most common changes related to synchronic epenthesis patterns, according to Blevins, are reinterpretation of vowel-to-vowel transitions and marking prosodic boundaries with laryngeal features, and less commonly the fortition of weak phonetically-natural epenthetic segments or rule inversion following the loss of weak coda consonants. None of these diachronic changes involves reference to syllable onsets or universal syllabification constraints. By breaking sound change into different types and exploring the mechanisms by which it occurs, some of the reasons behind these weights can also be discovered.

8.2.2 *The Micro Model*

Exploring the reasons behind the weights is done more directly in what is called the Micro Model, which is less focused on measuring the weights themselves. The Micro Model seeks to find out *why* some changes are more common than others, by hypothesizing about the factors that make some changes more likely than others, and then filling in the weights according to the hypothesis (which can then be tested with available typological and historical data). This approach is represented by Hume and Johnson's (2001c) model of the interplay of phonology with external factors (perception, production, categorization, and social identity) and also by approaches based in Universal Grammar, which posit impossible patterns which correspond to the zero weights in Fig. 8.3.

8.3 Combining models

The model described in this chapter is intended to include all of the sources of explanation discussed in earlier chapters, i.e. it is the union of all of the models implied in these approaches. The individual submodels can be derived from this model by omitting unused components and weighting the remaining ones. The purpose of constructing such a "Supermodel" is to allow a clear means of comparing different models in the same context and terminology, and of illustrating their assumptions and implications. With a clear understanding of what is claimed and predicted by these models, it will be easier to proceed to the next section, which tests some of the predictions. Since this model is being constructed for expository rather than scientific purposes, all that is necessary for a component to be included in the model is for it to have been argued for in the above literature, not for there to be clear evidence for its existence in reality.

For a simple mathematical metaphor, suppose that we are trying to uncover the nature of a mysterious function $L(x)$, and that three competing reductionist hypotheses, termed F, G, and H, have been proposed, which we formalize as $F(x)$, $G(x)$, and $H(x)$. We are certain that the correct characterization of $L(x)$ involves one of these three hypotheses, or some combination of them, and nothing else. Without knowing any more than this, we can make the true statement in (48).

(48) $L(x) = k_1 F(x) + k_2 G(x) + k_3 H(x)$

Now, stating the correct model is a matter of choosing the right coefficients (k_1, k_2, k_3) for the three competing hypotheses. Determining the coefficients may be a very complicated process, but the representation of the explanatory value of each hypothesis is simple. If the correct characterization of L turns out to be precisely Hypothesis F, and Hypotheses G and H are both completely wrong, then a more explicit version of (37) can be given as in (49):

(49) $L(x) = 1 \cdot F(x) + 0 \cdot G(x) + 0 \cdot H(x)$ i.e. $L(x) = F(x)$

If Hypothesis F is completely wrong, Hypothesis G explains 99 percent of L, and Hypothesis H explains the remaining 1 percent, then (50) is the correct model.

(50) $L(x) = 0 \cdot F(x) + \frac{99}{100} G(x) + \frac{1}{100} H(x)$ i.e. $L(x) = \frac{99}{100} G(x) + \frac{1}{100} H(x)$

Choosing the correct model here is a matter of choosing the correct coefficients. By constructing a general model of the emergence of linguistic structure, and in

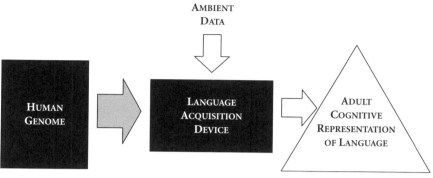

FIGURE 8.4 The human genome generates the language acquisition device, which generates the cognitive representation of language, with the help of ambient data

effect determining the "coefficients" of all the components, we can arrive at the correct model or at least get closer to it.

The model starts with a traditional view of language acquisition and the emergence of structure (Fig. 8.4). The adult cognitive representation of language results from the collision of the language acquisition device (UG) with ambient language data (e.g. Chomsky 1965). If no other explanation is available, we assume that the language acquisition device is highly structured, and that its structure is reflected in the cognitive representation of language that it generates. This highly structured language acquisition device must in turn be generated by the human genome. If another explanation for language structure is available, the language acquisition device could simply record the ambient data and impose no innate structures upon it.

In many of the approaches to distinctive features discussed in earlier chapters, the language acquisition device contains a small number of distinctive features, and phonological patterns must be statable in terms of these patterns in order to be learned. As a result, the phonological component of the cognitive representation of each language will be in terms of these features, and a typology will be predicted on the basis of what patterns are statable and what patterns are not. If innate, these features are by definition specified in the human genome, and to be in the human genome they would have resulted from natural selection.

If the structure responsible for recurrent patterns in language is hard-wired into humans, it must have evolved as a result of an advantage in terms of survival and/or reproduction which is held by humans with more highly developed Universal Grammars, as shown in Fig. 8.5.

Recognizing that there are many reasons to suspect that internal factors attributable to the human genome do not provide an exhaustive account of human

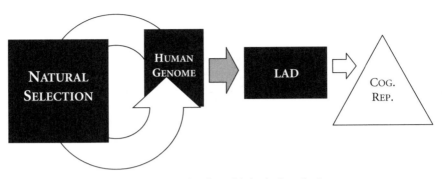

FIGURE 8.5 Innate language properties from biological evolution

language competence or performance, it is appropriate to explore some of the external factors commonly exploited in explanations for linguistic phenomena.

In the terms used above, the ambient data which allows the language acquisition device to generate the cognitive representation does not come from nowhere, but is generated by other cognitive representations, similar to the one being generated by the language acquisition device on the basis of this data (Fig. 8.6). This familiar scenario is discussed in such works as Andersen (1973), Anttila (1977), and Janda (2003).

Further, the data which are generated by other cognitive representations is not transmitted directly from the mind of the speaker to the mind of the learner/listener, but filtered and distorted by environmental factors (Fig. 8.7). These factors are not random, and some are likely to be universal.

The way internal and external factors relate to each other can be schematized as two loops, illustrated in Fig. 8.8. The result of the factors' influence is constantly fed back in to be influenced again. One loop involves the language acquisition device, which generates the cognitive representation of language, which generates data, which is the input on which the language acquisition device bases the generation of the cognitive representation. Noise in transmission is amplified as language data is constantly fed back through noise sources. The Noise in Transmission loop involves the external factors that are argued to influence language as it is used. When speech is transmitted from one speaker to another, the social, production, perception, and cognitive factors all impact the signal along the way, possibly causing the listener to develop a different representation of what the speaker produced, and leading to language change in a direction preferred by one or more of the external filters. The language acquisition device is generated by the human genome, and this requires a Genetic Change loop involving natural selection.

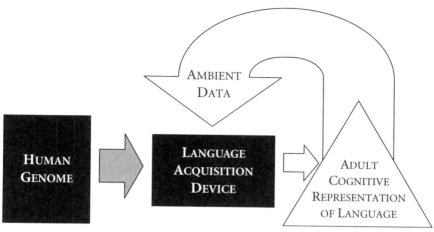

FIGURE 8.6 The ambient data does not come from outer space

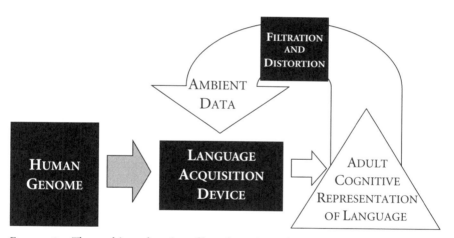

FIGURE 8.7 The ambient data is a filtered version of the output of the cognitive representation

A number of external factors participate in the filtration and distortion of the ambient data received by the learner/listener. These are constraints that are generally not assumed to be part of the "language faculty" proper, but act as external filters, as in Hume and Johnson (2001c). They include social and cognitive factors, as well as constraints on speech production and perception.

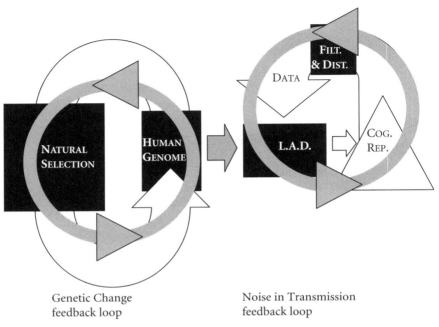

Genetic Change   Noise in Transmission
feedback loop   feedback loop

FIGURE 8.8 Feedback loops

8.3.1 *Production filters*

Factors involved in speech production may cause certain types of sound change to be more common than others. These factors may be viewed (following Hume and Johnson 2001c) as filters acting on the transmission of language (e.g. from one generation to the next). Production-oriented filters can be separated into universal factors and factors which may be influenced by the language being produced by the speaker. Aerodynamics and physiology are universal factors within a particular modality. The laws of physics are expected to apply to the vocal tracts of all spoken language speakers and the body parts of all signed language speakers. For example, articulators in both modalities are subject to inertia, and consequently to potential for gestural undershoot or gesture mistiming, which may be conventionalized by subsequent speakers. The Bernoulli Principle plays a role in the production of all spoken language, by causing narrow constrictions to be narrowed further by the drop in air pressure caused by fast-moving air, and leading to recurrent changes in the production of consonants. Because vocal fold vibration depends on the Bernoulli Principle, voicing is antagonistic with a complete closure in the vocal tract, which causes pressure build-up and ultimately stops the flow of air across the vocal folds (Ohala 1983, Keating 1984). Thus the tendency for stops with closure voicing to be more likely at fronter places of articulation is universal, if only conventionalized in certain languages (Maddieson 2001). The fact that pressure build-up can force an opening in a closed vocal tract is due to universal physical laws, and so is the crosslinguistic tendency for voiced velar stops to be devoiced or to be vented either in the oral cavity or in the nasal cavity, resulting in a universal tendency for velar stops to be devoiced, approximated, or nasalized, which is conventionalized in some languages.

The laws of physics which are expected to affect languages similarly are conceptualized as a filter/prism in Fig. 8.9. As a filter, it causes some aspects of the input to be less likely to be represented in the output; as a prism, it causes elements to appear in the output which may differ from the input. The filter/prism is very coarse, and allows most linguistic patterns to pass through unchanged. But repeated cycling, through language use and language transmission between generations, causes certain patterns which are favored by physical laws (e.g. velar approximants and nasals rather than voiced velar stops) to be more likely to remain. In addition to universal laws of physics, there are production-related factors which may differ from language to language. Gesture timing and mistiming may be influenced by the sound systems already present in a language.

The external factors represented as filter/prisms are to be interpreted as acting upon the speech stream, and consequently indirectly affecting the trajectory of language change. External factors do not direct language change in predictable directions, but disrupt the transmission of language from generation to generation. Among the changes which result, some are more

FIGURE 8.9 The laws of physics filter/prism

likely than others, and this likelihood can be understood in terms of filter/prisms on the language transmission process.

This account of the motivation for language change to move in certain directions is analogous to Einstein's (1905) explanation for Brownian motion—the erratic movement of floating dust particles which is attributed to collisions with smaller, less readily observable air molecules. The air molecules do not push the dust particles in predictable directions, but the movement of the dust particles can be understood on the basis of an understanding of the properties of the gas in which they are suspended.

8.3.2 *Perception filters*

Like production, the perception of language is subject to universal and language-specific factors which make some changes more likely than others. Among the universal factors are vision, which is relevant for perceiving both signed and spoken language, and audition, which is relevant for perceiving spoken language. Presumably the way in which light and sound waves are transmitted to the optical and auditory nerves are not influenced by specific languages, but the non-transparent way in which this happens may influence the path of language change. For example, the response of the auditory nerve to stimuli is nonlinear in more than one dimension. The ear is more sensitive to some frequencies than to others, and the auditory nerve is more sensitive to the onsets of stimuli than to the offsets. This asymmetry in the auditory system can explain asymmetries in sound patterns. All else being equal, consonant–vowel transitions are more salient than vowel–consonant transitions (Fujimura et al. 1978, Ohala 1992), and accordingly postvocalic consonants are more prone to alteration than prevocalic consonants (Steriade 1997, 2001). Similarly in sign languages, because the three-dimensional space in which signing occurs must be projected onto two dimensions to be viewed, information is lost as gestures obscure each other. The way in which language is converted into a nerve impulse thus helps direct the path of language change, due to the fact that certain features of language are more likely than others to be obscured, and therefore more prone to being changed.

At a higher level of processing, language-specific factors play a role in language perception. Speakers of different languages may attend to different aspects of a speech signal for cues to identifying sounds and signs. It is the role of attention that contributes to crosslinguistic differences in the perceptibility of contrasts. While the auditory (or optical) nerve may deliver the same signal in two different listeners, the way it is perceived depends on which parts of the signal are expected to contain distinctive information. For example, if a listener whose native language contrasts stops according to voice onset time and a listener whose native language contrasts stops according to closure voicing hear two utterances that differ only in the closure voicing stop, the first listener is less likely to notice the difference, because the change did not affect a cue that is important for distinguishing words in the listener's language. Consequently, this language is more likely to tolerate subtle changes in closure voicing, because these changes have a relatively small impact on word recognition. It has been shown experimentally that the precise nature of what counts as non-salient (and therefore goes unnoticed) varies according to the system in which the changes are viewed (e.g. Hume et al. 1999, Hume 2004a, Mielke 2003), and so the influence of perception on phonological patterns involves language-specific components.

To the extent that the mental representation of language is organized and/ or condensed, rather than consisting of a list of every utterance encountered, this organization impacts the way language is treated. A certain amount of stimulus generalization is necessary for a speaker to identify two different acoustic signals as examples of the same phoneme. Further, similar sounds, whether instances of the same phoneme or different phonemes which share properties, tend to pattern similarly. If a speaker expects this, then the categorization of sounds will cause sounds which are similar to tend to be treated similarly, even without explicit evidence to support similar treatment.

8.3.3 *Generalization*

If a speaker is more likely to assume that /t/ will pattern with /k/ than to assume that /t/ will pattern with /o/, then it is more likely that a sound pattern involving /k/ will be generalized to include /t/ than that a sound pattern involving /o/ will be generalized to include /t/. If this is the case, then generalization acts as a filter which favors processes in which similar sounds pattern similarly. This filter is expected to occasionally filter out processes which violate this expectation and introduce processes which meet it.

This is illustrated in the ability of language listeners to group together acoustically non-identical tokens of what is considered to be the same speech sound, and to be prepared to correctly categorize new tokens which are identical to none of the previously heard tokens. Generalization is necessary for learning abstract phonemes from clouds of actual tokens, and can easily be extended to the learning of phonologically significant classes from clusters of different phonemes.

The formation of stereotypes is also the result of generalization. Attributes observed in one person may be attributed to another who does not possess the attribute but shares a different salient attribute with the first person. Experimental evidence shows a cognitive basis for stereotype formation. For example, in work on stereotypes, Van Knippenberg and Dijksterhuis (1996) find that information that is inconsistent with a stereotype is more difficult to recall than information that is consistent with the stereotype. Snyder et al. (1982) and Johnston (1996) find that people tend to seek information that confirms stereotypes rather than information that disconfirms them. The mistaken overgeneralization that results in stereotypes is the result of the same adaptive strategies that allow knowledge to be generalized at all, as described by Fox (1992) in her work on prejudice as a residue from an earlier stage of adaptation.

Stereotypes which are inconsistent with observable facts (such as many stereotypes about people) may eventually disappear—i.e. overgeneralizations can be corrected, given enough time to coexist with the conflicting reality. Overgeneralizations about language are a different matter in an interesting way, because language is culturally transmitted and arbitrary. An overgeneralization about people, even if it is widely held, will always have the opportunity to be compared with reality and to possibly be corrected, but an overgeneralization about language structure that is widely held often *becomes* the reality that it would be compared to. Because language is arbitrary and many attributes of people are not, an overgeneralization in the domain of language structure stands a much greater chance of being a self-fulfilling prophecy. For example, if 75 percent of the population starts to believe (mistakenly) that the other 25 percent is good at math (based on evidence from only a small fraction of that 25 percent), there will always be opportunities for this belief to be challenged by facts and discredited. If a generation of speakers believes that all voiced consonants are devoiced word-finally, when in reality most of the population has only been devoicing word-final voiced *obstruents*, it is quite possible that when that generation reaches old age, it will be *true* that most of the population devoices all word-final consonants.

Another cognitive factor related to generalization is cognitive complexity. Culicover and Nowak (2003) argue that many typological observations about language (such as the preference for binary branching among syntactic constituents) are the result of differences in cognitive complexity. Patterns that are easier to process are favored slightly, and as a result of social factors which encourage some language varieties to overwhelm others, the more complex patterns are more likely to disappear.

The social context in which language is used also influences language patterns. For example, the tendency to conform to specific linguistic norms causes the outputs of individuals' grammars to become more like each other or more like the output of a particular set of grammars. In the course of conforming to an unfamiliar norm, an undergeneralization or overgeneralization may also occur. This is represented by the social identity filter filtering out phonological patterns according to the social identity of the speaker. Another observation that can be talked about in terms of these filters is Trudgill's (2002) suggestion that isolated communities with dense social networks are better able to sustain complex alternations and relatively non-natural sound changes that might not survive in communities with larger and less dense networks. Using the Hume and Johnson model, the elimination of complex alternations and non-natural sound changes can be attributed to an increased role of the generalization filters in communities with sparse networks, whereas the conformity filter would eliminate forms that deviate from the (perhaps phonetically unnatural) norms of a community with denser social networks. This is not to say that conformity cannot also lead to an increased role for complex or non-natural patterns, but the opportunity for these patterns to be eliminated in communities with sparse networks may be greater.

8.3.4 *Supermodel*

Putting all of the external factors together with the genetic factors results in the supermodel, shown in Fig. 8.10. The human genome provides a (not necessarily very detailed) mechanism for learning language, and this is represented in the initial states of language learners, whose cognitive representations of language are represented in Fig. 8.10 by triangles. The initial cognitive representation develops into the adult cognitive representation "p", and development is represented by movement to the right. An adult cognitive representation produces an output which passes through filter/prisms before becoming the ambient data available to the learner. This data is passed through further filter/prisms as it is received by the learner, and four of the six filter/prisms are influenced to some extent by the cognitive representation (indicated by the faint arrows in the figure), as discussed above. Such a model allows phonological patterning to be accounted for by external factors or by innate features. Specific submodels can be illustrated by removing or discounting components of the supermodel. Importantly, these possibly mutually exclusive models can be illustrated in the same terms.

The emergence of phonological patterns necessarily involves more than one filter/prism, but not necessarily in the sequence shown in Fig. 8.10. The filter/prisms in the figure are sequenced according to when they apply in the production and perception of speech. Representing the emergence of a phonological pattern may involve abstracting over many production–perception cycles, and so the pertinent actions of the filter/prisms represented in the figure do not necessarily occur in the same cycle. When a listener miscategorizes a speech

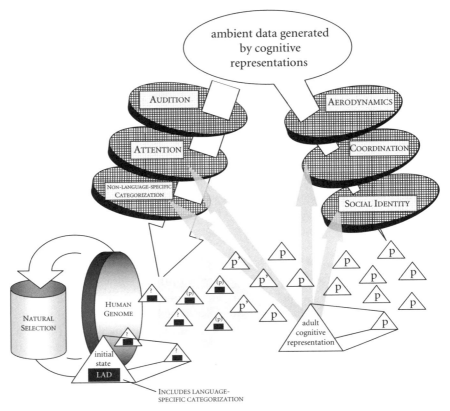

FIGURE 8.10 The supermodel of internal and external influences on language structure

sound as a consequence of a speaker's misarticulation, then both factors are present in the same loop. But whether this miscategorization spreads and becomes the norm for a community depends on the social identity filter/prisms of many other speakers at later points in time.

As an example, a vowel harmony process can emerge over time as a result of repeated cycling through the external factors shown in Fig. 8.10. First, coarticulation between vowels occurs as a result of gesture mistiming. Utterances produced with overlapping gestures are favored over those in which gestures associated with segments are completely segregated in time. This is represented by the coordination filter/prism, which tends to admit forms with gestural overlap. The result of this gesture mistiming may be phonetically rounded vowels which would be unrounded if not for the presence of a rounded vowel nearby. These phonetically rounded vowels are perceptually similar to contrastively rounded vowels, as a result of limitations of the human auditory system and the attention of the listener to specific points in the waveform. This is represented by the audition and attention filter/prisms. Because speakers group sounds into categories according to their phonetic properties, the vowels which are perceived as similar to phonologically rounded vowels may be categorized as rounded vowels by some speakers. The four factors invoked to this point would all be relevant in the same cycle. The result is that a speaker produces a vowel which is intended to be unrounded and the listener hears a rounded vowel. Over time, the rounding harmony takes on social significance and spreads throughout a community. Speakers choose to produce round vowels in the environments where they have appeared as a result of four other factors, and this choice is represented by the social identity filter/prism. In the end, the language contains a rule of vowel harmony.

This description has made use only of the Language Change loop, and bypassed the Genetic Change loop. The Genetic Change loop is also able to produce a story for the emergence of vowel harmony. Through the process of natural selection, humans with more highly developed innate language faculties are more fit for survival or reproduction. If a speaker has a cognitive entity [round] or [Labial] which refers to rounded vowels, she will have an easier time communicating with other people, and consequently, the argument goes, she will be more successful in other aspects of life, such as reproduction. After many generations come and go, the result is a human population with a set of phonological distinctive features. A vowel harmony rule may emerge as a result of the feature [round] which is associated with a particular vowel being related to another vowel. Whether this results from a superfluous association line in a speaker's head or from external events is not a concern of the innate features account based on genetic change. Ultimately, learners construct a vowel harmony rule or a constraint ranking that results in the feature [round] being associated with two segments.

In summary, the model in Fig. 8.12 contains redundancy. Both the Genetic Change and Language Change loops are independently able to produce a story for the emergence of vowel harmony and other linguistic patterns. This means that one or the other may be expendable. To evaluate the components of the supermodel, it is necessary to examine the submodels more closely.

8.3.5 *Submodels*

Models of phonology can be derived from the supermodel (Fig. 8.10) by omitting parts of it. Each proposed submodel addresses the question of how much of the observations about recurrent phonological patterns are attributable to the Noise in Transmission feedback loop and how much is the result of the Genetic Change feedback loop. More influence from the Genetic Change loop requires a more specific language acquisition device (Universal Grammar). More influence from the Noise in Transmission loop means that less information needs to be provided to the language learner by Universal Grammar.

A specific language acquisition device/strong Universal Grammar requires natural selection to cause the evolution of the genetic code needed to produce it. For this to be true, humans with more developed language acquisition devices must be more fit for survival and better able to produce offspring than humans with less developed language acquisition devices. This must also be the case for a long enough period of time for the LAD to be highly developed enough to generate the regularity attributed to it. The leading argument for Universal Grammar is that it explains facts that have no explanation elsewhere. Given the problems surrounding the account of biological evolution of the language faculty, if language change can explain the observed similarity between languages, this explanation is preferable to an explanation based on biological evolution.

Models of phonology which are rooted in innate distinctive features cancel out or diminish the importance of external factors and the Noise in Transmission feedback loop in favor of internal factors and the Genetic Change feedback loop. The human genome provides the language learner with an innate feature set which is used to construct a grammar based on the data received. Noise in transmission is of little importance for the core data for the theory, but may be invoked when the innate feature set fails to account for a particular phonological pattern. Therefore the Noise in Transmission loop is likely to be present for all theories of innate features, but it plays only a tangential role in determining what are likely phonological patterns. The null hypothesis is that it is absent, but much of the work on innate features makes clear that these factors are necessary in order to deal with exceptions.

Fig. 8.11 shows a submodel corresponding to the innate features approach. The language acquisition device is highly structured and contains the features necessary to categorize speech sounds and signs and to formulate rules. The external factors are de-emphasized, because they are not the primary source of explanation for generalizations about phonological patterns. But they are not removed completely, because they will be necessary to account for phonological patterns that innate features are unable to account for, as seen above.

This approach to phonology has allowed the formulation of many generalizations about phonological patterns. The innate features approach has not

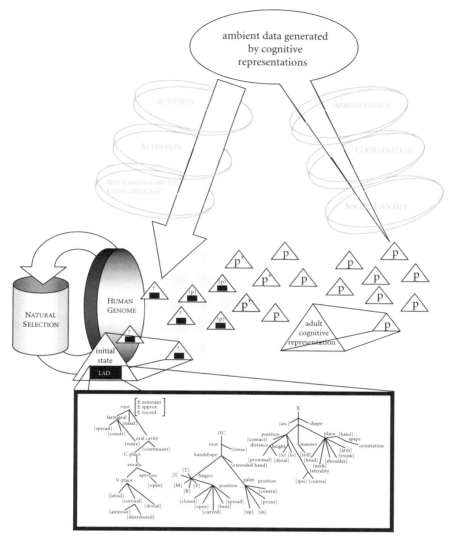

FIGURE 8.11 The innate features submodel

converged on a single set of features which are innate and universal. Even among the phenomena reported in the phonology literature, there are phonological patterns which require external explanation. By taking innate features as the null hypothesis, it is very difficult for this approach to discover how many phenomena which may be accounted for with innate features may also be accounted for with external factors. Most of the generalizations produced by innate feature theory are informative to an emergentist approach, because the phonetic facts in which the formal innate features model is grounded are covered by the external factors in the model.

The emergent features approach takes the external factors as the null hypothesis. Thus, emergentist approaches to phonology cancel out or diminish the importance of internal factors and the Genetic Change feedback loop in favor of external factors and the Noise in Transmission feedback loop, as shown in Fig. 8.12. Nothing needs to be hypothesized to be in Universal Grammar that has an independent explanation from noise in transmission and language change. However, it is not known at this time whether all constraints on phonological patterns can be accounted for in this way. If it is discovered that a certain type of phonological pattern which is not ruled out by any known external factors does not occur, and that its absence is statistically

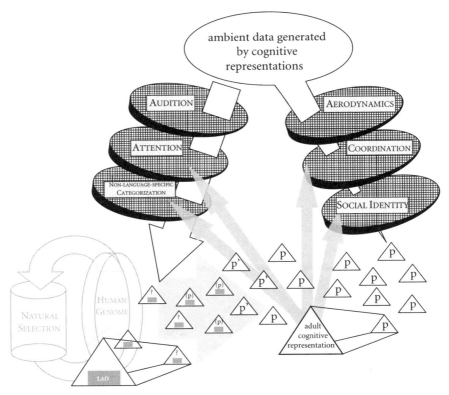

FIGURE 8.12 The emergent features submodel

significant, then this is better grounds for hypothesizing that Universal Grammar may be responsible. It is assumed, however, that most typological observations can be accounted for by external factors. The null hypothesis is that the Genetic Change feedback loop plays no role that is specific to language; but this possibility is left open.

8.4 Summary

This chapter has proposed a general framework in which natural classes, distinctive features, and other linguistic phenomena can be explored. Formalization of the cognitive representation of language is separated from explanation, and Markov chains are used as a means of formalizing typological observations without placing them in the cognitive representation. Two approaches to filling in and explaining transition weights in this model are the Macro Model, which investigates actual diachronic changes, and the Micro Model, which explores why some weights would be expected to be different from others. The Micro Model has many components with overlapping coverage, including components attributed to biological evolution and components attributable to language change. The relative importance of these components is investigated by testing the predictions they make about the nature of the linguistic patterns they both try to account for.

8.5 Conclusions

This book has proposed and argued for emergent feature theory. It has been shown that there are reasons to be suspicious of the idea that distinctive features are innate. There are major differences between features for signed and spoken languages which innate features account for; the common denominator between the features used in these two modalities is cognitive categories, and as Jakobson (e.g. 1942) demonstrated, cognitive categories are learned and exploited by non-human animals. The arguments for innate features have not been accompanied by sufficient evidence, in terms either of crosslinguistic phonological patterning or of a clear hypothesis about how much of this patterning should be accounted for by features and how much would be expected from other factors. It has been seen that about a quarter of phonologically active classes are not accounted for by innate feature theories, but many of them are predicted by emergent feature theory on the basis of phonetic similarity and phonetically driven sound change. Further, the classes which are accounted for by innate feature theory are just as easily accounted for by emergent feature theory. Given all of these facts, there is little reason to believe that innate features add insights that are not already provided by other sources of explanation; but the enterprise of innate feature theory has been quite successful in clarifying many of these other sources of explanation.

Just as it can be useful to neglect air resistance when making physics calculations, it is useful to neglect the language-specific differences in phonological features when developing a theory of crosslinguistic phonological tendencies until the field has advanced far enough that these simplifying assumptions can be abandoned. Indeed, innate feature theories have helped foster an understanding of the many external factors which they model abstractly, and the result is that it is now possible to move beyond innate features. The insights of innate features are portable and, as has been shown in this book, can be incorporated into emergent feature theory. Removing the assumptions of innateness allows feature theory to deal with the wide range of "exceptions" which can now be dealt with in just the same way as any other naturally occurring linguistic phenomena. Emergent feature theory is part of a larger theory of the emergence of linguistic structure, and part of a larger movement beyond some of the assumptions which were fundamental to advancing the study of language—assumptions which have worked so effectively that much of their work is now complete.

Appendix A   Languages in the survey

!Xóõ (Traill 1985)   Khoisan
Abujhmaria (Natarajan 1985)   Dravidian
Abun (Berry and Berry 1998)   West Papuan
Acehnese (Durie 1985)   Austronesian
Adyghe (Bzhedukh dialect) (Colarusso 1988)   North Caucasian
Af Tunni Somali (Tunni) (Tosco 1997)   Afro-Asiatic
Afar (Bliese 1981)   Afro-Asiatic
Afrikaans (Donaldson 1993)   Indo-European
    (including dialect spoken in the Transvaal and
    the Free State)
Agarabi (Bee et al. 1973)   Trans-New Guinea
Agta (Healey 1960)   Austronesian
Ainu (Tamura 2000, Shibatani 1990)   Language Isolate
Akan (Akuapem, Asante, and Fante)   Niger-Congo
    (Dolphyne 1988)
Alabama (Lupardus 1982)   Muskogean
Albanian (Bevington 1974)   Indo-European
Alyawarra (Yallop 1977)   Australian
Amele (Roberts 1987)   Trans-New Guinea
Amharic (Leslau 2000)   Afro-Asiatic
Angami (Giridhar 1980)   Sino-Tibetan
Anywa (Anuak) (Reh 1996)   Nilo-Saharan
Ao (Ao Naga) (Gowda 1991)   Sino-Tibetan
Aoma (Elugbe 1989)   Niger-Congo
Apatani (Abraham 1985)   Sino-Tibetan
Arabana (Hercus 1994)   Australian
Arabic, Abha (Nakshabandi 1988)   Afro-Asiatic
Arabic, Egyptian (Broselow 1976)   Afro-Asiatic
Arabic, Jordanian (Al-Sughayer 1990)   Afro-Asiatic
Arabic, Libyan (Abumdas 1985)   Afro-Asiatic
Arabic, Moroccan (Keegan 1986)   Afro-Asiatic
    (including Northern dialect)
Arabic, Muscat (Glover 1989)   Afro-Asiatic
Arabic, North Israel Bedouin (Rosenhouse 1984)   Afro-Asiatic
Arapesh (Fortune 1977)   Torricelli
Arbore (Hayward 1984)   Afro-Asiatic
Argobba (Leslau 1997)   Afro-Asiatic

Armenian (Vaux 1998) (including Agn, Agulis, Homshetsma, Karchevian, Kirzan, Marash, Standard Eastern Armenian)	Indo-European
Ashuku (Shimizu 1980a)	Niger-Congo
Asmat (Flamingo Bay Dialect) (Voorhoeve 1965)	Trans-New Guinea
Assiniboine (Levin 1961)	Siouan
Assyrian Neo-Aramaic (Fox 1997, Odisho 1988) (including Iraqi Koine and Jilu)	Afro-Asiatic
Auchi (Yekhee) (Elugbe 1989)	Niger-Congo
Auyana (McKaughan and Marks 1973)	Trans-New Guinea
Awa (Loving 1973)	Trans-New Guinea
Axininca Campa (Asháninca) (Payne 1981)	Arawakan
Aymara (Davidson 1977)	Aymaran
Azari, Iranian (South Azerbaijani) (Dehghani 2000)	Altaic
Bagri (Gusain 2000)	Indo-European
Balangao (Shetler 1976)	Austronesian
Banoni (Lincoln 1976)	Austronesian
Baré (Aikhenvald 1995)	Arawakan
Bari (Kukú dialect) (Cohen 2000)	Nilo-Saharan
Basque (Saltarelli et al. 1988)	Austronesian
Bata (Boyd 2002)	Afro-Asiatic
Batibo Moghamo (Meta') (Stallcup 1978)	Niger-Congo
Beaver, Halfway River (Randoja 1990)	Na-Dene
Belizian Creole (Greene 1999)	Creole
Bemba (van Sambeek 1966)	Niger-Congo
Bengali (Ray 1966)	Indo-European
Berbice Dutch Creole (Kouwenberg 1994)	Creole
Bikele (dialect of Kol) (Begne 1980)	Niger-Congo
Binumarien (Oatridge and Oatridge 1973)	Trans-New Guinea
Biri (Terrill 1998)	Australian
Bisu (Xu 2001)	Sino-Tibetan
Blackfoot (Frantz 1991)	Algic
Boko/Busa (including Kaiama dialect) (Jones 1998)	Niger-Congo
Boruca (Constenla 1981)	Chibchan
Brahui (Andronov 1980)	Dravidian
Breton (Press 1986)	Indo-European
Bribri (Constenla 1981)	Chibchan
Bukiyip (Conrad and Wogiga 1991)	Torricelli
Bukusu (Austen 1974)	Niger-Congo
Bulgarian (Scatton 1984)	Indo-European
Buriat (Poppe 1960)	Altaic
Burmese (Okell 1969)	Sino-Tibetan

Cabécar (Constenla 1981)	Chibchan
Cahuilla (Seiler 1977)	Uto-Aztecan
Cantonese (Hashimoto 1972)	Sino-Tibetan
Capanahua (Loos 1967)	Panoan
Casiguran Dumagat (Agta) (Vanoverbergh 1937)	Austronesian
Catalan (Wheeler 1979)	Indo-European
Cavineña (Key 1968)	Tacanan
Cayapa (Chachi) (Lindskoog and Brend 1962)	Barbacoan
Cebuano (Bunye and Yap 1971)	Austronesian
Chakosi (Anufo) (Stanford and Stanford 1970)	Niger-Congo
Chamorro (Topping 1973)	Austronesian
Chemehuevi (dialect of Ute-Southern Paiute) (Press 1975)	Uto-Aztecan
Cheremis, Eastern (Sebeok 1961)	Uralic
Cherokee (King 1975, Walker 1975) (including Oklahoma and Qualla dialects)	Iroquoian
Chomo (Dhu, Como Karim) (Shimizu 1980a)	Niger-Congo
Chori (Cori) (Dihoff 1976)	Niger-Congo
Chrau (Thomas 1971)	Austro-Asiatic
Ciyao (Yao) (Ngunga 2000)	Niger-Congo
Coatzospan Mixtec (Coatzospan Mixteco) (Gerfen 1999)	Oto-Manguean
Coeur d'Alene (Johnson 1975)	Salishan
Cofán (Borman 1962)	Chibchan
Comaltepec Chinantec (Anderson 1989)	Oto-Manguean
Comanche (Charney 1993)	Uto-Aztecan
Creole of São Tomé (Sãotomense) (Ferraz 1979)	Creole
Cuna (San Blas Cuna) (Sherzer 1975)	Chibchan
Czech (Harkins 1953)	Indo-European
Daga (Murane 1974)	Trans-New Guinea
Dàgáárè (Bodomo 2000)	Niger-Congo
Dagur (Martin 1961)	Altaic
Dahalo (Tosco 1991)	Afro-Asiatic
Dani, Lower Grand Valley (Bromley 1961)	Trans-New Guinea
Danish (Jones and Gade 1981)	Indo-European
Degema (Elugbe 1989, Kari 1997)	Niger-Congo
Delaware (Unami) (Goddard 1979)	Algic
Desano (Kaye 1970)	Tucanoan
Dhaasanac (Daasanach) (Tosco 2001)	Afro-Asiatic
Dhivehi (Maldivian) (Cain and Gair 2000)	Indo-European
Dholuo (Luo) (Okoth-Okombo 1982)	Nilo-Saharan
Dieri (Diyari) (Austin 1981)	Australian
Diola-Fogny (Jola-Fogny) (Sapir 1965)	Niger-Congo

Djinang/Djinba (Waters 1989)	Australian
Dominican Creole (Edward 1980)	Creole
Doyayo (Wiering 1994, Wiering and Wiering 1994b)	Niger-Congo
Dutch (Booij 1995)	Indo-European
(including Southern, Belgium, and other dialects)	
Dyirbal (Dixon 1972)	Australian
Edo (Elugbe 1989)	Niger-Congo
Efik (Ward 1933)	Niger-Congo
Egene (Engenni) (Elugbe 1989)	Niger-Congo
Ehueun (Elugbe 1989)	Niger-Congo
Ejagham (Watters 1981)	Niger-Congo
(including Eyumojok-Ndebaya sub-dialect)	
Ekigusii (Gusii) (Cammenga 2002)	Niger-Congo
Emhalhe (Somorika/Okpamheri) (Elugbe 1989)	Niger-Congo
English (Jensen 1993, McMahon 2002)	Indo-European
(including British and American dialects)	
Epie (Elugbe 1989)	Niger-Congo
Eruwa (Elugbe 1989)	Niger-Congo
Esse Ejja (Key 1968)	Tacanan
Estonian (Harms 1962)	Uralic
Evenki (Nedjalkov 1997)	Altaic
Ewe (Ansre 1961)	Niger-Congo
Faranah-Maninka (Spears 1965)	Niger-Congo
Faroese (Lockwood 1955)	Indo-European
(including more than one dialect)	
Fe'Fe'-Bamileke (Hyman 1972)	Niger-Congo
Fijian, Boumaa (Dixon 1988)	Austronesian
Finnish (Sulkala and Karjalainen 1992)	Uralic
(including more than one dialect)	
French (Valdman 1976, Casagrande 1984)	Indo-European
Fulfulde (dialect of Mali) (McIntosh 1984)	Niger-Congo
Fyem (Nettle 1998)	Niger-Congo
Gā (Zimmermann 1858)	Niger-Congo
Gade (Pieter 1977)	Niger-Congo
Gadsup (Frantz and Frantz 1973)	Trans-New Guinea
Ganda (Cole 1967)	Niger-Congo
Ganggulida (Holmer 1988)	Australian
Garawa (Bundjil/Wandji) (Holmer 1988)	Australian
Garo (Burling 1961)	Sino-Tibetan
Garwa (Holmer 1988)	Australian
Georgian (Cherchi 1999)	South Caucasian
German (Fox 1990)	Indo-European
German, Michigan (Born 1994)	Indo-European

Ghotuo (Elugbe 1989)	Niger-Congo
Gikuyu (Mugane 1997)	Niger-Congo
Giziga (Rossing 1978)	Afro-Asiatic
Godoberi (Kibrik 1996)	North Caucasian
Gondi, Adilabad (Subrahmanyam 1968)	Dravidian
Gondi, Koya (Subrahmanyam 1968)	Dravidian
Gooniyandi (McGregor 1990)	Australian
Grebo (Innes 1966)	Niger-Congo
Greek (Joseph and Philippaki-Warburton 1987)	Indo-European
Guatuso (Maléku Jaíka) (Constenla 1981)	Chibchan
Gugu-Bujun (Gugu Badhun) (Holmer 1988)	Australian
Gujarati (Cardona 1965)	Indo-European
Gunin/Kwini (Kwini) (McGregor 1993)	Australian
Gwari (Gbagyi) (Hyman and Magaji 1970)	Niger-Congo
Haitian Creole (Hall 1953)	Creole
Hakka/Kejia (Hashimoto 1973, Chung 1989)	Sino-Tibetan
Halkomelem, Chilliwack (Galloway 1977)	Salishan
Hatam (Reesink 1999)	West Papuan
Hausa (Jaggar 2001)	Afro-Asiatic
Hebrew (Bolozky 1972)	Afro-Asiatic
Higi (Kamwe) (Mohrlang 1972)	Afro-Asiatic
Hiligaynon (Spitz 2001)	Austronesian
Hindi (Shukla 2000)	Indo-European
Hixkaryana (Derbyshire 1985)	Carib
Hungarian (Abondolo 1988)	Uralic
Hurza/Ndreme/Vame (Pelasla) (Rossing 1978)	Afro-Asiatic
Ibilo (Elugbe 1989)	Niger-Congo
Icen (Etkywan) (Shimizu 1980a)	Niger-Congo
Igbo (Emananjo 1978)	Niger-Congo
Ijo, Kolkuma dialect (Williamson 1965)	Niger-Congo
Ikalanga (Mathingwane 1999)	Niger-Congo
Ilocano (Rubino 2000)	Austronesian
Indonesian (Lapowila 1981)	Austronesian
Ingessana (Gaam) (Crewe 1975)	Nilo-Saharan
Inor (dialect of West Gurage)	Afro-Asiatic
(Chamora and Hetzron 2000)	
Inuktitut, West Greenlandic (Fortescue 1984)	Eskimo-Aleut
Inupiaq, Barrow (North Alaskan Inupiatun)	Eskimo-Aleut
(Kaplan 1981)	
Iraqw (Nordbustad 1988)	Afro-Asiatic

Irish (Irish Gaelic) (Ó Siadhail 1989) (including   Indo-European
  various dialects of Clare, Connacht, Connemara,
  Donegal, Dunquin, Gweedore, Muskerry,
  Munster, and Ring)
Irula (Zvelebil 1973)   Dravidian
Isoko (Uzere dialect) (Elugbe 1989)   Niger-Congo
Italian (Castiglione 1957)   Indo-European
Izi (Meier et al. 1975)   Niger-Congo
Jacaltec (Day 1973)   Mayan
Jamaican Creole (Bailey 1966)   Creole
Japanese (Vance 1987)   Japanese
Jaqaru (Hardman 2000)   Aymaran
Javanese (Suharno 1982)   Austronesian
Jiru (Wuyar) (Shimizu 1980a)   Niger-Congo
Jukun (Jukun Takum) (Shimizu 1980a, 1980b)   Niger-Congo
  (including Wukari dialect)
Kabardian (Colarusso 1988)   North Caucasian
Kalengin (Toweett 1979) (including Nandi variety)   Nilo-Saharan
Kalispel (dialect of Kalispel-Pend d'Oreille)   Salishan
  (Vogt 1940)
Kamba (Lindblom 1925)   Niger-Congo
Kana (Khana) (Ikoro 1996)   Niger-Congo
Kanakuru (Dera) (Newman 1974)   Afro-Asiatic
Kannada (Sridhar 1990)   Dravidian
Kanuri (Cyffer 1998)   Nilo-Saharan
Kapampangan (Pampangan) (Forman 1971)   Austronesian
Karanga (Central and Victoria dialects)   Nilo-Saharan
  (Marconnès 1931)
Karao (Brainard 1994)   Austronesian
Karimojong (Karamojong) (Novelli 1985)   Nilo-Saharan
Karo Batak (Woollams 1996)   Austronesian
Kashaya (Buckley 1994)   Hokan
Kashmiri (Wali and Koul 1997)   Indo-European
Kayah Li, Eastern (Eastern Kayah) (Solnit 1997)   Sino-Tibetan
Kedang (Samely 1991)   Austronesian
Kharia (Bilgiri 1965)   Austro-Asiatic
Khmer (Gorgoniyev 1966)   Austro-Asiatic
Khmu? (Smalley 1961)   Austro-Asiatic
Kickapoo (Voorhis 1974)   Algic
Kihungan (Hungana) (Takizala 1974)   Niger-Congo
Kilivila/Kiriwina (Lawton 1993)   Austronesian
Kimatuumbi (Matumbi) (Odden 1996)   Niger-Congo
Kinnauri (Sharma 1988)   Sino-Tibetan

Kinyamwezi (Maganga and Schadeberg 1992)	Niger-Congo
Kinyarwanda (Rwanda) (Kimenyi 1979)	Niger-Congo
Kiowa (Watkins 1984)	Kiowa Tanoan
Kirghiz (Hebert and Poppe 1963)	Altaic
Kiribati (Groves et al. 1985) (including northern and southern varieties)	Austronesian
Kisar (Christenson and Christenson 1992)	Austronesian
Kisi (Childs 1990)	Niger-Congo
Klamath (White 1973)	Penutian
Koiari (Dutton 1996)	Trans-New Guinea
Kolami (Emeneau 1961)	Dravidian
Kombai (de Vreis 1993)	Trans-New Guinea
Koraga, Mudu (Bhat 1971)	Dravidian
Koraga, Onti (Bhat 1971)	Dravidian
Koraga, Tappu (Bhat 1971)	Dravidian
Korean (Yi 1989)	language isolate
Koromfé (Rennison 1997)	Niger-Congo
Korowai (van Enk and de Vries 1997)	Trans-New Guinea
Koyukon, Central Outer (Kroul 1980)	Na-Dene
Kpan (Kente dialect) (Shimizu 1980a)	Niger-Congo
Kpelle (Westerman and Melzian 1974)	Niger-Congo
Kporo (Shimizu 1980a)	Niger-Congo
Kristang (Malaccan Creole Portuguese) (Baxter 1988)	Creole
Kriyol (Upper Guinea Crioulo) (Kihm 1994)	Creole
Kui (Winfield 1928)	Dravidian
Kuku-Yalanji Kantyu/Koko-Yalandji (Holmer 1988)	Australian
Kumiái (Jamul Tiipay variety) (Miller 2001)	Hokan
Kumiái (Diegueño variety) (Gorbet 1976)	Hokan
Kurmanji (Kurdish) (Kahn 1976)	Indo-European
Kurux (Gordon 1976)	Dravidian
Kutep (Lissam dialect) (Shimizu 1980a)	Niger-Congo
Kuvi (Israel 1979)	Dravidian
Kwamera (Lindstrom and Lynch 1994)	Austronesian
Lakota (Patterson 1990)	Siouan
Lama (Ourso 1989)	Niger-Congo
Lango (Noonan 1992)	Nilo-Saharan
Lao (Morev et al. 1979)	Tai-Kadai
Larike (Laidig 1992)	Austronesian
Latvian (Mathiassen 1997)	Indo-European
Lealao Chinantec (Lealao Chinanteco) (Rupp 1989)	Oto-Manguean
Lele (Frajzyngier 2001)	Afro-Asiatic
Lezgian (Lezgi) (Haspelmath 1993)	North Caucasian
Limbu (Weidert and Subba 1985)	Sino-Tibetan

Lingala (Odhner 1981)	Niger-Congo
Lithuanian (Ambrazas et al. 1997)	Indo-European
Lomongo (Mongo-Nkundu)	Niger-Congo
(Ruskin and Ruskin 1934)	
Loniu (Hamel 1985, 1994)	Austronesian
Lorma (Loma) (Dwyer 1981)	Niger-Congo
Lotha (Lotha Naga) (Acharya 1983)	Sino-Tibetan
Louisiana Creole French (Klingler 1992)	Creole
Lumasaaba (Masaba) (Brown 1972)	Niger-Congo
Lusi (Counts 1969)	Austronesian
Maale (Male) (Amha 2001)	Afro-Asiatic
Maasai (Hollis 1971)	Nilo-Saharan
Macuxi (Macushi) (Carson 1982)	Carib
Mada (Rossing 1978)	Afro-Asiatic
Madurese (Davies 1999)	Austronesian
Maithili (Yadav 1996)	Indo-European
Malay (Teoh 1988)	Austronesian
Malayalam (Asher and Kumari 1997)	Dravidian
Maltese (Borg and Azzopardi-Alexander 1997)	Afro-Asiatic
Mam (Northern Mam) (England 1983)	Mayan
Mandan (Mixco 1997)	Siouan
Mandarin (Chao 1968, Bodman and Stimson 1961)	Sino-Tibetan
Mandikakan (Pakawu dialect) (Ngom 2000)	Niger-Congo
Mandinkakan (Guinea Bissau dialect) (Ngom 2000)	Niger-Congo
Mangap-Mbula (Bugenhagen 1995)	Austronesian
Manipuri (Meitei) (Bhat and Ningomba 1997)	Sino-Tibetan
Maori (Harlow 1996)	Austronesian
Marathi (Ghatage 1971, Jha 1980)	Indo-European
(Cochin and Kosti varieties)	
Margi (Marghi Central) (Hoffmann 1963)	Afro-Asiatic
Marshallese (Bender 1969)	Austronesian
Martuthunira (Dench 1995)	Australian
Marwari (Shekhawati dialect) (Gusain 2001)	Indo-European
Masalit (Edgar 1989)	Nilo-Saharan
Maya (Yucatan) (Straight 1976)	Mayan
Maya, Chontal (Tabasco Chontal) (Knowles 1984)	Mayan
Maya, Itzaj (Itzá) (Hofling 2000)	Mayan
Mbili (Bambili) (Ayuninjam 1998)	Niger-Congo
Melanesian Pidgin English (Tok Pisin) (Hall 1943)	Creole
Melayu Betawi (Ikranagara 1975)	Creole
Mende (Sengova 1984)	Niger-Congo
Menomini (Miner 1975)	Algic
Meriam (Mer) (Holmer 1988)	Trans-New Guinea

Mikasuki (Boynton 1982)	Muskogean
Mikir (Jeyapaul 1987)	Sino-Tibetan
Miogliola Ligurian (Ghini 2001)	Indo-European
Mishmi (Sastry 1984)	Sino-Tibetan
Mising (Prasad 1991)	Sino-Tibetan
Mixe, Lowland (Dieterman and Van Haitsma 1976, Wichmann 1995) (Coatlán, Guichicovi, San José El Paraíso, and San Juan el Paraíso varieties)	Mixe-Zoque
Mixe, Midland (Wichmann 1995) (including Atitlán, Cacalotepec, Cotzocón, Jaltepec, Juquila, Matamoros, Muxmetacán, and Puxmetacán varieties)	Mixe-Zoque
Mixe, North Highland (Totontepec) (Wichmann 1995)	Mixe-Zoque
Mixe, South Highland (Wichmann 1995) (Mixistlán, Tepantlali, Tepuxtepec, and Tlahuitoltepec varieties)	Mixe-Zoque
Mofu (Rossing 1978)	Afro-Asiatic
Mohawk (Michelson 1983)	Iroquoian
Mojave (Mohave) (Munro 1976)	Hokan
Mokilese (Harrison 1976)	Austronesian
Moloko (Melokwo) (Rossing 1978)	Afro-Asiatic
Mongolian (Halh Mongolian) (Bosson 1964)	Altaic
Montagnais (more than one dialect) (Cyr 1996)	Algic
Muktile (Matal) (Rossing 1978)	Afro-Asiatic
Mumuye (Zing dialect) (Shimizu 1983)	Niger-Congo
Muna (van den Berg 1989)	Austronesian
Mundari (Cook 1974)	Austro-Asiatic
Mupun (Mwaghavul) (Frajzyngier 1993) (including Jipari dialect)	Afro-Asiatic
Muruwari (Oates 1988)	Australian
Muyang (Rossing 1978)	Afro-Asiatic
Mwera (Harries 1950)	Niger-Congo
Nagamese (Naga Pidgin) (Boruah 1993)	Creole
Nahual, Michoacán (Michoacán Nahuatl) (Sischo 1979)	Uto-Aztecan
Nahuatl, Huasteca (Beller and Beller 1979)	Uto-Aztecan
Nahuatl, North Puebla (Brockway 1979)	Uto-Aztecan
Nahuatl, Tetelcingo (Tuggy 1979)	Uto-Aztecan
Nalik (Volker 1998)	Austronesian
Nangikurrunggurr (Hoddinott and Kofod 1988)	Australian
Navajo (Navaho) (Reichard 1974)	Na-Dene
Ndebele, Northern Transvaal (Ziervogel 1959)	Niger-Congo

Ndyuka (Huttar and Huttar 1994)	Creole
Ngiti (Kutsch Lojenga 1994)	Nilo-Saharan
Ngiyambaa (Donaldson 1980)	Australian
Nguna (North Efate) (Schütz 1969)	Austronesian
Ngura (Holmer 1988)	Australian
Nhanda (Yinggarda) (Blevins 2001)	Australian
Nigerian English (Nigerian Pidgin) (Faraclas 1996)	Creole
Nimboran (Anceaux 1965)	Trans-New Guinea
Nisgha (Nisga'a) (Tarpent 1987)	Penutian
Nkore-Kiga (Chiga) (Taylor 1985)	Niger-Congo
Noni (Noone) (Hyman 1981)	Niger-Congo
Noon (Soukka 2000)	Niger-Congo
Nuer (Crazzolara 1933)	Nilo-Saharan
Nuuchahnulth (Tsishaath Nootka) (Stonham 1999)	Wakashan
Nyangumata (O'Grady 1964)	Australian
Nyanja (Price 1958)	Niger-Congo
Nyanja (Chichewa dialect)	Niger-Congo
(Bentley and Kulemeka 2001)	
Nyulnyul (McGregor 1996)	Australian
Ojibwa, Central (Rhodes 1976)	Algic
Ojibwa, Eastern (Bloomfield 1956)	Algic
Okpe (Elugbe 1989)	Niger-Congo
Oloma (Elugbe 1989)	Niger-Congo
Oneida (Michelson 1983)	Iroquoian
Onondaga (Michelson 1983)	Iroquoian
O'odham (Saxton 1982)	Uto-Aztecan
Oriya, Kotia (Adivasi Oriya) (Gustafsson 1974)	Indo-European
Orma (Stroomer 1987)	Afro-Asiatic
Oromo, Boraana (Borana-Arsi-Guji) (Stroomer 1987)	Afro-Asiatic
Oromo, Harar (Eastern Oromo) (Owens 1985)	Afro-Asiatic
Oromo, Waata (Sanye) (Stroomer 1987)	Afro-Asiatic
Oshindonga (Ndonga) (Fivaz 1986)	Niger-Congo
Ostyak, Eastern (Khanty) (Gulya 1966)	Uralic
Pa'anci (Skinner 1979)	Afro-Asiatic
Paiute, Northern (Snapp et al. 1982)	Uto-Aztecan
Palauan (Josephs 1975)	Austronesian
Papiamentu (Kouwenberg and Murray 1994)	Creole
Passamaquoddy-Maliseet (Leavitt 1996)	Algic
Pawnee (Parks 1976)	Caddoan
Pech (Paya) (Holt 1999)	Chibchan
Pengo (Burrow and Bhattacharya 1970)	Dravidian
Pero (including Gwandum dialect)	Afro-Asiatic
(Frajzyngier 1989)	

Persian (Dehghani 2002)	Indo-European
Pileni (Næss 2000)	Austronesian
Pima Bajo (Fernández 1996)	Uto-Aztecan
Pitjantjatjara/Western Desert Language	Australian
(Douglas 1964)	
Polish (Swan 1983)	Indo-European
Popoluca, Oluta (Wichmann 1995)	Mixe-Zoque
Popoluca, Sayula (Wichmann 1995)	Mixe-Zoque
Portuguese (Mateus and d'Andrade 2000)	Indo-European
(Brazilian and European varieties)	
Pulaar (Paradis 1992)	Niger-Congo
Pulu Annian (Oda 1977)	Austronesian
Punjabi (Bhatia 1993)	Indo-European
Purik (Rangan 1979)	Sino-Tibetan
Quechua, Cuzco (Cuzco Kechua)	Quechuan
(Davidson 1977)	
Quechua, Ecuadorean Highland	Quechuan
(Lombeida-Naranjo 1976)	
Quechua, Huallaga (Huanaco) (Weber 1983)	Quechuan
Quechua, Junín (Adelaar 1977)	Quechuan
(San Pedro de Cajas variety)	
Quechua, Tarma (Adelaar 1977)	Quechuan
Quichoa, Chimborazo (Beukema 1975)	Quechuan
Quichua, Ecuador (Puyo Pongo (E. Ecuador))	Quechuan
(Orr 1962)	
Quichua, Imbabura Highland (Carpenter 1982)	Quechuan
Rabaul Creole German (Unserdeutsch) (Volker 1982)	Creole
Rao (Stanhope 1980)	Sepik-Ramu
Rapanui (Du Feu 1996)	Austronesian
Resígaro (Allin 1976)	Arawakan
Romani, Burgenland-Romani (Halwachs 2002)	Indo-European
Romanian (Chitoran 2002)	Indo-European
Rotuman (Vamarasi 2002)	Austronesian
Runyankore (Nyankore) (Morris and Kirwan 1957)	Niger-Congo
Runyoro-Rutooro (Nyoro/Tooro) (Rubongoya 1999)	Niger-Congo
Russian (Unbegaun 1957)	Indo-European
Saami, Central South(-Lappish) (Hasselbrink 1965)	Uralic
Sacapultec (Sacapulteco) (Dubois 1981)	Mayan
Sahaptin, Northern (Jacobs 1931)	Penutian
Saibai (Kala Lagaw Ya) (Holmer 1988)	Australian
Salish, Straits (Samish dialect) (Galloway 1990)	Salishan
Sango (Samarin 1967)	Creole
Santali (Neukom 2001)	Austro-Asiatic

Sawai (Whisler 1992)	Austronesian
Secoya (Johnson and Peeke 1962)	Tucanoan
Sekani (Hargus 1988)	Na-Dene
Selepet (McElhanon 1970)	Trans-New Guinea
Sema (Sreedhar 1980)	Sino-Tibetan
Senoufo, Cebaara Senoufo (Mills 1984)	Niger-Congo
Senoufo, Supyire (Carlson 1994)	Niger-Congo
Sentani (including Central dialect) (Cowan 1965)	Trans-New Guinea
Sepečides-Romani (Cech and Heinschink 1996)	Indo-European
Serbo-Croatian (Cres Čakavian) (Houtzagers 1985)	Indo-European
Shambala (Besha 1989)	Niger-Congo
Shilluk (Gilley 1992)	Nilo-Saharan
Shiriana Yanam (Ninam) (Gómez 1990)	Yanomam
Shona (Zezuru, Central and Eastern varieties) (Doke 1931)	Niger-Congo
Shoshoni, Western (Crum and Dayley 1993)	Uto-Aztecan
Si-Luyana (Luyana) (Givon 1970)	Niger-Congo
Sie (Crowley 1998)	Austronesian
Sinaugoro (Tauberschmidt 1999)	Austronesian
Siona (Wheeler and Wheeler 1962)	Tucanoan
Slavey, North (Rice 1989) (including Bearlake, Hare, and Mountain varieties)	Na-Dene
Slavey, South (Slavey) (Rice 1989)	Na-Dene
Slovak (Rubach 1993)	Indo-European
Slovene (Herrity 2000)	Indo-European
So (Soo) (Carlin 1993)	Nilo-Saharan
Somali (Pia 1963, Saeed 1987)	Afro-Asiatic
Sonora Yaqui (Dedrick and Casad 1999)	Uto-Aztecan
Sotho (Southern dialect) (Doke and Mofokeng 1957)	Niger-Congo
Spanish (European) (Cressey 1978)	Indo-European
Sre (Manley 1972)	Austro-Asiatic
Sri Lanka Creole Portuguese (Smith 1981)	Creole
St Lucian Creole (Carrington 1984)	Creole
Svan (Tuite 1997)	South Caucasian
Swahili (Ashton 1969)	Niger-Congo
Swazi (Swati) (Ziervogel 1952)	Niger-Congo
Swedish (McClean 1987)	Indo-European
Tacana (Key 1968)	Tacanan
Tagalog (Ramos 1971)	Austronesian
Talysh, Northern (Schulze 2000)	Indo-European
Tamasheq (including Tadraq variety) (Sudlow 2001)	Afro-Asiatic
Tamazight (Abdel-Massih 1968, Jilali 1976) (Ait Ayache and Ayt Ndhir varieties)	Afro-Asiatic

Tamil (Schiffman 1999)	Dravidian
Tangale (Kidda 1985)	Afro-Asiatic
Tangkhul (Tangkhul Naga) (Arokianathan 1987)	Sino-Tibetan
Tarangan, West (including River variety) (Nivens 1992)	Austronesian
Tashlhiyt (Dell and Elmedlaoui 2002) (including Haha and Imdlawn varieties)	Afro-Asiatic
Tauya (MacDonald 1990)	Trans-New Guinea
Tawala (Ezard 1997)	Austronesian
Telugu (Lakshmi 1982)	Dravidian
Temne (Wilson 1961)	Niger-Congo
Tepecano (Mason 1917)	Uto-Aztecan
Tepehuan, Northern (Bascom 1982)	Uto-Aztecan
Tepehuan, Southeastern (Willett 1988)	Uto-Aztecan
Tepetotutla Chinantec (Westley 1991)	Oto-Manguean
Teribe (Quesada 2000)	Chibchan
Tetun, Fehan (van Klinken 1999)	Austronesian
Thai (Palikupt 1983) (Central and Northeastern varieties)	Tai-Kadai
Thompson (Thompson and Thompson 1992)	Salishan
Tibetan (Dawson 1980)	Sino-Tibetan
Tigre (Raz 1983)	Afro-Asiatic
Tigrinya (Pam 1973)	Afro-Asiatic
Tiri/Tinrin (Osumi 1995)	Austronesian
Tiriyó (Trió) (Meira 2000)	Carib
Tirmaga (Suri) (Bryant 1999)	Nilo-Saharan
Tiv (Abraham 1968)	Niger-Congo
Toba (Klein 2001)	Mataco-Guaicuru
Tojolabal Maya (Brody 1982)	Mayan
Tokelauan (Hooper 1996)	Austronesian
Totonac, Misantla (MacKay 1999) (including San Marcos and Yecuatla varieties)	Totonacan
Tsakhur (Schulze 1997)	North Caucasian
Tsimshian, Coast (Dunn 1979[1995])	Penutian
Tswana (Cole 1955)	Niger-Congo
Tukang Besi (Donohue 1999)	Austronesian
Turkana (Dimmendaal 1983)	Nilo-Saharan
Turkish (Lewis 1967)	Altaic
Turkmen (Frank 1995)	Altaic
Tuvaluan (Besnier 2000)	Austronesian
Tyvan (Tuvin) (Anderson and Harrison 1999)	Altaic
Tzotzil (Cowan 1968)	Mayan

Tzutujil (Western Tzutujil) (Dayley 1981)	Mayan
(including San Juan and Santiago Atitlán varieties)	
Ubykh (Colarusso 1988)	North Caucasian
Uhami (Okpamheri) (Elugbe 1989)	Niger-Congo
Ukrainian (Bidwell 1967–68)	Indo-European
Ukue (Elugbe 1989:99)	Niger-Congo
Umbundu (Schadeberg 1990)	Niger-Congo
Uneme (Elugbe 1989)	Niger-Congo
Ura (Crowley 1996, 1999)	East Papuan
Urdu, Dakkhini (Mustafa 2000)	Indo-European
Urhobo (Elugbe 1989)	Niger-Congo
Usarufa (Bee and Glasgow 1973)	Trans-New Guinea
Uvbie (Elugbe 1989)	Niger-Congo
Vei (Vai) (Koelle 1968[1854])	Niger-Congo
Venda (Poulos 1990)	Niger-Congo
Vietnamese (Nguyên 1997)	Austro-Asiatic
Waffa (Stringer and Hotz 1973)	Trans-New Guinea
Wambaya (Nordlinger 1998)	Australian
Wangkangurru (Hercus 1994)	Australian
(including Eastern variety)	
Waorani (Saint and Pike 1962)	Unclassified
Warembori (Donohue 1996)	Lower Mamberamo
Warlpiri (Nash 1986)	Australian
Warrwa (McGregor 1994)	Australian
Welsh (Thorne 1993)	Indo-European
(including North and South varieties)	
Wichita (Rood 1976)	Caddoan
Wirangu (Hercus 1998)	Australian
Wisa (Lala-Bisa) (Madan 1906)	Niger-Congo
Wiyot (Reichard 1925)	Algic
Wolaytta (Lamberti and Sottile 1997)	Afro-Asiatic
Woleaian (Sohn 1975)	Austronesian
Wolio (Anceaux 1952)	Austronesian
Wolof (Ka 1994)	Niger-Congo
Xakas (Khakas) (Anderson 1998)	Altaic
Xhosa (McLaren 1906)	Niger-Congo
Yapese (Jensen 1977)	Austronesian
Yavapai (Shaterian 1983, Hardy 1979)	Hokan
(including Western/Tolkapaya variety)	
Yiddish (Katz 1987)	Indo-European
Yidiɲ (Dixon 1977)	Australian
Yinggarda (Dench 1998)	Australian
Yir-Yoront (Alpher 1991)	Australian

Yom (Pila) (Beacham 1968)	Niger-Congo
Yoruba (Awobuluyi 1978)	Niger-Congo
Yuchi (Ballard 1975)	Language Isolate
Yukuben (Shimizu 1980a)	Niger-Congo
Yupik, Central (St. Clair 1974)	Eskimo-Aleut
Yurok (Robins 1958)	Algic
Zina Kotoko (Odden 2002b)	Afro-Asiatic
Zulgo (Zulgwa) (Rossing 1978)	Afro-Asiatic
Zulu (Malcolm 1966)	Niger-Congo
Zway (Leslau 1999)	Afro-Asiatic

Appendix B   Detailed survey results

TABLE B.1 The most common natural classes (*Preliminaries*)

Rank	No.	Class description	Example	Features
1	306	[non-consonantal, vocalic]	/i u e o a/	2
2	164	[nasal]	/m n ŋ/	1
3	88	[diffuse, tense]	/i u/	2
4	85	[unvoiced]	/p t k s ʃ h/	1
5	65	[acute, tense]	/i e/	2
6	61	[flat]	/u ʊ o ɔ/	1
	61	[compact, grave, non-vocalic]	/k g/	3
8	59	[grave, vocalic]	/u i o a/	2
9	48	[non-diffuse, vocalic]	/e o ɛ ɔ a/	2
10	47	[interrupted, unvoiced]	/p t k tʃ/	2
11	46	[continuant, vocalic]	/i u a l/ (*/ɾ/)	2
12	41	[acute, non-compact, non-consonantal]	/i ɪ e ɛ/	3
	41	[LONG]	/i: u: e: o: a:/	1
14	39	[interrupted, non-vocalic, oral, voiced]	/b d dʒ g/ (*/l r ɾ/)	3
15	37	[vocalic]	/i u e o a l r/	1
	37	[non-diffuse, tense]	/e o/	2
	37	[non-compact, tense]	/i u e o/	2
18	36	[consonantal, vocalic]	/l r/	2
19	34	[consonantal]	/b d t k s n l/ (*/j/)	1
20	32	[tense]	/i u e o/	1
	32	[non-consonantal, plain (vs. flat), vocalic]	/i i e æ a/ (*/u o/)	3
22	30	[consonantal, unvoiced]	/p t k s/ (*/h/)	2
	30	[SHORT, non-consonantal, vocalic]	/i u a/ (*/l r i: u: a:/)	3
24	29	[grave, interrupted, non-compact]	/p b/ (*/t k g ɸ/)	3
25	27	[nasal, vocalic]	/ĩ ũ ẽ õ ã/	2
26	26	[lax]	/ɪ ʊ ɛ ɔ a/ (*/i u e/)	1
27	25	[voiced]	/b d g z n l i u a/	1
	25	[plain (vs. flat), tense]	/e i/	2
	25	[non-consonantal, non-vocalic, voiced]	/j w/ (*/h ʍ/)	3

	25	[interrupted, non-vocalic, oral]	/p t k b d g/ (*/ɾ/)	3
	25	[grave, strident]	/f v/, /q G χ ħ/	2
32	23	[non-vocalic]	/p t ʔ b g s h z n j/	1
33	22	[consonantal, interrupted, unvoiced]	/p t k/	3
34	22	[compact, strident]	/tʃ dʒ ʃ ʒ/	2
	21	[continuant, non-diffuse, non-vocalic]	/j w/	3
36	21	[acute, compact]	/ʈ c ɟ ɳ ɲ ʎ ʎ j/	2
37	20	[non-consonantal, unvoiced]	/j w i u ɪ ʊ e o ɛ ɔ/	2
38	20	[grave, unvoiced]	/p k f x/	2
39	19	[grave, non-compact, non-vocalic]	/p b f w/	3

TABLE B.2 The most common natural classes (*SPE*)

Rank	No.	Class description	Example	Features
1	433	[+syl]	/i u e o a m̩ ŋ̩/	1
2	180	[−syl]	/p t k s h m n l r j w/	1
3	162	[+nasal]	/m n ŋ/	1
4	86	[+high, +tense]	/i u/	2
5	80	[+tense, −back]	/i e/	2
6	77	[+round]	/u ʊ o ɔ/	1
7	73	[−voice]	/p t k s ʃ h/	1
8	64	[+syl, −back]	/i ɪ e ɛ/	2
9	62	[+back, −son]	/k g x ŋ/	2
10	57	[+tense]	/i u e o/	1
	57	[+back, +voc]	/ɨ u ʊ ə o ɔ a/	2
12	53	[−son]	/p t k b d g tʃ dʒ s z/	1
13	46	[+voice, −cons, −voc]	/j w/	3
14	44	[+syl, −high]	/e o ɛ ɔ a/	2
15	43	[+voice, −son]	/b d g dʒ z/	2
16	40	[+LONG]	/iː uː eː oː aː/	1
17	37	[+syl, −round]	/i ɨ e/	2
	37	[+syl, −LONG]	/i u a/ (*/iː uː aː/)	2
19	36	[−cont, −voice]	/p t k ʔ tʃ/	2
	36	[+tense, −high]	/e o/	2
21	35	[−movement of glottal closure]	/p t k b d g tʃ (*/pʼ ɓ.../)	1
	35	[−cont, −son]	/p t k b d g tʃ dʒ/	2
23	33	[+cor, +voc]	/l r/	2
24	32	[+voc, −tense]	/ɪ ʊ ɛ ɔ a/ (*/i u e/)	2
	32	[+cor, −movement of glottal closure]	/t d tʃ dʒ/ (*/tʼ ɗ/)	2
26	30	[+voice, −syl]	/b d g z m n l r j w/	2
	30	[+high, +voc]	/i ɨ ɪ ɯ u ʊ/	2

(*Continued*)

TABLE B.2 (*Continued*)

Rank	No.	Class description	Example	Features
28	29	[+voice, −movement of glottal closure]	/b d g/ (*/ɓ ɗ ɠ/)	2
	29	[+cons]	/t k b d s n l r/ (*/h j/)	1
	29	[+ant, −tense]	/m n/	2
31	28	[+delayed release]	/ts dz tʃ dʒ/	1
32	27	[+nasal, +voc]	/ĩ ũ ẽ õ ã/	2
33	25	[+voice]	/b d g z n l i u a/	1
34	24	[+ant, −cor]	/p b f v m w/	2
35	23	[+back, +cons]	/k g ŋ/	2
36	21	[+high, −back, −syl]	/tʃ dʒ ɲ ʎ j/	3
37	20	[−cons, −syl]	/j w/	2
	20	[+syl, −nasal]	/i u a/ (*/ĩ ũ ã/)	2
	20	[+son, −voice]	/ʔ h ʍ/	2
	20	[+cor]	/t d c ɟ s z ç ɲ n l r j/	1

TABLE B.3 The most common natural classes (UFT)

Rank	No.	Class description	Example	Features
1	401	[+SYLLABIC]	/i u e o a m̩ n̩/	1
2	185	[−SYLLABIC]	/p t k s h m n l r j w/	1
3	163	[+nasal]	/m n ŋ/	1
4	124	[+SYLLABIC, Coronal]	/i e/	2
5	91	[+SYLLABIC, Labial]	/u o/	2
6	86	[C-place Lingual, Dorsal]	/k g x ŋ/	2
7	78	[−voice]	/p t k s ʃ h/	1
8	70	[+vocoid, −SYLLABIC]	/j w/	2
9	61	[+SYLLABIC, −open2]	/i u e o/	2
10	55	[−continuant, −sonorant]	/p t k b d g tʃ dʒ/	2
11	48	[−sonorant]	/p t k b d g tʃ dʒ s z/	1
	48	[+SYLLABIC, −open3]	/i u ɪ ʊ e o/	2
13	46	[+SYLLABIC, Lingual]	/i u e o/	2
14	44	[+SYLLABIC, −LONG]	/i u a/ (*/i: u: a:/)	2
15	43	[+voice, −sonorant]	/b d g dʒ z/	2
16	42	[+vocoid]	/j w i u ɪ ʊ e o ɛ ɔ/	1
17	41	[+LONG]	/i: u: e: o: a:/	1
18	40	[+open2, V-place]	/e o/	2
19	36	[+voice, −SYLLABIC]	/b d g z m n l r j w/	2
20	35	[−continuant, −voice]	/p t k ʔ tʃ/	2
21	33	[C-place Labial]	/p b f v m w/	1
	33	[+open2]	/ɛ ɔ a/	1
23	32	[+approx, −vocoid]	/l r ɾ/	2
24	29	[−vocoid]	/t k d g s z n l r/	1
	29	[−sonorant, Dorsal]	/k g x/	2

	29	[+SYLLABIC, +nasal]	/m̥ t̪/ or /ĩ ũ ã/	2
27	28	[+strident, −continuant]	/ts tʃ dz dʒ/	2
28	26	[+approx, −SYLLABIC]	/l r ɾ j w/	2
29	25	[−continuant, −sonorant, Coronal]	/t d tʃ dʒ/	3
	25	[+voice, −continuant, −sonorant]	/b d g dʒ/	3
31	24	[+voice]	/b d g z n l i u a/	1
	23	[+open3]	/æ a/	1
33	21	[−continuant, −sonorant, Labial]	/p b/	3
34	20	[−SYLLABIC, Labial]	/p b f v m w/	2
	20	[−SYLLABIC, −anterior]	/ʈ ɖ c ɟ tʃ dʒ ʂ z̦ ç ʝ/	2
	20	[+SYLLABIC, −nasal]	/i u a/ (*/ĩ ũ ã m̥ t̪/)	2

TABLE B.4 The most common features occurring in natural classes (*Preliminaries*)

Rank	No.	Feature	Rank	No.	Feature
1	855	vocalic	16	269	plain (vs. flat)
2	644	non-consonantal	17	259	voiced
3	623	non-vocalic	18	239	continuant
4	540	interrupted	19	209	flat
5	524	acute	20	205	mellow
6	499	grave	21	168	lax
7	462	oral	22	159	strident
8	456	tense	23	129	SHORT
9	442	unvoiced	24	65	LONG
10	407	non-compact	25	54	unchecked
11	390	consonantal	26	38	plain (vs. sharp)
12	298	compact	27	24	checked
13	288	diffuse	28	11	sharp
14	286	non-diffuse	29	6	NON-EXTRA
15	272	nasal	30	2	EXTRA

TABLE B.5 The most common features occurring in natural classes (*SPE*)

Rank	No.	Feature	Rank	No.	Feature
1	731	+syllabic		153	−low
2	456	−sonorant	27	140	−vocalic
3	447	−syllabic	28	131	−LONG
4	419	+tense	29	118	+distributed
5	402	+high	30	111	−anterior
6	395	−back	31	97	−strident
7	379	−voice	32	94	−glottal closure
8	375	+coronal	33	80	+strident
9	373	+voice	34	79	−hi subglottal pressure
10	333	+vocalic	35	64	+LONG
11	307	+back	36	52	−distributed
12	282	−high	37	37	+delayed release
13	251	+anterior	38	36	−delayed release
14	245	+nasal	39	22	−lateral
15	215	+sonorant	40	20	+low
16	211	−continuant	41	17	+glottal closure
17	204	−mov. glottal closure	42	9	+lateral
18	195	−coronal	43	8	+mov. glottal closure
19	185	+continuant		8	+hi subglottal pressure
20	180	+consonantal	45	6	−EXTRA
21	175	−round	46	2	+EXTRA
22	173	+round	47	1	−del rel 2nd closure
23	166	−consonantal	48	0	+covered
24	164	−nasal			−covered
25	153	−tense		0	+del rel 2nd closure

TABLE B.6 The most common features occurring in natural classes (UFT)

Rank	No.	Feature	Rank	No.	Feature
1	1058	+SYLLABIC	36	53	−lateral
2	536	−SYLLABIC	37	49	vocalic
3	486	−sonorant	38	42	C-place Labial
4	417	−continuant	39	33	+constricted glottis
5	390	Coronal	40	31	−open4
6	285	−voice	41	29	−ATR
7	274	Labial	42	25	+ATR
8	256	+nasal	43	21	Pharyngeal
9	250	+voice		21	+open4
10	185	Dorsal	45	17	C-place Pharyngeal
11	170	−strident		17	+spread glottis
	170	+sonorant	47	14	−open1
13	158	−open2		14	+lateral

14	152	−distributed	49	13	+open1
15	151	−nasal	50	7	−open6
16	144	C-place Lingual	51	5	−open5
17	132	+continuant	52	4	−EXTRA
18	126	−vocoid	53	3	+C-place distributed
19	124	Lingual	54	2	+open6
20	122	+vocoid		2	+EXTRA
21	121	−anterior	56	1	V-place Lingual
	121	+strident		1	V-place Labial
23	118	−LONG		1	C-place Coronal
24	115	C−place		1	−C-place distributed
25	114	−open3		1	+open5
26	106	−constricted glottis	61	0	V-place Dorsal
27	102	+approx		0	−C-place anterior
28	100	+open2		0	+V-place distributed
29	98	−approximant		0	C-place Dorsal
30	80	V−place		0	V-place Pharyngeal
31	76	+anterior		0	V-place Coronal
32	74	+open3		0	+C-place anterior
33	64	−spread glottis		0	−V-place distributed
34	62	+LONG		0	+V-place anterior
35	60	+distributed			

TABLE B.7 Place groupings

Rank	No.	Class Description
1	175	labial and coronal (127 are anterior)
2	132	coronal and velar (lingual)
3	101	labial and velar (grave)
4	18	velar and laryngeal
5	13	coronal, velar, and laryngeal
6	10	labial, velar, and laryngeal
7	8	coronal and laryngeal
8	7	labial, coronal, and laryngeal
9	6	labial and laryngeal
10	5	velar and uvular
11	4	labial, coronal, and uvular
	4	coronal and pharyngeal
	4	velar and pharyngeal
	4	velar and laryngeal
	4	uvular and pharyngeal
	4	uvular and laryngeal
	4	pharyngeal and laryngeal
18	3	coronal, velar, uvular, and laryngeal
	3	coronal, velar, and pharyngeal

(*Continued*)

TABLE B.7 (*Continued*)

Rank	No.	Class Description
20	2	labial, velar, and uvular
	2	labial and uvular
	2	coronal, velar, and laryngeal
	2	velar, uvular, and laryngeal
	2	uvular, pharyngeal, and laryngeal
25	1	labial, coronal, and pharyngeal
	1	labial and pharyngeal
	1	coronal, uvular, pharyngeal, and laryngeal
	1	coronal, pharyngeal, and laryngeal
	1	velar, uvular, pharyngeal, and laryngeal
	1	velar, pharyngeal, and laryngeal
	1	labial, velar, uvular, and laryngeal
	1	labial, velar, pharyngeal, and laryngeal
	1	labial, uvular, and pharyngeal
	1	labial, uvular, pharyngeal, and laryngeal

TABLE **B.8** Frequency and availability of features (*Preliminaries*)

Feature	Frequency		Availability (%)	Adjusted frequency
	+	−		
tense/lax	456	168	6.5	4,836.0
nasal/oral	272	462	9.7	3,792.3
flat/plain	209	269	6.5	3,704.5
vocalic	855	623	29.0	2,545.4
consonantal	390	644	35.5	1,457.0
grave/acute	499	524	38.7	1,321.4
voiced/unvoiced	259	442	35.5	987.8
interrupted/continuant	540	239	48.4	805.0
compact/non-compact	298	407	45.2	780.5
strident/mellow	159	205	25.8	705.3
diffuse/non-diffuse	288	288	45.2	637.7
checked/unchecked	24	54	9.8	403.0
sharp/plain	11	38	6.5	379.8
LONG	65	129	0	n/a
EXTRA	2	6	0	n/a

TABLE **B.9** Frequency and availability of features (*SPE*)

Feature	Frequency		Availability (%)	Adjusted frequency
	+	−		
round	173	175	6.5	2,697.0
distributed	118	52	3.2	2,635.0
syllabic	731	447	22.6	2,608.4
nasal	245	164	9.7	2,113.2
tense	419	153	16.1	1,773.2
back	307	395	29.0	1,209.0
movement of gl. clos.	8	204	9.7	1,095.3
voice	373	379	35.5	1,059.6
low	20	153	9.7	893.8
vocalic	333	140	29.0	814.6
high	402	282	45.2	757.3
sonorant	215	456	48.4	693.4
coronal	375	195	41.9	679.6
consonantal	180	166	35.5	487.5
lateral	9	22	3.2	480.5
anterior	251	111	38.7	467.6
glottal (3ary) closure	17	94	12.9	430.1
continuant	185	211	48.4	409.2
strident	80	97	25.8	342.9
delayed prim. release	37	1	9.7	196.3
del. rel. of 2nd closure	0	0	0	n/a
hi subglottal pressure	8	79	0	n/a
covered	0	0	0	n/a
LONG	64	131	0	n/a
EXTRA	2	6	0	n/a

TABLE **B.10** Frequency and availability of features (UFT)

Feature	Frequency		Availability (%)	Adjusted frequency
	+	−		
SYLLABIC	1,058	536	22.6	3,529.6
nasal	256	151	9.7	2,102.8
open2	100	158	6.5	1,999.5
spread	17	64	3.2	1,255.5
lateral	14	53	3.2	1,038.5
C-place	115		6.5	891.2
voice	250	285	35.5	753.9

(*Continued*)

TABLE B.10 (*Continued*)

Feature	Frequency		Availability (%)	Adjusted frequency
	+	−		
open3	74	114	12.9	728.5
labial	274		19.4	707.8
sonorant	170	486	48.4	677.9
continuant	132	426	48.4	576.6
strident	121	170	25.8	563.8
constricted	33	106	12.9	538.6
dorsal	185		19.4	477.9
C-place lingual	144		16.1	446.4
coronal	390		45.2	431.8
vocoid	122	126	29.0	427.1
ATR	25	29	6.5	418.5
open1	13	14	3.2	418.5
V-place	80		9.7	413.3
anterior	76	121	25.8	381.7
approximant	102	98	35.5	281.8
lingual	124		25.8	240.3
C-place labial	42		9.7	217.0
vocalic	49		29.0	84.4
V-place labial	1		9.7	5.2
C-place coronal	1		25.8	1.9
C-place dorsal	0		9.7	n/a
V-place dorsal	0		9.7	n/a
C-place anterior	0	0	19.4	n/a
V-place coronal	0		9.7	n/a
C-place pharyngeal	17		0	n/a
open4	21	31	0	n/a
open5	1	5	0	n/a
open6	2	7	0	n/a
V-place lingual	1		0	n/a
V-place pharyngeal	0		0	n/a
pharyngeal	21		0	n/a
C-place distributed	34	12	0	n/a
distributed	60	152	0	n/a
V-place anterior	0	0	0	n/a
V-place distributed	0	0	0	n/a
LONG	62	118	0	n/a
EXTRA	2	4	0	n/a

TABLE B.11 The most common complex classes (*Preliminaries*)

Rank	No.	Components			
		Rank among natural classes	No. of natural classes	Class	Description
1	40	116	6	[consonantal, oral]	consonants
		32	23	∨ [non-vocalic]	
2	31	19	34	[consonantal]	consonants
		32	23	∨ [non-vocalic]	
3	17	335	1	[consonantal, mellow]	non-strident
		32	23	∨ [non-vocalic]	consonants
4	10	20	32	[non-consonantal, plain	vowels
		20	32	(vs. flat), vocalic]	
				∨ [tense]	
5	9	19	34	[consonantal] ∨	consonants
		96	7	[non-vocalic, oral]	
	9	18	36	[consonantal, vocalic]	nasals and
		2	164	∨ [nasal]	liquids
7	8	n/a	0	[consonantal, plain (vs.	non-labialized
		32	23	flat)] ∨ [non-vocalic]	consonants, etc.
	8	228	2	[consonantal, non-	labial, dental,
		32	23	compact] ∨ [non-	and alveolar
				vocalic]	consonants
9	7	3	88	[diffuse, tense]	high tense
		26	26	∨ [lax]	vowels and lax vowels
	7	19	34	[consonantal] ∨	consonants
		4	85	[unvoiced]	(including /h ʔ/)
	7	109	6	[acute, nasal] ∨	liquids and
		18	36	[consonantal, vocalic]	coronal nasals

TABLE B.12 The most common complex classes (*SPE*)

Rank	No.	Components			
		Rank among natural classes	No. of natural classes	Class	Description
1	6	4	86	[+high, +tense]	/i u a/ or /i u ɛ ɔ a/
		24	32	∨ [+vocalic, −tense]	
2	5	40	20	[+coronal]	dental/alveolar and palatal consonants
		80	9	∨ [−anterior, −back, −syllabic]	
	5	245	2	[+coronal, −tense]	dental/alveolar and palatal nasals
		245	2	∨ [+high, +nasal]	
4	4	156	4	[+low, +vocalic]	low vowels and tense vowels
		10	57	∨ [+tense]	
	4	156	4	[+lateral] ∨ [+nasal]	laterals and nasals
		3	162		
	4	58	12	[+high, +vocalic, −round]	unrounded high vowels and lax vowels
		24	32	∨ [+vocalic, −tense]	
	4	4	86	[+high, +tense]	round vowels and high tense vowels
		6	77	∨ [+round]	
	4	n/a	0	[+back, −low, −round] −	velar consonants, unrounded non-low back and tense vowels
		24	32	[+vocalic, −tense]	
	4	196	3	[+back, +voice, −sonorant] ∨	voiced velar obstruents and coronal implosive
		n/a	0	[+coronal, +voice, +movement of glot clos]	
	4	n/a	0	[+back, +voice, −low, −round] ∨	voiced velar consonants, unrounded non-low back and tense vowels
		10	57	[+tense]	
	4	379	1	[+anterior, −coronal, −voice] ∨	voiceless labials and velars
		134	5	[+back, −voice]	

TABLE **B.13** The most common complex classes (UFT)

Rank	No.	Components			
		Rank among natural classes	No. of natural classes	Class	Description
1	31	5	91	[+SYLLABIC, Labial] ∨ [+open1]	round back vowels and /a/
		55	11		
2	27	4	124	[+SYLLABIC, Coronal] ∨ [+open1]	unrounded front vowels and /a/
		55	11		
3	20	55	11	[+open1] ∨ [+open2, Labial]	round non-high back vowels and /a/
		180	3		
4	17	55	11	[+open1] ∨ [+open2, Coronal]	unrounded non-high front vowels and /a/
		103	6		
5	12	24	29	[−son, Dorsal] ∨ [−son, Labial]	grave obstruents
		51	12		
6	12	9	61	[+SYLLABIC, −open2] ∨ [+open1]	high and low vowels
		55	11		
	10	n/a	0	[+distributed, −open6] ∨ [−open6, Labial]	front and round non-low vowels
		180	3		
8	10	47	14	[+SYLLABIC, Dorsal] ∨ [+open1]	back vowels and /a/
		55	11		
9	8	322	1	[+nasal, Coronal] ∨ [+nasal, Labial]	coronal and labial nasals
		322	1		
	8	n/a	0	[+nasal, −distributed] ∨ [+nasal, Labial]	alveolar and labial nasals
		322	1		
	8	42	18	[+SYLLABIC, −open2, Coronal] ∨ [+open1]	front and low vowels
		55	11		

TABLE B.14 The ten most common components of complex classes (*Preliminaries*)

Rank	No.	Rank among natural classes	No. of natural classes	Class
1	150	32	23	[non-vocalic]
2	123	18	36	[consonantal, vocalic]
3	98	2	164	[nasal]
4	89	19	34	[consonantal]
5	77	125	5	[interrupted, vocalic]
6	63	143	4	[consonantal, continuant, vocalic]
7	51	59	13	[acute, diffuse, tense]
8	50	109	6	[consonantal, oral]
9	49	37	20	[non-consonantal, unvoiced]
	49	109	6	[acute, nasal]

TABLE B.15 The ten most common components of complex classes (*SPE*)

Rank	No.	Rank among natural classes	No. of natural classes	Class
1	51	245	2	[+coronal, −tense]
2	41	156	4	[+lateral]
3	34	245	2	[+vocalic, −lateral]
4	33	1	433	[+syllabic]
	33	3	162	[+nasal]
	33	4	86	[+high, +tense]
	33	134	5	[+back, −voice]
8	29	156	4	[+low, +vocalic]
	29	n/a	0	[+coronal, −movement of glottal closure]
10	27	71	10	[+high, +round]

TABLE B.16   The ten most common components of complex classes (UFT)

Rank	No.	Rank among natural classes	No. of natural classes	Class
1	203	55	11	[+open1]
2	63	322	1	[+nasal, Labial]
3	60	5	91	[+SYLLABIC, Labial]
4	54	1	401	[+SYLLABIC]
5	52	6	86	[Dorsal, C-place Lingual]
6	50	51	12	[−sonorant, Labial]
	50	4	124	[+SYLLABIC, Coronal]
8	43	8	70	[+vocoid, −SYLLABIC]
9	41	62	10	[+lateral]
10	39	322	1	[+spread glottis]

Appendix C   Detailed phonetic similarity results

TABLE C.1 Five phonetic dimensions based on a MDS analysis of Wang and Bilger's (1973) confusion matrices

Consonant	1	2	3	4	5
p	2.1971	−0.2245	−0.2685	0.2126	0.5442
t	1.6899	0.9856	0.2222	−0.019	−0.313
k	−0.4668	−0.9313	1.6769	−1.1242	−1.5968
b	0.135	0.1403	−1.585	−0.1685	0.9983
d	−0.6007	0.9871	−0.5486	−1.2595	−0.7856
g	−0.2727	−0.7603	0.019	−1.3472	−0.2326
tʃ	1.4799	0.5594	0.417	1.4956	−1.16
dʒ	−0.4668	−0.9313	1.6769	−1.1242	−1.5968
f	1.2601	0.1347	−1.321	0.5386	0.5863
θ	0.5124	0.3567	−1.6357	0.4913	−0.4406
s	0.8298	−0.7117	−1.3018	1.5072	−0.3333
ʃ	0.5451	−0.0148	0.5705	1.8838	−1.0385
h	1.9862	−0.0132	−0.0509	0.6395	1.3597
v	−1.3551	−0.1245	−0.9896	0.018	0.9307
ð	−1.3185	0.2025	−1.4942	−0.2456	−0.1715
z	−1.7014	−0.4442	−0.5025	0.4631	−0.0811
ʒ	−1.557	−0.8806	0.3357	−0.1338	−0.7621
m	−0.4174	2.1854	0.4043	−0.1509	0.7004
n	−1.2158	1.9007	0.437	0.4317	0.5388
ŋ	−0.7017	1.908	1.3051	−0.2257	0.6335
l	−0.7273	−0.2966	0.135	−2.3354	0.4682
r	−1.6106	−0.8786	1.413	−1.5881	0.1598
j	−0.4668	−0.9313	1.6769	−1.1242	−1.5968
ʍ	0.205	−1.7658	1.0611	0.7069	1.2041
w	−0.8369	−1.4551	1.6261	0.2103	0.8945

TABLE C.2 Four phonetic dimensions based on a MDS analysis of Wang and Bilger's (1973) confusion matrices and one artificial dimension based on place of articulation

consonant	1	2	3	4	place
p	2.0672	−0.3226	−0.1127	0.3974	2
t	1.6384	0.561	0.2322	−0.03	0.25
k	1.6462	0.1001	−0.788	0.2464	−1
b	0.1099	−1.1066	0.4613	1.1769	2
d	−0.8865	0.6735	0.3082	0.5008	0.25
g	−0.5574	0.4428	−0.8944	0.5666	−1
tʃ	1.8815	−0.3452	0.3365	−1.3485	−0.25
dʒ	−0.0487	−0.0824	−0.8453	−1.4504	−0.25
f	1.1991	−1.1841	0.3203	0.6757	1.5
θ	0.5653	−1.3404	−0.1661	0.2496	0.75
s	1.1397	−1.6482	−0.4573	−0.6091	0.25
ʃ	0.9697	−0.4734	0.0552	−1.8084	−0.25
h	1.9136	−0.328	0.1809	1.1234	−2
v	−1.2442	−0.9172	0.2457	0.7115	1.5
ð	−1.2065	−1.1332	0.0708	0.5476	0.75
z	−1.3718	−0.7649	−0.273	−0.4026	0.25
ʒ	−1.5278	−0.2681	−0.6768	−0.9585	−0.25
m	−0.3581	0.3035	2.1646	0.1436	2
n	−1.0701	−0.2371	1.8616	−0.469	0.25
ŋ	−0.693	1.273	1.8297	−0.214	−1
l	−1.2228	1.5877	0.6704	0.8532	0.25
r	−1.8048	1.7443	−0.6744	−0.0041	0.25
j	−0.6232	1.9828	−0.7387	−1.442	−0.25
ʍ	0.3348	0.602	−1.5976	1.0295	2
w	−0.8504	0.8807	−1.5131	0.5146	2

TABLE C.3   Scaled average scores according to three models

	5 dimensions		4 dim. + place		SPE	
	real	random	real	random	real	random
Berbice Dutch	1.237	2.285	0.630	1.876	0.178	1.451
Agta (Casiguran Dumagat)	0.287	1.792	0.333	1.319	0.000	1.082
Daga	0.000	1.015	0.000	0.633	0.000	0.674
Desano	0.665	1.900	0.414	1.643	0.636	1.082
Jamaican Creole	0.000	0.719	0.000	0.863	0.000	1.400
Kickapoo	0.730	1.459	0.105	1.659	0.000	0.891
Lingala	0.314	1.686	1.222	1.380	0.000	0.923
Meriam	0.000	1.407	0.000	1.164	0.000	0.636
Mishmi	1.040	2.062	1.126	1.564	0.420	1.374
Montagnais	0.000	0.867	0.000	0.985	1.273	0.891
Ndyuka	0.892	2.389	0.703	1.903	0.127	1.451
Nyanja	0.000	1.391	0.000	1.126	0.000	1.693
Sawai	0.813	2.671	2.643	2.108	0.000	1.909
Sentani	0.000	0.083	0.398	1.631	0.000	0.547
Sentani (Central)	0.000	1.385	0.000	1.266	0.000	0.509
Xakas	0.692	2.220	1.106	2.201	0.477	1.686

References

Abdel-Massih, Ernest T. (1968) *Tamazight Verb Structure: A Generative Approach.* Bloomington/The Hague: Indiana University Press/Mouton.

Abondolo, D. M. (1988) *Hungarian Inflectional Morphology.* Budapest: Akadémiai Kiadó.

Abraham, P. T. (1985) *Apatani Grammar.* Mysore: Central Institute of Indian Languages.

Abraham, R. C. (1968) *The Principles of Tiv.* Farnborough, UK: Gregg.

Abumdas, Abdul Hamid Ali (1985) *Libyan Arabic Phonology.* Ann Arbor: UMI.

Acharya, K. P. (1983) *Lotha Grammar.* Mysore: Central Institute of Indian Languages.

Adelaar, W. F. H. (1977) *Tarma Quechua Grammar, Texts, Dictionary.* Lisse: de Ridder.

Aikhenvald, Alexandra (1995) *Bare.* Munich: Lincom Europa.

Allin, Trevor R. (1976) *A Grammar of Resígaro.* High Wycombe, UK: Summer Institute of Linguistics.

Alpher, Barry (1991) *Yir-Yoront Lexicon: Sketch and Dictionary of an Australian Language.* New York: Mouton de Gruyter.

Al-Sughayer, Khalil Ibrahim (1990) *Aspects of Comparative Jordanian and Modern Standard Arabic Phonology.* Ann Arbor: UMI.

Ambrazas, Vytautas, Emma Geniušienė, Aleksas Girdenis, Nijolė Sližienė, Dalija Tekorienė, Adelė Valeckienė, and Elena Valiulytė (1997) *Lithuanian Grammar.* Lithuania: Baltos Lankos.

Amha, Azeb (2001) *The Maale Language.* Leiden: Research School of Asian, African, and Amerindian Studies, Universiteit Leiden.

Anceaux, J. C. (1952) *The Wolio Language.* The Hague: Nijhoff.

—— (1965) *The Nimboran Language.* The Hague: Nijhoff.

Andersen, Henning (1972) Diphthongization. *Language* 48: 11–50.

—— (1973) Abductive and deductive change. *Language* 49: 765–93.

Anderson, Gregory D. S. (1998) *Xakas.* Munich: Lincom Europa.

—— and K. David Harrison (1999) *Tyvan.* Munich: Lincom Europa.

Anderson, John M., and Colin J. Ewen (1987) *Principles of Dependency Phonology.* Cambridge: Cambridge University Press.

Anderson, Judi Lynn (1989) *Comaltepec Chinantec Syntax.* Arlington: Summer Institute of Linguistics and the University of Texas at Arlington.

Anderson, Stephen R. (1976) Nasal consonants and the internal structure of segments. *Language* 52: 326–44.

—— (1981) Why phonology isn't 'Natural'. *Linguistic Inquiry* 12: 493–539.

Andronov, M. S. (1980) *The Brahui Language.* Moscow: Nauka.

Ansre, Gilbert (1961) The tonal structure of Ewe. MA thesis, Hartford Seminary Foundation.

Anttila, Raimo (1977) *Analogy.* The Hague: Mouton.
—— (2003) Analogy: the warp and woof of cognition. In Joseph and Janda (2003: 425–40).
—— and Warren A. Brewer (1977) *Analogy: A Basic Bibliography.* Amsterdam: Benjamins.
Arokianathan, S. (1987) *Tangkhul Naga Grammar.* Mysore: Central Institute of Indian Languages.
Aronoff, Mark (1994) *Morphology by Itself.* Cambridge, Mass.: MIT Press.
Asher, R. E., and T. C. Kumari (1997) *Malayalam.* New York: Routledge.
Ashton, E. O. (1969) *Swahili Grammar.* London: Longmans.
Aslin, Richard N., and David B. Pisoni (1980) Some developmental processes in speech perception. In Grace H. Yeni-Komshian, F. Kavanaugh James, and Charles A. Ferguson (eds.), *Child Phonology, vol. 2: Perception.* New York: Academic Press, pp. 67–96.
Austen, Cheryl Lynn (1974) *Aspects of Bukusu Syntax and Phonology.* Ann Arbor: University of Michigan Press.
Austin, Peter (1981) *A Grammar of Diyari, South Australia.* Cambridge: Cambridge University Press.
Avery, Peter, and William J. Idsardi (2001) Laryngeal dimensions, completion and enhancement. In Hall (2001: 41–70).
Awobuluyi, Oladele (1978) *Essentials of Yoruba.* Ibadan: Oxford University Press Nigeria.
Ayuninjam, Funwi F. (1998) *A Reference Grammar of Mbili.* Lanham, Md.: University Press of America.
Bach, Emmon, and Robert T. Harms (1972) How do languages get crazy rules? In R. P. Stockwell and R. K. S. Macauley (eds.), *Linguistic Change and Generative Theory.* Bloomington: Indiana University Press, pp. 1–21.
Bailey, Beryl Loftman (1966) *Jamaican Creole Syntax: A Transformational Approach.* Cambridge: Cambridge University Press.
Ballard, W. L. (1975) Aspects of Yuchi morphophonology. In Crawford (1975: 163–87).
Bascom, Burton (1979) Northern Tepehuan. In Langacker (1982: 267–393).
Baxter, Alan N. (1988) *A Grammar of Kristang (Malacca Creole Portuguese). Pacific Linguistics Series B,* 95. Canberra: Pacific Linguistics.
Beacham, Charles Gordon Jr. (1968) *The Phonology and Morphology of Yom.* Ann Arbor: UMI.
Beckman, Mary, and Janet Pierrehumbert (2003) Interpreting "phonetic interpretation" over the lexicon. In J. Local, R. Ogden, and R. Temple (eds.), *Papers in Laboratory Phonology VI.* Cambridge: Cambridge University Press, pp. 13–37.
Beckman, Mary E., Kiyoko Yoneyama, and Jan Edwards (2003) Language-specific and language-universal aspects of lingual obstruent productions in Japanese-acquiring children. *Journal of the Phonetic Society of Japan* 7: 18–28.
Beddor, Patrice Speeter (1991) Predicting the structure of phonological systems. *Phonetica* 48: 83–107.
Bee, Darlene, and Kathleen Barker Glasgow (1973) Usarufa tone and segmental phonemes. In McKaughan (1973: 190–203).

Bee, Darlene, Lorna Luff, and Jean Goddard (1973) Notes on Agarabi Phonology. In McKaughan (1973: 414–23).

Begne, Leopold Prosper (1980) *The Phonology of Bikele, a Cameroonian Language.* Ann Arbor: UMI.

Beller, Richard, and Patricia Beller (1979) Huastaca Nahauatl. In Langacker (1979: 199–306).

Bender, Byron W. (1969) *Spoken Marshallese.* Honolulu: University of Hawai'i Press.

Benkő, Loránd, and Samu Imre (eds.) (1972) *The Hungarian Language.* The Hague: Mouton.

Bentley, Mayrene, and Andrew Kulemeka (2001) *Chichewa.* Munich: Lincom Europa.

Berry, Keith, and Christine Berry (1998) *A Description of Abun: A West Papuan Language of Irian Jaya.* Canberra: Pacific Linguistics.

Besha, Ruth Mfumbwa (1989) *A Study of Tense and Aspect in Shambala.* Berlin: Reimer.

Besnier, Niko (2000) *Tuvaluan.* New York: Routledge.

Best, Catherine T., Gerald W. McRoberts, and Nomathemba M. Sithole (1988) Examination of perceptual reorganization for nonnative speech contrasts: Zulu click discrimination by English-speaking adults and infants. *Journal of Experimental Psychology: Human Perception and Performance* 14: 345–60.

Beukema, Ronald William (1975) *A Grammatical Sketch of Chimborazo Quichoa.* Ann Arbor: UMI.

Bevington, Gary Loyd (1974) *Albanian Phonology.* Wiesbaden: Harrassowitz.

Bhat, D. N. S. (1971) *The Koraga Language.* Poona: Deccan College Postgraduate and Research Institute.

—— and M. S. Ningomba (1997) *Manipuri Grammar.* Newcastle: Lincom Europa.

Bhatia, Tej K. (1993) *Punjabi.* New York: Routledge.

Bidwell, Charles E. (1967–68) *Outline of Ukrainian Morphology.* University of Pittsburgh.

Bilgiri, H. S. (1965) *Kharia: Phonology, Grammar, and Vocabulary.* Poona: Deccan College Postgraduate and Research Institute.

Blevins, Juliette (2001) *Nhanda, an Aboriginal Language of Western Australia.* Honolulu: University of Hawai'i Press.

—— (2004) *Evolutionary Phonology.* Cambridge: Cambridge University Press.

—— (to appear) Consonant epenthesis: natural and unnatural histories. In J. Good (ed.), *Proceedings of the Workshop on Explaining Linguistic Universals.* Oxford: Oxford University Press.

—— and Andrew Garrett (1998) The origins of consonant-vowel metathesis. *Language* 74: 508–56.

Bliese, Loren F. (1981) *A Generative Grammar of Afar.* Arlington: Summer Institute of Linguistics and the University of Texas at Arlington.

Bloomfield, Leonard (1956) *Eastern Ojibwa: Grammatical Sketch, Texts, and Word List.* Ann Arbor: University of Michigan Press.

Bodman, Nicholas C., and Hugh M. Stimson (1961) *Mandarin Chinese: units 1–6.* Washington, DC: Center for Applied Linguistics of the Modern Language Association of America.

Bodomo, Adams B. (2000) *Dàgáàrè.* Munich: Lincom Europa.

Bolozky, Shmuel (1972) *Categorial Limitations on Rules in the Phonology of Modern Hebrew.* Ann Arbor: UMI.

Booij, Geert (1995) *The Phonology of Dutch.* Oxford: Clarendon Press.

Borg, Albert, and Marie Azzopardi-Alexander (1997) *Maltese.* New York: Routledge.

Borman, M. B. (1962) Cofan phonemes. In Elson (1962: 45–59).

Born, Renate (1994) *Michigan German in Frankenmuth: Variation and Change in an East Franconian Dialect.* Columbia, SC: Camden House.

Boruah, B. K. (1993) *Nagamese: The Language of Nagaland.* New Delhi: Mittal.

Bosson, James E. (1964) *Modern Mongolian: A Primer and Reader.* Bloomington/The Hague: Indiana University Press/Mouton.

Bowern, Claire (1998) The case of Proto Karnic: morphological change and reconstruction in the nominal and pronominal system of Proto Karnic (Lake Eyre Basin). BA thesis, Australian National University.

—— and Harold Koch (eds.) (2004) *Australian Languages: Classification and the Comparative Method.* Amsterdam: Benjamins.

Bowers, Nora, Rick Bowers, and Kenn Kaufman (2004) *Mammals of North America.* New York: Houghton Mifflin.

Boyd, Raymond (2002) *Bata Phonology: A Reappraisal.* Munich: Lincom Europa.

Boynton, Sylvia S. (1982) *Mikasuki Grammar in Outline.* Ann Arbor: UMI.

Bradshaw, Mary (1999) A crosslinguistic study of consonant–tone interaction. Ph.D. dissertation, Ohio State University.

Brainard, Sherri (1994) *The Phonology of Karao, the Philippines.* Canberra: Pacific Linguistics.

Breen, Gavan (2001) The Wonders of Arandic Phonology. In Simpson, Jane, David Nash, Mary Laughren, Peter Austin, and Barry Alpher (eds.) *Forty years on: Ken Hale and Australian languages.* Canberra: Pacific Linguistics.

Brentari, Diane (1990) Licensing in ASL handshape. In C. Lucas (ed.), *Sign Language Research: Theoretical Issues.* Washington, DC: Gallaudet University Press, pp. 57–68.

—— (1995) Sign language phonology: ASL. In John A. Goldsmith (ed.), *The Handbook of Phonological Theory.* Cambridge, Mass.: Blackwell, pp. 615–39.

—— (1998) *A Prosodic Model of Sign Language Phonology.* Cambridge, Mass.: MIT Press.

Bright, William (1972) The enunciative vowel. *International Journal of Dravidian Linguistics* 1:1 26–55.

Brockway, Earl (1979) North Puebla Nahuatl. In Langacker (1979: 141–98).

Brody, Mary Jill (1982) *Discourse Processes of Highlighting in Tojolabal Maya Morphosyntax.* Ann Arbor: UMI.

Bromley, H. Myron (1961) *The Phonology of Lower Grand Valley Dani.* The Hague: Nijhoff.

Broselow, Ellen I. (1976) Phonology of Egyptian Arabic. Ph.D. dissertation, University of Massachusetts.

Browman, Catherine, and Louis Goldstein (1992) Articulatory phonology: an overview. *Phonetica* 49: 155–80.

Brown, Gillian (1972) *Phonological Rules and Dialect Variation.* Cambridge: Cambridge University Press.

Brown, Roger (1973) *A First Language.* Cambridge, Mass.: Harvard University Press.

Bryant, Michael Grayson (1999) *Aspects of Tirmaga Grammar.* Ann Arbor: UMI.

Buckley, Eugene (1994) *Theoretical Aspects of Kashaya Phonology and Morphology.* Stanford, Calif.: CSLI.

—— (2000) What should phonology explain? Handout from SUNY Buffalo Linguistics Colloquium, March 17, 2000.

Bugenhagen, Robert D. (1995) *A Grammar of Mangap-Mbula: An Austronesian Language of Papua New Guinea.* Canberra: Pacific Linguistics.

Bunye, Maria Victoria R., and Elsa Paula Yap (1971) *Cebuano Grammar Notes.* Honolulu: University of Hawai'i Press.

Burling, Robbins (1961) *A Garo Grammar.* Poona: Deccan College Postgraduate and Research Institute.

Burquest, Donald A., and Wyn D. Laidig (eds.) (1992) *Phonological Studies in Four Languages of Maluku.* Arlington, Tex.: Summer Institute of Linguistics.

Burrow, T., and S. Bhattacharya (1970) *The Pengo Language.* Oxford: Clarendon Press.

Butcher, Andrew (2006) Australian Aboriginal languages: consonant-salient phonologies and the "place-of-articulation imperative". In J. Harrington and M. Tabain (eds.), *Speech Production: Models, Phonetic Processes, and Techniques.* London: Psychology Press, pp. 187–210.

Bybee, Joan L. (1985) *Morphology: A Study into the Relation between Meaning and Form.* Amsterdam: Benjamins.

—— (1998) Usage-based phonology. In M. Darnell, E. Moravcsik, F. Newmeyer, M. Noonan, and K. Wheatley (eds.), *Functionalism and Formalism in Linguistics,* vol. 1: *General Papers.* Amsterdam: Benjamins, pp. 211–42.

—— (2001) *Phonology and Language Use.* Cambridge: Cambridge University Press.

Cain, Bruce D., and James W. Gair (2000) *Dhiveni (Maldivian).* Munich: Lincom Europa.

Cammenga, Jelle (2002) *Phonology and Morphology of Ekigusii.* Cologne: Köppe.

Cardona, George (1965) *A Gujarati Reference Grammar.* Philadelphia: University of Pennsylvania Press.

Carlin, Eithne (1993) *The So Language.* Cologne: Institut für Afrikanistik, Universität zu Köln.

Carlson, Robert (1994) *A Grammar of Supyire.* Berlin: Mouton de Gruyter.

Carpenter, Lawrence Kidd (1982) *Ecuadorian Quichua: Descriptive Sketch and Variation.* Ann Arbor: University of Michigan Press.

Carrington, Lawrence D. (1984) *St. Lucian Creole: A Descriptive Analysis of its Phonology and Morph-Syntax.* Hamburg: Buske.

Carson, Neusa Martins (1982) *Phonology and Morphosyntax of Macuxi (Carib).* Ann Arbor: UMI.

Carstairs-McCarthy, Andrew (1994) Inflection classes, gender and the Principle of Contrast. *Language* 70, 737–88.

Casagrande, Jean (1984) *The Sound System of French*. Washington, DC: Georgetown University Press.

Castiglione, Pierina Borrani (1957) *Italian Phonetics, Diction and Intonation*. New York: Vanni.

Cech, Petra, and Mozes F. Heinschink (1996) *Sepečides-Romani*. Munich: Lincom Europa.

Chalmers, David J. (1990) Thoughts on emergence. http://www.u.arizona.edu/~chalmers/notes/emergence.html

Chambers, J. K. (1995) *Sociolinguistic Theory: Linguistic Variation and its Social Significance*. Cambridge, Mass.: Blackwell.

Chamora, Berhanu, and Robert Hetzron (2000) *Inor*. Munich: Lincom Europa.

Chao, Yuen Ren (1968) *A Grammar of Spoken Chinese*. Berkeley: University of California Press.

Charney, Jean Ormsbee (1993) *A Grammar of Comanche*. Lincoln: University of Nebraska Press.

Chen, Matthew (1973) On the formal expression of natural rules in phonology. *Journal of Linguistics* 9: 223–49.

Cherchi, Marcello (1999) *Georgian*. Munich: Lincom Europa.

Childs, George Tucker (1990) *Phonology and Morphology of Kisi*. Ann Arbor: University of Michigan Press.

Chitoran, Ioana (2002) *The Phonology of Romanian: A Constraint-Based Approach*. New York: Mouton de Gruyter.

Chomsky, Noam (1957) *Syntactic Structures*. The Hague: Mouton.

—— (1965) *Aspects of the Theory of Syntax*. Cambridge, Mass.: MIT Press.

—— (1968) *Language and Mind*. San Diego, Calif.: Harcourt Brace Jovanovich.

—— and Morris Halle (1968) *The Sound Pattern of English*. Cambridge, Mass.: MIT Press.

Christenson, John, and Sylvia Christenson (1992) Kisar phonology. In Burquest and Laidig (1992: 33–65).

Chung, Raung-Fu (1989) Aspects of Kejia phonology. UIUC dissertation, UMI.

Clements, G. N. (1985) The geometry of phonological features. *Phonology Yearbook* 2: 225–52.

—— (1990) Place of articulation in consonants and vowels: a unified theory. Expanded version of a paper presented at NELS 21.

—— (1999) Affricates as noncontoured stops. In O. Fujimura, B. D. Joseph, and B. Palek (eds.), *Proceedings of LP'98*. Prague: Karolinum Press, 271–99.

—— (2001) Representational economy in constraint-based phonology. In Hall (2001: 71–146).

—— and Elizabeth V. Hume (1995) The internal organization of speech sounds. In J. Goldsmith (ed.), *The Handbook of Phonological Theory*. Cambridge, Mass.: Blackwell, pp. 245–306.

Cohen, Kevin Bretonnel (2000) *Aspects of the Grammar of Kukú*. Munich: Lincom Europa.

Colarusso, John (1988) *The Northwest Caucasian Languages: A Phonological Survey.* New York: Garland.

Cole, Desmond T. (1955) *An Introduction to Tswana Grammar.* New York: Longmans, Green.

——(1967) *Some Features of Ganda Linguistic Structure.* Johannesburg: Witwatersrand University Press.

Cole, R. A., R. N. Haber, and B. D. Sales (1973) Mechanisms of aural encoding, VI: Consonants and vowels are remembered as subsets of distinctive features. *Perception and Psychophysics* 13: 870–92.

Conrad, Robert J., and Kepas Wogiga (1991) *An Outline of Bukiyip Grammar.* Canberra: Pacific Linguistics.

Constenla, Adolfo (1981) *Comparative Chibchan Phonology.* Ann Arbor: UMI.

Cook, Revd Walter Anthony, SJ (1974) *Structure of the Mundari Language.* Ann Arbor: Xerox University Microfilms.

Corina, David P., and Elizabeth Sagey (1989) Are Phonological Hierarchies Universal? Evidence from American Sign Language. In K. de Jong and Yongkyoon No (eds.), *Proceedings of the Sixth Eastern States Conference on Linguistics,* pp. 73–83.

Counts, David R. (1969) *A Grammar of Kaliai-Kove.* Honolulu: University of Hawai'i Press.

Cowan, H. K. J. (1965) *Grammar of the Sentani Language.* The Hague: Nijhoff.

—— Marion M. (1968) *Tzotzil Grammar.* Norman: Summer Institute of Linguistics of the University of Oklahoma.

Crawford, James M. (ed.) (1975) *Studies in Southeastern Indian Languages.* Athens: University of Georgia Press.

Crazzolara, Father J. P. (1933) *Outlines of a Nuer Grammar.* Vienna: Verlag der Internationalen Zeitschrift.

Cressey, William W. (1978) *Spanish Phonology and Morphology: A Generative View.* Washington, DC: Georgetown University Press.

Crewe, W. J. (1975) *The Phonological Features of the Ingessana Language.* University of Khartoum: Institute of African and Asian Studies.

Croft, William (2001) *Radical Construction Grammar: Syntactic Theory in Typological Perspective.* Oxford: Oxford University Press.

Crowley, Terry (1996) *Ura.* Munich: Lincom Europa.

——(1998) *An Erromangan (Sye) Grammar.* Honolulu: University of Hawai'i Press.

——(1999) *Ura: A Disappearing Language of Southern Vanuatu.* Canberra: Pacific Linguistics.

Crum, Beverly, and John P. Dayley (1993) *Western Shoshoni Grammar.* Boise, Ida.: Dept of Anthropology, Boise State University.

Culicover, Peter W., and Andrzej Nowak (2003) Markedness, antisymmetry and complexity of constructions. In Pierre Pica and Johann Rooryk (eds.), *Variation Yearbook.* Amsterdam: Benjamins, pp. 5–30.

—— and—— (2004). *Dynamical Grammar.* Oxford: Oxford University Press.

Cyffer, Norbert (1998) *A Sketch of Kanuri.* Cologne: Rüdiger Köppe Verlag.

Cyr, Danielle (1996) *Montagnais: An Ethnogrammatical Description.* In Maurais (1996: 174–203).

Darley, Vincent (1994) Emergent phenomena and complexity. In *Proceedings of the Alife IV Workshop,* Cambridge, Mass.

Davidson, Joseph O., Jr. (1977) *A Contrastive Study of the Grammatical Structures of Aymara and Cuzco Kechua.* Ann Arbor: UMI.

Davies, William (1999) *Madurese.* Newcastle: Lincom Europa.

Dawson, Willa (1980) *Tibetan Phonology.* Ann Arbor: UMI.

Day, Christopher (1973) *The Jacaltec Language.* Bloomington The Hague: Indiana University Press/Mouton.

Dayley, Jon Philip (1981) *Tzutujil Grammar.* Ann Arbor: UMI.

de Boer, Bart (2000) *The Origins of Vowel Systems.* Oxford: Oxford University Press.

de Boysson-Bardies, B., and Marilyn May Vihman (1991). Adaptation to language: evidence from babbling and first words in four languages. *Language* 67: 297–319.

de Hoon, Michiel Jan Laurens (2002) The C Clustering Library for cDNA microarray data. Laboratory of DNA Information Analysis, Human Genome Center, Institute of Medical Science, University of Tokyo.

de Vreis, Lourens (1993) *Forms and Functions in Kombai, an Awyu Language of Irian Jaya.* Canberra: Pacific Linguistics.

Dedrick, John M., and Eugene H. Casad (1999) *Sonora Yaqui Language Structures.* Tucson: University of Arizona Press.

Dehghani, Yavar (2000) *A Grammar of Iranian Azari.* Munich: Lincom Europa.

—— (2002) *Persian.* Munich: Lincom Europa.

Dell, François, and Mohamed Elmedlaoui (2002) *Syllables in Tashlhiyt Berber and Moroccan Arabic.* Boston: Kluwer Academic.

Dench, Alan (1998) *Yingkarta.* Munich: Lincom Europa.

—— (1995) *Martuthunira: A Language of the Pilbara Region of Western Australia.* Canberra: Pacific Linguistics.

Derbyshire, Desmond C. (1985) *Hixkaryana and Linguistic Typology.* Arlington: Summer Institute of Linguistics and the University of Texas at Arlington.

Dieterman, Julia, and Willard Van Haitsma (1976) *A Hierarchical Sketch of Mixe as Spoken in San José El Paraíso.* Norman: Summer Institute of Linguistics of the University of Oklahoma.

Dihoff, Ivan Raymond (1976) *Aspects of the Tonal Structure of Chori.* Ann Arbor: UMI.

Dimmendaal, Gerritt Jan (1983) *The Turkana Language.* Cinnaminson, NJ: Foris.

Disner, Sandra (1983) Vowel quality: the contribution of language particular and language universal factors. *UCLA Working Papers in Linguistics* 58: 1–154.

Dixon, R. M. W. (1972) *The Dyirbal Language of North Queensland.* Cambridge: Cambridge University Press.

—— (1977) *A Grammar of Yidiɲ.* New York: Cambridge University Press.

—— (1988) *A Grammar of Boumaa Fijian.* Chicago: University of Chicago Press.

—— (2002) *Australian Languages: Their Nature and Development.* Cambridge: Cambridge University Press.

Doke, C. M., and S. M. Mofokeng (1957) *Textbook of Southern Sotho Grammar*. New York: Longmans, Green.

—— (1931) *A Comparative Study in Shona Phonetics*. Johannesburg: University of the Witwatersrand Press.

Dolbey, A. E., and G. Ó. Hansson (1999) The source of naturalness in synchronic phonology. *CLS* 35, vol. 1. Chicago: Chicago Linguistic Society, pp. 59–69.

Dolphyne, Florence Abena (1988) *The Akan (Twi-Fante) Language: Its Sound Systems and Tonal Structure*. Accra: Ghana Universities Press.

Donaldson, Bruce C. (1993) *A Grammar of Afrikaans*. New York: Mouton de Gruyter.

Donaldson, Tamsin (1980) *Ngiyambaa: The Language of the Wangaaybuwan*. New York: Cambridge University Press.

Donohue, Mark (1996) *Warembori*. Munich: Lincom Europa.

—— (1999) *A Grammar of Tukang Besi*. New York: Mouton de Gruyter.

Douglas, W. H. (1964) *An Introduction to the Western Desert Language*. Sydney: University of Sydney Press.

Dresher, Elan (2003) Contrast and asymmetries in inventories. In A. M. Di Sciullo (ed.), *Asymmetry in Grammar*. Amsterdam: Benjamins, pp. 239–57.

Dubois, John William (1981) *The Sacapultec Language*. Ann Arbor: UMI.

Du Feu, Veronica (1996) *Rapanui*. New York: Routledge.

Dunn, John Asher (1979[1995]) *Sm'algyax: A Reference Dictionary and Grammar for the Coast Tsimshian Language*. Seattle: University of Washington Press.

Duponceau, Peter Stephen (1830) "The translator's preface" and "Concluding note by the translator" in "A grammar of the language of the Lenni Lenape or Delaware Indians...presented to the Society 2d December 1816", Transactions of the American Philosophical Society 3.

Durie, Mark (1985) *A Grammar of Acehnese on the Basis of a Dialect of North Aceh*. Cinnaminson, NJ: Foris.

Dutton, Tom E. (1996) *Koiari*. Munich: Lincom Europa.

Dwyer, David James (1981) *A Reference Handbook of Lorma*. East Lansing: Michigan State University Press.

Edgar, John (1989) *A Masalit Grammar*. Berlin: Reimer.

Edward, Amastae Jon (1980) *Dominican Creole Phonology*. Ann Arbor: UMI.

Eimas, P. D., E. R. Siqueland, P. Jusczyk, and J. Vigorito (1971) Speech perception in infants. *Science* 171: 303–6.

Einstein, Albert (1905) *Investigations on the Theory of the Brownian Movement*. 1956 reprint of 1926 English translation, New York: Dover.

Elson, Benjamin (ed.) (1962) *Studies in Ecuadorian Indian Languages*, 1. Norman: Summer Institute of Linguistics of the University of Oklahoma.

Elugbe, Ben Ohiomamhe (1989) *Comparative Edoid: Phonology and Lexicon*. Port Harcourt: University of Port Harcourt Press.

Emananjo, E. Nolue (1978) *Elements of Modern Igbo Grammar: A Descriptive Approach*. Ibadan: Oxford University Press.

Emeneau, M. B. (1961) *Kolami: A Dravidian Language*. Annamalainagar: Annamalai University.

England, Nora C. (1983) *A Grammar of Mam, a Mayan Language*. Austin: University of Texas Press.

Engstrand, Olle (1997) Why are clicks so exclusive?. Papers from FONETIK-97, the Ninth Swedish Phonetics Conference, held in Umeå. *Reports from the Department of Phonetics, Umeå University (PHONUM)* 4: 191–4.

Eulitz, C., and A. Lahiri (2004) Neurobiological evidence for abstract phonological representations in the mental lexicon during speech recognition. *Journal of Cognitive Neuroscience* 16: 577–83.

Ezard, Bryan (1997) *A Grammar of Tawala: An Austronesian Language of the Milne Bay Area, Papua New Guinea*. Canberra: Pacific Linguistics.

Faraclas, Nicholas G. (1996) *Nigerian Pidgin*. New York: Routledge.

Fernández, Zarina Estrada (1996) *Pima Bajo*. Munich: Lincom Europa.

Ferraz, Luiz Evans (1979) *The Creole of São Tomé*. Johannesburg: Witwatersrand University Press.

Fivaz, Derek (1986) *A Reference Grammar of Oshindonga (Wambo)*. Windhoek: Star Binder & Printers.

Flemming, Edward (2002) *Auditory Representations in Phonology*. New York: Routledge.

—— (2005) Deriving natural classes in phonology. *Lingua* 115: 287–309.

Forman, Michael L. (1971) *Kapampangan Grammar Notes*. Honolulu: University of Hawai'i Press.

Fortescue, Michael (1984) *West Greenlandic*. Sydney: Croom Helm.

Fortune, R. F. (1977) *Arapesh*. New York: Augustin.

Fox, Anthony (1990) *The Structure of German*. Oxford: Clarendon Press.

Fox, Robyn (1992) Prejudice and the unfinished mind: a new look at an old failing. *Psychological Inquiry* 3: 137–52.

Fox, Samuel Ethan (1997) *The Neo-Aramaic Dialect of Jilu*. Wiesbaden: Harrassowitz.

Frajzyngier, Zygmunt (1989) *A Grammar of Pero*. Berlin: Reimer.

—— (1993) *A Grammar of Mupun*. Berlin: Reimer.

—— (2001) *A Grammar of Lele*. Palo Alto, Calif.: CSLI.

Frank, Allen J. (1995) *Turkmen Reader*. Kensington, Md.: Dunwoody Press.

Frantz, Chester, and Marjorie Frantz (1973) Gadsup phoneme and toneme units. In McKaughan (1973: 1–11).

Frantz, Donald G. (1991) *Blackfoot Grammar*. Toronto: University of Toronto Press.

Fromkin, Victoria A. (ed.) (1973) *Speech Errors as Linguistic Evidence*. The Hague: Mouton.

Fromkin, Victoria A. (1988) Grammatical aspects of speech errors. In F. J. Newmeyer (ed.), *Linguistics: The Cambridge Survey*, vol. 2: *Linguistic Theory: Extensions and Implications*. Cambridge: Cambridge University Press, pp. 117–138.

Fujimura, Osamu, Marian J. Macchi, and L. A. Streeter (1978) Perception of stop consonants with conflicting transitional cues: a cross-linguistic study. *Language and Speech* 21: part 4.

Galloway, Brent D. (1977) *A Grammar of Chilliwack Halkomelem.* Ann Arbor: UMI.

—— (1990) A phonology, morphology, and classified word list for the Samish dialect of Straits Salish. Canadian Ethnology Service, Mercury Series Paper 116.

Garrett, Andrew, and Juliette Blevins (2004) Analogical morphophonology. In *The nature of the word: Essays in honor of Paul Kiparsky,* ed. by Kristin Hanson and Sharon Inkelas. Cambridge, Mass.: MIT Press.

Gerfen, Chip (1999) *Phonology and Phonetics in Coatzospan Mixtec.* Dordrecht: Kluwer Academic.

Ghatage, A. M. (1971) *Marathi Dialect Texts,* 1: *Dialect of Cochin.* Poona: Deccan College.

Ghini, Mirco (2001) *Asymmetries in the Phonology of Miogliola.* New York: Mouton de Gruyter.

Gierut, J. A. (1996) Categorization and feature specification in phonological acquisition. *Journal of Child Language.* 23: 397–415.

Gilley, Leoma G. (1992) *An Autosegmental Approach to Shilluk Phonology.* Arlington, Tex.: Summer Institute of Linguistics.

Giridhar, P. P. (1980) *Angami Grammar.* Mysore: Central Institute of Indian Languages.

Givon, Talmy (1970) *The Si-Luyana Language: A Preliminary Linguistic Description.* University of Zambia, Institute for Social Research.

Glover, Bonnie Carol (1989) *The Morphophonology of Muscat Arabic.* Ann Arbor: UMI.

Goddard, Ives (1979) *Delaware Verbal Morphology: A Descriptive and Comparative Study.* New York: Garland.

Goldinger, Stephen D. (1997) Words and voices: perception and production in an episodic lexicon. In K. Johnson and J. W. Mullenix (eds.), *Talker Variability in Speech Processing.* San Diego, Calif.: Academic Press, pp. 33–66.

—— (1998) Echoes of Echoes? An Episodic Theory of Lexical Access. *Psychological Review* 105: 251–79.

Goldstein, Louis (1977) Categorical features in speech perception and production. Prepared for the Working Group on Slips of the Tongue, 12th International Congress of Linguists, Vienna.

Gómez, Gale Goodwin (1990) *The Shiriana Dialect of Yanam (Northern Brazil).* Ann Arbor: UMI.

Gorbet, Larry Paul (1976) *A Grammar of Diegueño Nominals.* New York: Garland.

Gordon, Kent H. (1976) *A Phonology of Dhangar-Kurux.* Kathmandu: Tribhuvan University Press.

Gorgoniyev, Y. A. (1966) *The Khmer Language.* Moscow: Nauka.

Gowda, K. S. Gurubasave (1991) *Ao Grammar.* Mysore: Central Institute of Indian Languages.

Graham, L. W., and A. S. House (1971) Phonological oppositions in children: a perceptual study. *Journal of the Acoustical Society of America* 49: 559–66.

Green, Lisa (1998) Aspect and predicate phrases in African-American vernacular English. In S. S. Mufwene (ed.), *African-American English: Structure, History, and Use.* New York: Routledge, pp. 85–109.

Greenberg, Joseph H. (1966) Synchronic and diachronic universals in phonology. *Language* 42: 508–17.

——(1978) Diachrony, synchrony, and language universals. In Joseph H. Greenberg (ed.), *Universals of Human Language*, vol. 1: *Method and Theory*. Palo Alto, Calif.: Stanford University Press, pp. 61–91.

Greene, Laurie A. (1999) *A Grammar of Belizean Creole: Compilations from Two Existing United States Dialects*. New York: Lang.

Grimes, Barbara F., Joseph E. Grimes, and Richard S. Pittman (eds.) (2000) *Ethnologue: Languages of the World*, 14th edn. http://www.ethnologue.com. Summer Institute of Linguistics.

Groves, Terab'ata R., Gordon W. Groves, and Roderick Jacobs (1985) *Kiribatese*. Canberra: Pacific Linguistics.

Gulya, János (1966) *Eastern Ostyak Chrestomathy*. Bloomington/The Hague: Indiana University/Mouton.

Gusain, Lakhan (2000) *Bagri*. Munich: Lincom Europa.

——(2001) *Shekhawati*. Munich: Lincom Europa.

Gustafsson, Uwe (1974) *Kotia Oriya Phonemic Summary*. Nagpur, India: Summer Institute of Linguistics.

Guy, Gregory R. (2003) Variationist approaches to phonological change. In Joseph and Janda (2003: 369–400).

Hajek, John (1997) *Universals of Sound Change in Nasalization*. Oxford: Blackwell.

Hale, Mark (2003) Neogrammarian sound change. In Joseph and Janda (2003: 343–68).

——and Charles Reiss (2000) Phonology as cognition. In N. Burton-Roberts, P. Carr, and G. Docherty (eds.), *Phonological Knowledge: Conceptual and Empirical Foundations*. Oxford: Oxford University Press, pp. 161–84.

Hall, Robert A., Jr (1943) *Melanesian Pidgin English: Grammar, Texts, Vocabulary*. Baltimore, Md.: Waverly Press.

——(1953) *Haitian Creole: Grammar—Texts—Vocabulary*. Philadelphia: American Folklore Society.

Hall, T. Alan (ed.) (2001) *Distinctive Feature Theory*. New York: Mouton de Gruyter.

Halle, Morris (1962) Phonology in a generative grammar. *Word* 18: 54–72.

——(1988) The immanent form of phonemes. In W. J. Hurst (ed.), *The Making of Cognitive Science*. Cambridge: Cambridge University Press, pp. 167–83.

——(1989) The intrinsic structure of speech sounds. MS, MIT.

——(1992) Phonological features. In W. Bright (ed.), *International Encyclopedia of Linguistics*, vol. 3. Oxford: Oxford University Press, pp. 207–12.

——and G. N. Clements (1983) *Problem Book in Phonology*. Cambridge, Mass.: MIT Press.

——and Kenneth N. Stevens (1979) Some reflections on the theoretical bases of phonetics. in B. Lindblom and S. Öhman (eds.), *Frontiers of Speech Communication Research*. London: Academic Press, pp. 335–53.

—— Bert Vaux, and Andrew Wolfe (2000) On feature spreading and the representation of place of articulation. *Linguistic Inquiry* 31: 387–444.

Halwachs, Dieter W. (2002) *Burgenland-Romani*. Munich: Lincom Europa.

Hamel, Patricia J. (1985) *A Grammar of Loniu*. Ann Arbor: UMI.

—— (1994) *A Grammar and Lexicon of Loniu, Papua New Guinea*. Canberra: Pacific Linguistics.

Hankins, Daniel G., and Julia A. Rosekrans (2004) Overview, prevention, and treatment of rabies. *Mayo Clinic Proceedings* 2004 (79): 671–6.

Hardman, M. J. (2000) *Jaqaru*. Munich: Lincom Europa.

Hardy, Heather Kay (1979) *Tolkapaya Syntax: Aspect, Modality, and Adverbial Modification in a Yavapai Dialect*. Ann Arbor: UMI.

Hargus, Sharon (1988) *The Lexical Phonology of Sekani*. New York: Garland.

Harkins, William E. (1953) *A Modern Czech Grammar*. New York: King's Crown Press.

Harlow, Ray (1996) *Māori*. Munich: Lincom Europa.

Harms, Robert T. (1962) *Estonian Grammar*. Bloomington/The Hague: Indiana University/Mouton.

Harries, Revd Lyndon (1950) *A Grammar of Mwera*. Johannesburg: Witwatersrand University Press.

Harris, James W. (1984) Theories of phonological representation and nasal consonants in Spanish. In. P. Baldi (ed.) *Papers from the 12th Linguistic Symposium on Romance Languages*. Amsterdam: Benjamins, pp. 153–68.

Harris, John (1994) *English Sound Structure*. Cambridge, Mass.: Blackwell.

—— and Geoff Lindsey (1995) The elements of phonological representation. In Jacques Durand and Francis Katamba (eds.), *Frontiers of Phonology: Atoms, Structures, Derivations*. Harlow, Essex: Longman, pp. 34–79.

Harrison, Sheldon P. (1976) *Mokilese Reference Grammar*. Honolulu: University of Hawai'i Press.

Hashimoto, Mantaro J. (1973) *The Hakka Dialect: A Linguistic Study of its Phonology, Syntax, and Lexicon*. Cambridge: Cambridge University Press.

—— Oi-kan Yue (1972) *Phonology of Cantonese*. Cambridge: Cambridge University Press.

Haspelmath, Martin (1993) *A Grammar of Lezgian*. New York: Mouton de Gruyter.

—— Matthew S. Dryer, David Gil, and Bernard Comrie (eds.) (2005) *World Atlas of Language Structures*. Oxford: Oxford University Press.

Hasselbrink, Gustav (1965) *Alternative Analyses of the Phonemic System in Central South-Lappish*. Bloomington/The Hague: Indiana University/Mouton.

Hauser, M., N. Chomsky, and T. Fitch (2002) The faculty of language: what is it, who has it, and how did it evolve? *Science* 298: 1569–79.

Hayward, Dick (1984) *The Arbore Language: A First Investigation, Including a Vocabulary*. Hamburg: Buske.

Healey, Phyllis M. (1960) *An Agta Grammar*. Manila: Bureau of Printing.

Hebert, Raymond J., and Nicholas Poppe (1963) *Kirghiz Manual*. Bloomington/The Hague: Indiana University/Mouton.

Hercus, Luise A. (1994) *A Grammar of the Arabana-Wangkangurru Language, Lake Eyre Basin, South Australia.* Canberra: Pacific Linguistics.

—— (1998) *A Grammar of the Wirangu Language from the West Coast of South Australia.* Canberra: Pacific Linguistics.

Herrity, Peter (2000) *Slovene: A Comprehensive Grammar.* New York: Routledge.

Hoard, James E. (1971) The new phonological paradigm. *Glossa* 5: 222–68.

Hock, Hans Henrich (2003) Analogical change. In Joseph and Janda (2003: 441–60).

Hoddinott, W. G., and F. M. Kofod (1988) *The Ngankikurungkurr Language.* Canberra: Pacific Linguistics.

Hoffmann, Carl (1963) *A Grammar of the Margi Language.* London: Oxford University Press.

Hofling, Charles Andrew (2000) *Itzaj Maya Grammar.* Salt Lake City: University of Utah Press.

Hollis, Alfred C. (1971) *The Masai: Their Language and Folklore.* Freeport, NY: Books for Libraries Press.

Holmer, Nils M. (1988) *Notes on Some Queensland Languages.* Canberra: Pacific Linguistics.

Holt, Dennis (1999) *Pech (Paya).* Munich: Lincom Europa.

Hombert, Jean-Marie, John J. Ohala, and William G. Ewan (1979) Phonetic explanations for the development of tones. *Language* 55: 37–58.

Hooper, Robin (1996) *Tokelauan.* Munich: Lincom Europa.

Houtzagers (1985) *The Čakavian Dialect of Orlec on the Island of Cres.* Amsterdam: Rodopi.

Hualde, José Ignacio (1988) Affricates are not contour segments. *Proceedings of WCCFL VII:* 143–57.

—— (1991) *Basque Phonology.* New York: Routledge.

Huang, Tsan (2001) The interplay of perception and phonology in tone 3 sandhi in Chinese Putonghua. In Hume and Johnson (2001b: 23–43).

Hume, Elizabeth V. (1994) *Front Vowels, Coronal Consonants and Their Interaction in Nonlinear Phonology.* New York: Garland.

—— (2004a) The indeterminacy/attestation model of metathesis. *Language* 80: 203–37.

—— (2004b) Deconstructing markedness: a predictability-based approach. *BLS* 30: 182–93.

—— and Keith Johnson (eds.) (2001a) *The Role of Speech Perception in Phonology.* New York: Academic Press.

—— and —— (eds.) (2001b) *Studies on the interplay of speech perception and phonology. Ohio State University Working Papers in Linguistics* 55.

—— and —— (2001c) A model of the interplay of speech perception and phonology. In Hume and Johnson (2001a: 4–26).

Hume, Elizabeth V. Keith Johnson, Misun Seo, Georgios Tserdanelis, and Stephen Winters (1999) A cross-linguistic study of stop place perception. *ICPhS* 14: 2070–73.

—— and David Odden (1996) Reconsidering [consonantal]. *Phonology* 13: 345–76.

—— and Georgios Tserdanelis (2002) Labial unmarkedness in Sri Lankan Portuguese Creole. *Phonology* 19/1: 441–58.

Huttar, George L., and Mary L. Huttar (1994) *Ndyuka.* New York: Routledge.

Hyman, Larry M. (1972) *A Phonological Study of Fe'Fe'-Bamileke*. Ann Arbor: UMI.

—— (1981) Noni grammatical structure. *Southern California Occasional Papers in Linguistics* 9.

—— (2001) The limits of phonetic determinism in phonology: *NC revisited. In Hume and Johnson (2001a: 141–85).

—— and Daniel J. Magaji (1970) *Essentials of Gwari Grammar*. Ibadan: Ibadan University Press.

—— and Russel G. Schuh (1974) Universals of tone rules: evidence from West Africa. *Linguistic Inquiry* 5: 81–115.

Ikoro, Suano M. (1996) *The Kana Language*. Leiden: Research School, CNWS.

Ikranagara, Kay (1975) *Melayu Betawi Grammar*. Ann Arbor: UMI.

Imre, Samu (1972) *Hungarian Dialects* (trans. Gombos Imre). In Benkő and Imre (1972: 299–326).

Ingram, D. (1978) The acquisition of word-initial fricatives and affricates by normal and linguistically deviant children. In A. Caramazza and E. B. Zurif (eds.), *Language Acquisition and Language Breakdown: Parallels and Divergences*. Baltimore, Md.: Johns Hopkins University Press, pp. 63–85.

Innes, Gordon (1966) *An Introduction to Grebo*. London: Luzac.

Israel, M. (1979) *A Grammar of the Kuvi Language*. Vanchiyoor: Dravidian Linguistics Association.

Jacobs, Melville (1931) *A Sketch of Northern Sahaptin Grammar*. Seattle: University of Washington Press.

Jaggar, Philip J. (2001) *Hausa*. Philadelphia: Benjamins.

Jakobson, Roman (1942) The concept of phoneme. Repr. 1990 in L. R. Waugh and M. Moville-Burston (eds.), *On Language*. Cambridge, Mass.: Harvard University Press, pp. 218–41.

—— C. Gunnar M. Fant, and Morris Halle (1954) *Preliminaries to Speech Analysis: The Distinctive Features and Their Correlates*. Cambridge, Mass.: MIT Press.

—— and Morris Halle (1956) *Fundamentals of Language*. The Hague: Mouton.

Janda, Richard D. (1999) Accounts of phonemic split have been exaggerated—but not enough. *ICPhS* 14: 329–32.

—— (2001) Beyond 'Pathways' and 'Unidirectionality': on the discontinuity of language transmission and the counterability of grammaticalization. *Language Sciences* 23: 265–340.

—— (2003) 'Phonologization' as the start of dephoneticization—or, on sound-change and its aftermath: of extension, generalization, lexicalization, and morpho-logization. In Joseph and Janda (2003: 401–22).

Janda, Richard D. and Brian D. Joseph (2001). Reconsidering the canons of sound-change: towards a Big Bang theory. MS, Ohio State University.

—— and —— (2003) On language, change, and language change—or, of history, linguistics, and historical linguistics. Introduction to Joseph and Janda (2003: 3–180).

Jensen, John T. (1993) *English Phonology*. Philadelphia: Benjamins.

Jensen, John Thayer (1977). *Yapese Reference Grammar*. Honolulu: University of Hawai'i Press.

Jeyapaul, V. Y. (1987) *Karbi Grammar*. Mysore: Central Institute of Indian Languages.

Jha, Aparna (1980) *Kosti: A Dialect of Marathi*. Pune: Deccan College Post-Graduate and Research Institute.

Jilali, Saib (1976) *A Phonological Study of Tamazight Berber: Dialect of the Ayt Ndhir*. Ann Arbor: UMI.

Johnson, Keith (1997) *Acoustic and Auditory Phonetics*. Cambridge, Mass.: Blackwell.

Johnson, Orville E., and Catherine Peeke (1962) Phonemic units in the Secoya word. In Elson (1962: 78–95).

—— Robert Erik (1975) *The Role of Phonetic Detail in Coeur d'Alene Phonology*. Ann Arbor: UMI.

Johnston, Lucy (1996) Resisting change: information-seeking and stereotype change. *European Journal of Social Psychology* 26: 799–825.

Jones, Ross McCallum (1998) *The Boko/Busa Language Cluster*. Munich: Lincom Europa.

Jones, W. Glyn, and Kirsten Gade (1981) *Danish: A Grammar*. Copenhagen: Gyldendal.

Joseph, Brian D., and Richard D. Janda (eds.) (2003) *The Handbook of Historical Linguistics*. Cambridge, Mass.: Blackwell.

—— and Irene Philippaki-Warburton (1987) *Modern Greek*. Wolfeboro, NH: Croom Helm.

Josephs, Lewis S. (1975) *Palauan Reference Grammar*. Honolulu: University of Hawai'i Press.

Ka, Omar (1994) *Wolof Phonology and Morphology*. Lanham, Md.: University Press of America.

Kahn, Margaret (1976) *Borrowing and Variation in a Phonological Description of Kurdish*. Ann Arbor: UMI.

Kaisse, Ellen M. (1992) Can [consonantal] spread? *Language* 68: 313–32.

—— (2000) Laterals are [−continuant]. Handout of talk presented at the University of Washington, June 2, 2000.

—— (2002) Laterals are [−continuant]. MS, University of Washington.

Kalman, B. (1972) Hungarian historical phonology. In L. Benko and S. Imre (1972).

Kaplan, Lawrence D. (1981) *Phonological Issues in North Alaskan Inupiaq*. Fairbanks: Alaska Native Language Center Research Papers.

Kari, Ethelbert E. (1997) *Degema*. Munich: Lincom Europa.

Katz, Dovid (1987) *Grammar of the Yiddish Language*. London: Duckworth.

Kaye, Jonathan Derek (1970) *The Desano Verb: Problems in Semantics, Syntax, and Phonology*. Ann Arbor: UMI.

Keating, Patricia (1984) Physiological effects on stop consonant voicing. *UCLA Working Papers in Phonetics* 59: 29–34.

Keegan, John M. (1986) *The Phonology and Morphology of Moroccan Arabic*. Ann Arbor: UMI.

Keel, William (1982) *Atomic Phonology and Phonological Variation.* Tübingen: Narr.

Kenstowicz, Michael, and Charles Kisseberth (1979) *Generative Phonology.* San Diego: Academic Press.

Key, Mary Ritchie (1968) *Comparative Tacanan Phonology.* The Hague: Mouton.

Kibrik, Alexander E. (1996) *Godoberi.* Munich: Lincom Europa.

Kidda, Mairo Elinor (1985) *Tangale Phonology: A Descriptive Analysis.* Ann Arbor: UMI

Kihm, Alain (1994) *Kriyol Syntax: The Portuguese-Based Creole Language of Guinea-Bissau.* Philadelphia: Benjamins.

Kim, H. (1997). The phonological representation of affricates: evidence from Korean and other languages. Ph.D., Cornell University.

Kimenyi, Alexandre (1979) *Studies in Kinyarwanda and Bantu Phonology.* Edmonton, Alberta: Linguistic Research.

King, Duane Harold (1975) *A Grammar and Dictionary of the Cherokee Language.* Ann Arbor: UMI.

—— (2003) The phonological basis of sound change. In Joseph and Janda (2003: 313–42).

Kisseberth, C. W., and M. I. Abasheikh (1975) The perfect stem in Chi-Mwi:ni and global rules. *Studies in African Linguistics* 6: 249–66.

Klein, Harriet E. Manelis (2001) *Toba.* Munich: Lincom Europa.

Klingler, Thomas A. (1992) *A Descriptive Study of the Creole Speech of Pointe Coupee Parish, Louisiana, with Focus on the Lexicon.* Ann Arbor: UMI.

Knowles, Susan Marie (1984) *A Descriptive Grammar of Chontal Maya (San Carlos Dialect).* Ann Arbor: UMI.

Koch, Harold (2004) The Arandic subgroup of Australian languages. In Bowern and Koch (2004: 127–50).

Kochetov, Alexei (2002) *Production, Perception, and Emergent Phonotactic Patterns: A Case of Contrastive Palatalization.* New York: Routledge.

Koelle, S. W. (1968[1854]) *Outlines of a Grammar of the Vei Language: Together with a Vei–English Vocabulary and an Account of the Discovery and Nature of the Vei Mode of Syllabic Writing.* Farnborough, UK: Gregg International.

Kouwenberg, Silvia (1994) *A Grammar of Berbice Dutch Creole.* New York: Mouton de Gruyter.

—— and Eric Murray (1994) *Papiamentu.* Munich: Lincom Europa.

Kroul, Mary Valentine (1980) *The Phonology and Morphology of the Central Outer Koyukon Athapaskan Language.* Ann Arbor: UMI.

Kuhl, P. K. and J. D. Mill (1975) Speech perception by the chinchilla: Voiced-voiceless distinction in the alveolar-plosive consonants. *Science* 190: 69–72.

—— and —— (1978) Speech perception by the chinchilla: identification functions for synthetic VOT stimuli. *Journal of the Acoustical Society of America* 63: 905–17.

Kutsch Lojenga, Constance (1994) *Ngiti: A Central-Sudanic Language of Zaire.* Cologne: Köppe.

Labov, William (1994) *Principles of Linguistic Change: Internal Factors.* Oxford: Blackwell.

—— (2001) *Principles of Linguistic Change: Social Factors.* Oxford: Blackwell.

LaCharité, Darlene (1993). The internal structure of affricates. Ph.D., University of Ottawa.

Ladefoged, Peter (1984) "Out of chaos comes order": physical, biological, and structural patterns in phonetics. In M. P. R. Van den Broecke and A. Cohen (eds.), *Proceedings of ICPhS 10*. Dordrecht: Foris, pp. 83–95.

—— (1985) Introduction (interview with V. A. Fromkin). In V. A. Fromkin, *Phonetic Linguistics*. New York: Academic Press, p. 11.

—— and Daniel Everett (1996) The status of phonetic rarities. *Language* 72: 794–800.

Laidig, Carol J. (1992) Segments, syllables, and stress in Larike. In Burquest and Laidig (1992: 67–126).

Lakshmi, V. Swarajya (1982) *A Descriptive Grammar of Cuddapah Dialect*. Hyderabad: Tekugu Akademi.

Lamberti, Marcello, and Roberto Sottile (1997) *The Wolaytta Language*. Cologne: Köppe.

Langacker, Ronald W. (ed.) (1979) *Studies in Uto-Aztecan grammar 2: Uto-Aztecan grammatical sketches*. Summer Institute of Linguistics Publications in Linguistics, 56(3). Dallas: Summer Institute of Linguistics and the University of Texas at Arlington.

—— ed. (1982) *Studies in Uto-Aztecan grammar 3: Modern Aztec grammatical sketches*. Summer Institute of Linguistics Publications in Linguistics, 56(2). Dallas: Summer Institute of Linguistics and the University of Texas at Arlington.

Lapowila, Hans (1981) *A Generative Approach to the Phonology of Bahasa Indonesia*. Canberra: Pacific Linguistics.

Lass, Roger (1975) How intrinsic is content? Markedness, sound change, and "family universals". In D. Goyvaertz and G. Pullum (eds.), *Essays on The Sound Pattern of English*. Ghent: Story-Scientia.

Lawton, Ralph (1993) *Topics in the Description of Kiriwina*. Canberra: Pacific Linguistics.

Leavitt, Robert M. (1996) *Passamaquoddy-Maliseet*. Munich: Lincom Europa.

Leslau, Wolf (1941) *Documents Tigrinya*. Paris: Klincksieck.

—— (1997) *Ethiopic Documents: Argobba Grammar and Dictionary*. Wiesbaden: Harrassowitz.

—— (1999) *Zway Ethiopic Documents: Grammar and Dictionary*. Wiesbaden: Harrassowitz.

—— (2000) *Introductory Grammar of Amharic*. Wiesbaden: Harrassowitz.

Levin, Norman Balfour (1961) *The Assiniboine Language*. Ann Arbor: UMI.

Lewis, G. L. (1967) *Turkish Grammar*. Oxford: Clarendon Press.

Liddell, Scott (1984) THINK and BELIEVE: sequentiality in American Sign Language. *Language* 60: 372–92.

—— and Robert Johnson (1989) American Sign Language: the phonological base. *Sign Language Studies* 64: 197–277.

Lincoln, Peter Craig (1976) *Describing Banoni, an Austronesian Language of Southwest Bougainville*. Ann Arbor: UMI.

Lindblom, Björn (1983) Economy of speech gestures. In P. F. MacNeilage (ed.), *The Production of Speech*. New York: Springer, pp. 217–46.

—— (1984). Can the models of evolutionary biology be applied to phonetic problems? In M. P. R. Van den Broecke and A. Cohen (eds.), *Proceedings of the Tenth International Congress of Phonetic Sciences*. Dordrecht: Foris, pp. 67–81.

—— (1986) Phonetic universals in vowel systems. In J. J. Ohala and J. J. Jaeger (eds.), *Experimental Phonology*. New York: Academic Press, pp. 13–44.

—— (1990a) On the notion of "possible speech sound". *Journal of Phonetics* 18: 135–52.

—— (1990b) Explaining phonetic variation: a sketch of the H&H theory. In W. J. Hardcastle and A. Marchal (eds.), *Speech Production and Speech Modelling*. Dordrecht: Kluwer, pp. 403–39.

—— (1999) Emergent phonology. MS, University of Stockholm/University of Texas at Austin.

—— (2000) Developmental origins of adult phonology: the interplay between phonetic emergents and the evolutionary adaptations of sound patterns. MS, University of Stockholm/University of Texas at Austin.

Lindblom, Gerhard (1925) *Notes on the Kamba Language*. Uppsala: Appelbergs.

Lindskoog, John N., and Ruth M. Brend (1962) Cayapa phonemics. In Elson (1962: 31–44).

Lindstrom, Lamont, and John Lynch (1994) *Kwamera*. Munich: Lincom Europa.

Lockwood, W. B. (1955) *An Introduction to Modern Faroese*. Copenhagen: Munskgaard.

Lombardi, Linda (1990) The nonlinear organization of the affricate. *Natural Language and Linguistic Theory* 8: 375–426.

Lombeida-Naranjo, Ernesto Balmodero (1976) *Ecuadorean Highland Quechua Phonology*. Ann Arbor: UMI.

Loos, Eugene Emil (1967) *The Phonology of Capanahua and its Grammatical Basis*. Norman: Summer Institute of Linguistics of the University of Oklahoma.

Loving, Richard (1973) Awa phonemes, tonemes, and tonally differentiated allomorphs. In McKaughan (1973: 10–18).

Lubker, J. (1968) An EMG-cinefluorographic investigation of velar function during normal speech production. *Cleft Palate Journal* 5: 1–18.

Lupardus, Karen Jacque (1982) *The Language of the Alabama Indians*. Ann Arbor: UMI.

MacDonald, Lorna (1990) *Tauya*. Berlin: Mouton de Gruyter.

MacKay, Carolyn J. (1999) *A Grammar of Misantla Totonac*. Salt Lake City: University of Utah Press.

MacWhinney, Brian (1998) Emergent language. In M. Darnell, E. Moravcsik, F. Newmeyer, M. Noonan, and K. Wheatley (eds.), *Functionalism and Formalism in Linguistics, vol. 1: General Papers*. Amsterdam: Benjamins, pp. 361–86.

Madan, A. C. (1906) *Wisa Handbook*. Oxford: Clarendon Press.

Maddieson, Ian (2001) Typological patterns: geographical distribution and phonetic explanation. Paper presented at the Conference on the Phonetics–Phonology Interface, Berlin, October 2001.

Maganga, Clement, and Thilo C. Schadeberg (1992) *Kinyamwezi: Grammar, Texts, Vocabulary*. Cologne: Köppe.

Maiden, Martin (1992) Irregularity as a determinant of morphological change. *Journal of Linguistics* 28: 285–312.

Makashay, Matthew J. (2001) Lexical effects in the perception of obstruent ordering. In Hume and Johnson (2001b: 88–116).

Malcolm, D. McK. (1966) *A New Zulu Manual* (revised by D. N. Bang). Cape Town: Longmans.

Manley, Timothy M. (1972) *Outline of Sre Structure*. Honolulu: University of Hawai'i Press.

Marconnès, Revd Francisque (1931) *A Grammar of Central Karanga*. Johannesburg: Witwatersrand University Press.

Martin, Samuel Elmo (1961) *Dagur Mongolian Grammar, Texts, and Lexicon; Based on the Speech of Peter Onon*. Bloomington: Indiana University.

Martinet, André (1968) Phonetics and linguistic evolution. In B. Malmberg (ed.), *Manual of Phonetics*. Amsterdam: North-Holland, pp. 464–87.

Mascaró, J. (1984) Continuant spreading in Basque, Catalan, and Spanish. In M. Aronoff et al. (eds.), *Language Sound and Structure*. Cambridge, Mass.: MIT Press, pp. 287–98.

Mason, J. Alden (1917) *Tepecano, a Piman Language of Western Mexico*. New York: New York Academy of Sciences.

Mateus, Maria Helena, and Ernesto d'Andrade (2000) *The Phonology of Portuguese*. New York: Oxford University Press.

Mathiassen, Terje (1997) *A Short Grammar of Latvian*. Columbus, OH: Slavica.

Mathingwane, Joyce T. (1999) *Ikalanga Phonetics and Phonology: A Synchronic and Diachronic Study*. Stanford, Calif.: CSLI.

Maurais, Jacques (ed.) (1996) *Quebec's Aboriginal Languages: History, Planning and Development*. Philadelphia: Multilingual Matters.

McCarthy, John J. (1991) Semitic gutturals and distinctive feature theory. In E. Dunlap and J. Padgett (eds.), *University of Massachusetts Occasional Papers 14* , pp. 29–50.

—— (1994) The phonetics and phonology of Semitic pharyngeals. In P. Keating (ed.), *Phonological Structure and Phonetic Form: Papers in Laboratory Phonology III*. Cambridge: Cambridge University Press, pp. 191–251.

—— and Alan Prince (1995) Faithfulness and Reduplicative Identity. In J. N. Beckman et al. (eds.), *Papers in Optimality Theory*. Amherst: University of Massachusetts, pp. 249–384.

McCawley, James D. (1968) *The Phonological Component of a Grammar of Japanese*. The Hague: Mouton.

McClean, R. J. (1987) *Swedish*. London: Hodder & Stoughton.

McElhanon, K. A. (1970) *Selepet Phonology*. Canberra: Pacific Linguistics.

McGregor, William (1990) *A Functional Grammar of Gooniyandi*. Philadelphia: Benjamins.

—— (1993) *Gunin/Kwini*. Munich: Lincom Europa.

—— (1994) *Warrwa*. Munich: Lincom Europa.

—— (1996) *Nyulnyul*. Munich: Lincom Europa.

McIntosh, Mary (1984) *Fulfulde Syntax and Verbal Morphology*. Boston: KPI.

McKaughan, Howard (ed.) (1973) *The Languages of the Eastern Family of the East New Guinea Highland Stock*. Seattle: University of Washington Press.

——and Doreen Marks (1973) Notes on Auyana phonology and morphology. In McKaughan (1973: 181–9).

McLaren, J. (1906) *A Grammar of the Kaffir Language*. New York: Longmans, Green.

McMahon, April (2002) *An Introduction to English Phonology*. Oxford: Oxford University Press.

Meier, Paul, Inge Meier, and John Bendor-Samuel (1975) *A Grammar of Izi: An Igbo Language*. Norman, Okla.: Summer Institute of Linguistics.

Meira, Sérgio (2000) *Reduplication in Tiriyó (Cariban)*. Munich: Lincom Europa.

Menn, Lise (1980) Phonological theory and child phonology. In G. H. Yeni-Komshian et al. (eds.), *Child Phonology*, vol. 1. New York: Academic Press, pp. 23–41.

Michelson, Karin Eva (1983) *A Comparative Study of Accent in the Five Nations Iroquoian Languages*. Ann Arbor: UMI.

Mielke, Jeff (2001) Explaining directional asymmetry in Turkish [h] deletion: a cross-linguistic study of perceptibility. In Hume and Johnson (2001b: 117–71).

——(2003) The interplay of speech perception and phonology: experimental evidence from Turkish. *Phonetica* 60: 208–29.

Mill, John Stuart (1843). *A System of Logic*. London: Longmans, Green, Reader, & Dyer.

Miller, Amy (2001) *A Grammar of Jamul Tiipay*. New York: Mouton de Gruyter.

Miller, George A., and Patricia E. Nicely (1955) An analysis of perceptual confusions among some English consonants. *Journal of the Acoustical Society of America* 27: 338–52.

Mills, Elizabeth (1984) *Senoufo Phonology, Discourse to Syllable (A Prosodic Approach)*. Arlington, Tex.: Summer Institute of Linguistics.

Milroy, Lesley (1980) *Language and Social Networks*. Oxford: Blackwell.

Miner, Kenneth Lee (1975) *Interference Relations in Menomini Phenology*. Ann Arbor: UMI.

Mixco, Maurice (1997) *Mandan*. Munich: Lincom Europa.

Mohrlang, Roger (1972) *Studies in Nigerian Languages, 2: Higi Phonology*. Zaria: Institute for Linguistics.

Moll, K. L. (1962) Velopharyngeal closure in vowels. *Journal of Speech and Hearing Research* 5: 30–37.

Morev, L. N., A. A. Moskalev, and Y. Y. Plam (1979) *The Lao Language*. Moscow: USSR Academy of Sciences, Institute of Oriental Studies.

Morris, H. F., and B. E. R. Kirwan (1957) *A Runyankore Grammar*. Nairobi: Eagle Press.

Mugane, John M. (1997) *Paradigmatic Grammar of Gĩkũyũ*. Palo Alto, Calif.: CSLI.

Munro, Pamela (1976) *Mojave Syntax*. New York: Garland.

Murane, Elizabeth (1974) *Daga Grammar from Morpheme to Discourse*. Glendale, Calif.: Church Press.

Mustafa, Khateeb S. (2000) *A Descriptive Grammar of Dakkhini*. New Delhi: Manoharlal.

Mutonyi, Nasiombe (2000) *Aspects of Bukusu Morphology and Phonology*. Ohio State University dissertation.

Myers, Scott (2002) Gaps in factorial typology: the case of voicing in consonant clusters. MS, University of Texas at Austin. ROA-509.

Næss, Åshild (2000) *Pileni*. Munich: Lincom Europa.

Nakshabandi, Anwar Mohammed H. (1988) *A Descriptive Study of the Phonology and Morphology of the Abha Dialect*. Ann Arbor: UMI.

Nash, David (1986) *Topics in Warlpiri Grammar*. New York: Garland.

Natarajan, G. V. (1985) *Abujhmaria Grammar*. Mysore: Central Institute of Indian Languages.

Nedjalkov, Igor (1997) *Evenki*. New York: Routledge.

Nettle, Daniel (1998) *The Fyem Language of Northern Nigeria*. Munich: Lincom Europa.

Neukom, Lukas (2001) *Santali*. Munich: Lincom Europa.

Newman, Paul (1974) *The Kanakuru Language*. Ilkley: Scolar Press.

Newmeyer, Frederick (1998) *Language Form and Language Function*. Cambridge, Mass.: MIT Press.

Ngom, Fallou (2000) *Phonetic and Phonological Description of Mandinkakan Phonemes as spoken in Kajor (Ziguinchor)*. Munich: Lincom Europa.

Ngunga, Armindo (2000) *Phonology and Morphology of the Ciyao Verb*. Palo Alto, Calif.: CSLI.

Nguyên Dình-Hoà (1997) *Vietnamese*. Amsterdam: Benjamins.

Nielsen, Kuniko (2007) Implicit phonetic imitation is constrained by phonemic contrast. In Jürgen Trouvain and William J. Barry (eds.) *Proceedings of the 16th International Congress of the Phonetic Sciences*. Dudweiler: Pirrot GmbH, pp. 1961–4.

Nivens, Richard (1992) A Lexical phonology of West Tarangan. In Burquest and Laidig (1992: 127–227).

Noonan, Michael (1992) *A Grammar of Lango*. New York: Mouton de Gruyter.

Nordbustad, Frøydis (1988) *Iraqw grammar: an analytical study of the Iraqw*. Berlin: Reimer.

Nordlinger, Rachel (1998) *A Grammar of Wambaya*. Canberra: Pacific Linguistics.

Novelli, Bruno (1985) *A Grammar of the Karimojong Language*. Berlin: Reimer.

Ó Siadhail, Mícheál (1989) *Modern Irish: Grammatical Structure and Dialectal Variation*. New York: Cambridge University Press.

Oates, Lynette F. (1988) *The Muruwari Language*. Canberra: Pacific Linguistics.

Oatridge, Desmond, and Jennifer Oatridge (1973) Phonemes of Binumarien. In McKaughan (1973: 13–21).

Obleser, J., A. Lahiri, and C. Eulitz (2004) Magnetic brain response mirrors extraction of phonological features from spoken vowels. *Journal of Cognitive Neuroscience* 16: 31–9.

Oda, Sachiko (1977) *The Syntax of Pulu Annian: A Nuclear Micronesian Language*. Ann Arbor: UMI.

Odden, David (1996) *The Phonology and Morphology of Kimatuumbi*. Oxford: Clarendon Press.

—— (2002a) Consonant–tone interaction in Zina Kotoko. Paper presented at MCWOP, Indiana University.

—— (2002b) The verbal tone system of Zina Kotoko. In B. K. Schmidt et al., *Aspects of Zina Kotoko Grammar*. Munich: Lincom Europa, pp. 15–34.

Odhner, John D. (1981) *English–Lingala Manual*. Washington, DC: University Press of America.

Odisho, Edward Y. (1988) *Sound System of Modern Assyrian (Neo-Aramaic)*. Wiesbaden: Harrassowitz.

O'Grady, Geoffrey N. (1964) *Nyangumata Grammar*. Sydney: University of Sydney.

Ohala, John J. (1981) The listener as a source of sound change. In C. S. Masek et al., (eds.), *Papers from the Parasession on Language and Behavior: Chicago Linguistic Society*. Chicago: CLS, 178–203.

—— (1983) The origin of sound patterns in vocal tract constraints. In P. F. MacNeilage (ed.), *The Production of Speech*. New York: Springer, pp. 189–216.

—— (1992) Alternatives to the sonority hierarchy for explaining segmental sequential constraints. In *Chicago Linguistic Society: Papers from the Parasession on the Syllable*. Chicago: CLS, pp. 319–38.

—— (1993a) The phonetics of sound change. In C. Jones (ed.), *Historical Linguistics: Problems and Perspectives*. London: Longman, pp. 237–78.

—— (1993b) Sound change as nature's speech perception experiment. *Speech Communication* 13: 155–61.

—— (2003) *Phonetics and Historical Phonology*. In Joseph and Janda (2003: 667–86).

Okell, John (1969) *A Reference Grammar of Colloquial Burmese*. London: Oxford University Press.

Okoth-Okombo, Duncan (1982) *Dholuo Morphophonemics in a Generative Framework*. Berlin: Reimer.

Onishi, Kristine H., Kyle E. Chambers, and Cynthia Fisher (2002) Learning phonotactic constraints from brief auditory experience. *Cognition* 83: B13–B23.

Orr, Carolyn (1962) Equador Quichua Phonology. In Elson (1962: 60–77).

Osumi, Midori (1995) *Tinrin Grammar*. Honolulu: University of Hawai'i Press.

Ourso, Meterwa (1989) *Lama Phonology and Morphology*. Ann Arbor: UMI.

Owens, Jonathan (1985) *A Grammar of Harar Oromo (Northeastern Ethiopia)*. Hamburg: Buske.

Palikupt, Deeyoo (1983) *Central Thai and Northeastern Thai: A Linguistic and Attitudinal Study*. Ann Arbor: UMI.

Pam, Martin David (1973) *Tigrinya Phonology*. Ann Arbor: UMI.

Paradis, Carole (1992) *Lexical Phonology and Morphology: The Nominal Classes in Fula*. New York: Garland.

Paradis, Carole, and Darlene LaCharité (2001) Guttural deletion in loanwords. *Phonology* 18: 225–300.

Parks, Douglas R. (1976) *A Grammar of Pawnee*. New York: Garland.

Parsons, T., and R. F. Bales (1955). *Family, Socialization and Interaction Process*. Glencoe, Ill.: Free Press.

Pasteur, Louis (1885) Method for preventing rabies after a bite. *Comptes rendus de l'Académie des Sciences, séance du 26 octobre 1885*, CI, pp. 765–73, 774. *Bulletin de l'Académie de médecine, séance du 27 octobre 1885*, 2e sér., XIV, pp. 1431–9. Trans. E. T. and C. V. Cohn.

Pater, Joe (2004) Exceptionality as constraint indexation. Paper presented at 2004 MOT phonology workshop, Ottawa, February 2004.

Patterson, Trudi Alice (1990) *Theoretical Aspects of Dakota Morphology and Phonology*. Ann Arbor: UMI.

Payne, David L. (1981) *The Phonology and Morphology of Axininca Campa*. Arlington: Summer Institute of Linguistics and University of Texas at Arlington.

Peperkamp, S. and E. Dupoux (2007) Learning the mapping from surface to underlying representations in an artificial language In J. Cole and J. Hualde (eds.), *Change in Phonology (Lab Phon 9)*: 315–38.

Perlmutter, David M. (1992) Sonority and syllable structure in American Sign Language. *Linguistic Inquiry* 23: 407–42.

Phillips, Colin, Thomas Pellathy, and Alec Marantz (2000) Phonological feature representations in auditory cortex. MS, University of Delaware and MIT.

Pia, J. Joseph (1963) An outline of the structure of Somali. MS, Michigan State University.

Pierrehumbert, Janet (2001) Why phonological constraints are so coarse-grained. In J. McQueen and A. Cutler (eds.), *SWAP* special issue, Language and Cognitive Processes, 16: 691–8.

—— (2003) Probabilistic phonology: discriminability and robustness. In R. Bod et al. (eds.), *Probabilistic Linguistics*. Cambridge, Mass.: MIT Press, pp. 177–228.

Pieter, Sterk Jan (1977) *Elements of Gade Grammar*. Ann Arbor: UMI.

Pinker, Steven (1994) *The Language Instinct*. New York: Morrow.

—— (1999) *Words and Rules*. New York: Basic Books.

Pitt, Mark, Keith Johnson, Elizabeth Hume, Scott Keisling, and William Raymond (2004) The Buckeye Corpus of Conversational Speech: labeling conventions and a test of transcriber reliability. MS, Ohio State University.

Poppe, Nikolai Nikolaevich (1960) *Buriat Grammar*. Bloomington: Indiana University.

Port, Robert F. (1996) The discreteness of phonetic elements and formal linguistics: response to A. Manaster Ramer. *Journal of Phonetics* 24: 491–511.

Poulos, George (1990) *A Linguistic Analysis of Venda*. Pretoria: Via Afrika.

Prasad, Bal Ram (1991) *Mising Grammar*. Mysore: Central Institute of Indian Languages.

Press, Ian (1986) *A Grammar of Modern Breton*. New York: Mouton de Gruyter.

Press, Margaret Lauritsen (1975) *A Grammar of Chemehuevi*. Ann Arbor: UMI.

Price, Thomas (1958) *The Elements of Nyanja*. Blantyre: Church of Scotland Mission.

Prince, Alan, and Paul Smolensky (1993) Optimality Theory: constraint interaction in generative grammar. Ms, Rutgers University, New Brunswick, and University of Colorado, Boulder.

Pulleyblank, Douglas (2003) Covert Feature Effects. In G. Garding and Mimu Tsujimura (eds.), *Proceedings of WCCFL 22*. Somerville, Mass.: Cascadilla Press, pp. 398–422.

Pye, C., D. Ingram, and H. List (1987) A comparison of initial consonant acquisition in English and Quiche. In K. E. Nelson and A. Van Kleeck (eds.), *Children's Language* 6. Hillsdale, NJ: Erlbaum, pp. 175–90.

Pyles, Thomas, and John Algeo (1993) *The Origins and Development of the English Language*, 4th edn. Fort Worth, Tex.: Harcourt Brace Jovanovich.

Quesada, J. Diego (2000) *A Grammar of Teribe*. Munich: Lincom Europa.

Ramos, Teresita V. (1971) *Tagalog Structures*. Honolulu: University of Hawai'i Press.

Randoja, Tiina (1990) *The Phonology and Morphology of Halfway River Beaver*. Ann Arbor: UMI.

Rangan, K. (1979) *Purki Grammar*. Mysore: Central Institute of Indian Languages.

Ray, Punya Sloka (1966) *Bengali Language Handbook*. Washington, DC: Center for Applied Linguistics.

Raymond, William D., Robin Dautricourt, and Elizabeth Hume (2006) Word-medial /t–d/ deletion in spontaneous speech: Modeling the effects of extra-linguistic, lexical, and phonological factors. *Language Variation and Change* 18: 55–97.

Raz, Shlomo (1983) *Tigre Grammar and Texts*. Malibu, Calif.: Undena.

Reesink, Ger P. (1999) *A grammar of Hatam, Bird's Head Peninsula, Irian Jaya*. Canberra: Pacific Linguistics.

Reh, Mchthild (1996) *Anywa Language*. Cologne: Köppe.

Reichard, Gladys A. (1925) *Wiyot Grammar and Texts*. Berkeley: University of California Press.

Reichard, Gladys A. (1974) *Navaho Grammar*. New York: Augustin.

Reiss, Charles (2003) Quantification in structural descriptions: Attested and unattested patterns.

Rennison, John R. (1997) *Koromfe*. New York: Routledge.

Rhodes, Richard Alan (1976) *Morphosyntax of the Central Ojibwa Verb*. Ann Arbor: UMI.

Rice, Keren (1989) *A Grammar of Slave*. New York: Mouton de Gruyter.

—— (1992) On deriving sonority: a structural account of sonority relationships. *Phonology* 9: 61–99.

—— (1999) Featural markedness in phonology: variation. MS, University of Toronto.

—— and Peter Avery (1989). On the interaction between sonorancy and voicing. In B. Brunson, S. Burton, and T. Wilson (eds.), *Toronto Working Papers in Linguistics* 10: 65–82.

—— and —— (1995) Variability in a deterministic model of language acquisition: a theory of segmental elaboration. In J. Archibald (ed.), *Phonological Acquisition and Phonological Theory*. Hillsdale, NJ: Erlbaum, pp. 23–42.

Roberts, John R. (1987) *Amele*. New York: Croom Helm.

Robins, R. H. (1958) *The Yurok Language: Grammar, Texts, Lexicon*. Berkeley: University of California Press.

Rood, David S. (1976) *Wichita Grammar*. New York: Garland.

Rosenhouse, Judith (1984) *Bedouin Arabic Dialects*. Wiesbaden: Harrassowitz.

Rossing, Melvin Olaf (1978) *Mafa-Mada*. Ann Arbor: UMI.

Rubach, Jerzy (1993) *The Lexical Phonology of Slovak*. Oxford: Clarendon Press.
—— (1994) Affricates as strident stops in Polish. *Linguistic Inquiry* 25: 119–43.
Rubino, Carl Ralph Galvez (2000) *Ilocano Dictionary and Grammar*. Honolulu: University of Hawai'i Press.
Rubongoya, L. T. (1999) *A Modern Runyoro-Rutooro Grammar*. Cologne: Köppe.
Rupp, James E. (1989) *Lealao Chinantec Syntax: Studies in Chinantec Languages*, vol. 2. Arlington: Summer Institute of Linguistics and the University of Texas at Arlington.
Ruskin, E. A., and L. Ruskin (1934) *A Grammar of the Lomongo Language*. Bongandanga: CBM Press.
Saeed, John Ibrahim (1987) *Somali Reference Grammar*. Wheaton, Md.: Dunwoody Press.
Saffran, J. R., and Thiessen E. D. (2003). Pattern induction by infant language learners. *Developmental Psychology*, 39, 1926–8.
Sagey, Elizabeth (1990[1986]) *The Representation of Features in Non-linear Phonology: The Articulator Node Hierarchy*. New York: Garland.
Saint, Rachel, and Kenneth L. Pike (1962) Auca phonemics. In Elson (1962: 2–3a).
Saltarelli, Mario, Miren Azkarate, David Farwell, Jon Ortiz de Urbina, and Lourdes Oñederra (1988) *Basque*. New York: Croom Helm.
Samarin, William J. (1967) *A Grammar of Sango*. The Hague: Mouton.
Samely, Ursula (1991) *Kedang (Eastern Indonesia): Some Aspects of its Grammar*. Hamburg: Buske.
Sandler, Wendy (1989) *Phonological Representation of the Sign: Linearity and Nonlinearity in American Sign Language*. Dordrecht: Foris.
—— and Diane Lillo-Martin (2006) *Sign Language and Linguistic Universals*. Cambridge: Cambridge University Press.
Sapir, J. David (1965) *A Grammar of Diola-Fogny*. Cambridge: Cambridge University Press.
Sastry, G. Devi Prasada (1984) *Mishmi Grammar*. Mysore: Central Institute of Indian Languages.
Saxton, Dean (1982) Papago. In Langacker (1982).
Scatton, Ernest A. (1984) *A Reference Grammar of Modern Bulgarian*. Columbus, OH: Slavica.
Schadeberg, Thilo C. (1990) *A Sketch of Umbundu*. Cologne: Köppe.
Schafer, Robin (1995) Headedness in the representation of affricates. *Linguistic Review* 12: 61–87.
Scherer, Wilhelm (1868) *Zur Geschichte der deutschen Sprache*. Berlin: Duncker.
Schiffman, Harold F. (1999) *A Reference Grammar of Spoken Tamil*. New York: Cambridge University Press.
Schmidt, Bodil Kappel, David Odden, and Anders Holmberg (eds.) (2002) *Some Aspects of the Grammar of Zina Kotoko*. Munich: Lincom Europa.
Schulze, Wolfgang (1997) *Tsakhur*. Munich: Lincom Europa.
—— (2000) *Northern Talysh*. Munich: Lincom Europa.

Schütz, Albert J. (1969) *Nguna Grammar*. Honolulu: Oceanic Linguistics.

Sebeok Thomas A. (1961) *An Eastern Cheremis Manual*. Bloomington/The Hague: Indiana University/Mouton.

Seiler, Hansjakob (1977) *Cahuilla Grammar*. Banning, Calif.: Malki Museum Press.

Selkirk, Elisabeth (1988) Dependency, place and the notion "Tier". MS, University of Massachusetts.

—— (1991) Major place in the vowel space: vowel height features. MS, University of Massachusetts.

—— (1993) [Labial] relations. MS, University of Massachusetts.

Sengova, Matthew Joko (1984) *Tense, Aspect, and Time Specification in the Verb System of Mende*. Ann Arbor: UMI.

Seo, Misun (2001) A perception-based study of sonorant assimilation in Korean. In Hume and Johnson (2001b: 43–69).

Shalizi, Cosma Rohilla (2001) Emergent properties. http://www.santafe.edu/~shalizi/notebooks/emergent-properties.html

Shannon, C. E., and W. Weaver (1949) *The Mathematical Theory of Communication*. Urbana: University of Illinois Press.

Sharma, D. D. (1988) *A Descriptive Grammar of Kinnauri*. Delhi: Mittal.

Shaterian, Alan William (1983) *Phonology and Dictionary of Yavapai*. Ann Arbor: UMI.

Shattuck-Hufnagel, S., and Dennis H. Klatt (1975) An analysis of 1500 phonetic errors in spontaneous speech. *Journal of the Acoustical Society of America* 58 (supplement 1): 66 (A).

Shattuck-Hufnagel, Stefanie, and Dennis H. Klatt (1979) The limited use of distinctive features and markedness in speech production: evidence from speech error data. *Journal of Verbal Learning and Verbal Behavior* 18: 41–55.

Sherzer, Joel (1975) A problem in Cuna phonology. *Journal of the Linguistic Association of the Southwest* 1: 45–53.

Shetler, Joanne (1976) *Notes on Balangao Grammar*. Huntington Beach, Calif.: Summer Institute of Linguistics.

Shibatani, Masayoshi (1990) *The Languages of Japan*. Cambridge: Cambridge University Press.

Shimizu, Kiyoshi (1980a) *Comparative Jukunoid*, vol. 1. Vienna: Beiträge zur Afrikanistik.

—— (1980b) *A Jukun Grammar*. Vienna: Institut für Afrikanistik.

—— (1983) *Zing Dialect of Mumuye: A Descriptive Grammar*. Hamburg: Buske.

Shukla, Shaligram (2000) *Hindi Phonology*. Munich: Lincom Europa.

Simpson, Jane, and Luise Hercus (2004) Thura-Yura as a subgroup. In Bowern and Koch (2004: 179–206).

Simpson, John (2004) *The Oxford English Dictionary*, 3rd edn. Oxford: Oxford University Press.

Singh, Sadanand, and John Black (1966) Study of twenty-six intervocalic consonants as spoken and recognized by four language groups. *Journal of the Acoustical Society of America* 39: 372–87.

Sischo, William R. (1979) Michoacán Nahauatl. In Langacker (1979: 307–80).

Skinner, Margaret Gardner (1979) *Aspects of Pac'anci Grammar*. Ann Arbor: UMI.

Smalley, William A. (1961) *Outline of Khmu̓ Structure*. New Haven, Conn.: American Oriental Society.

Smith, Ian Russell (1978) *Sri Lanka Creole Portuguese phonology*. Vanchiyoor: Dravidian Linguistics Association.

——(1981) *Sri Lanka Portuguese Creole Phonology*. Ann Arbor: UMI.

Snapp, Allen, John Anderson, and Joy Anderson (1982) Northern Paiute. In Langacker (1982: 1–92).

Snyder, M., B. H. Campbell, and E. Preston (1982) Testing hypotheses about human nature: assessing the accuracy of social stereotypes. *Social Cognition* 1: 256–72.

Sohn, Ho-Min (1975) *Woleaian Reference Grammar*. Honolulu: University of Hawai'i Press.

Solnit, David B. (1997) *Eastern Kayah Li: Grammar, Texts, Glossary*. University of Hawai'i Press.

Soukka, Maria (2000) *A Descriptive Grammar of Noon*. Munich: Lincom Europa.

Spear, Norman E., and David C. Riccio (1987) *Memory: Phenomena and Principles*. Boston: Allyn & Bacon.

Spears, Richard Alan (1965) *The Structure of Faranah-Maninka*. Ann Arbor: UMI.

Spitz, Walter L. (2001) *Hiligaynon/Ilonggo*. Munich: Lincom Europa.

Sreedhar, M. V. (1980) *A Sema Grammar*. Mysore: Central Institute of Indian Languages.

Sridhar, S. N. (1990) *Kannada*. New York: Routledge.

St. Clair, Robert N. (1974) *Theoretical Aspects of Eskimo Phonology*. Ann Arbor: UMI.

Stallcup, Kenneth Lyell (1978) *A Comparative Perspective on the Phonology and Noun Classification of Three Cameroon Grassfields Bantu Languages: Moghamo, Ngie, and Oshie*. Ann Arbor: UMI.

Stampe, David (1979) *A Dissertation on Natural Phonology*. Bloomington, Ind.: IULC.

Stanford, Ronald, and Lyn Stanford (1970) *Collected Field Reports on the Phonology and Grammar of Chakosi*. Collected Language Notes No. 11. Accra: University of Ghana, Institute of African Studies.

Stanhope, John M. (1980) *The Language of the Rao People, Grengabu, Madang Province, Papua New Guinea*. Canberra: Pacific Linguistics.

Steels, Luc (1997) The synthetic modelling of language origins. *Evolution of Communication* 1: 1–34.

Steriade, Donca (1997) Similarity and lexical conservatism in surface analogy. MS, UCLA.

——(2001). Directional asymmetries in place assimilation: a perceptual account. In Hume and Johnson (2001a:

Stevens, Kenneth (1972) The quantal nature of speech: evidence from articulatory-acoustic data. In E. E. David, and P. B. Denes (eds.), *Human Communication: A Unified View*. New York: McGraw-Hill, pp. 51–66.

——(1989) On the quantal nature of speech. *Journal of Phonetics* 17: 3–45.

Stokoe, William (1960) Sign language structure: an outline of the visual communication of the American deaf. *Studies in Linguistics*, Occasional Papers 8.

Stonham, John (1999) *Aspects of Tsishaath Nootka Phonetics and Phonology*. Munich: Lincom Europa.

Straight, H. Stephen (1976) *Acquisition of Maya Phonology*. New York: Garland.

Stringer, Mary, and Joyce Hotz (1973) *Waffa Phonemes*. In McKaughan (1973: 523–9).

Stroomer, Harry (1987) *A Comparative Study of Three Southern Oromo Dialects in Kenya*. Hamburg: Buske.

Studdert-Kennedy, M., and D. Shankweiler (1970) Hemispheric specialization for speech perception. *Journal of the Acoustical Society of America* 48: 579–94.

—— —— and D. Pisoni (1972) Auditory and phonetic processes in speech perception: evidence from a dichotic study. *Cognitive Psychology* 3: 455–66.

Subrahmanyam, P. S. (1968) *A Descriptive Grammar of Gondi*. Annamalainagar: Annamalai University.

Sudlow, David (2001) *The Tamasheq of North-East Burkina Faso*. Cologne: Köppe.

Suharno, Ignatius (1982) *A Descriptive Study of Javanese*. Canberra: Pacific Linguistics.

Sulkala, Helena, and Merja Karjalainen (1992) *Finnish*. New York: Routledge.

Swan, Oscar E. (1983) *A Concise Grammar of Polish*. Lanham, Md.: University Press of America.

Szigetvári, Péter (1997) On affricates. In A. B. Farkas (ed.), *Proceedings of the First Symposium of Doctoral Students in Linguistics*. Budapest: Theoretical Linguistics Programme, pp. 1–12.

Takizala, Alexis (1974) *Studies in the Grammar of Kihungan*. Ann Arbor: UMI.

Tamura, Suzuko (2000) *The Ainu language*. Tokyo: Sanseido.

Tarpent, Marie-Lucie (1987) *A Grammar of the Nisgha Language*. Ann Arbor: UMI.

Tauberschmidt, Gerhard (1999) *A Grammar of Sinaugoro*. Canberra: Pacific Linguistics.

Taylor, Charles (1985) *Nkore-Kiga*. Dover, NH: Croom Helm.

Teoh, Boon Seng (1988) *Aspects of Malay Phonology Revisited: A Non-linear Approach*. Ann Arbor: UMI.

Terravecchia, Gian Paolo (2002) Free on line dictionary of philosophy. http://www.swif.uniba.it/lei/foldop/

Terrill, Angela (1998) *Biri*. Munich: Lincom Europa.

Thomas, David D. (1971) *Chrau Grammar*. Honolulu: University of Hawai'i Press.

Thompson, Laurence C., and M. Terry Thompson (1992) *The Thompson Language*. University of Montana Occasional Papers in Linguistics 8.

Thorne, David A. (1993) *A Comprehensive Welsh Grammar*. Cambridge, Mass.: Blackwell.

Thornley, David H. (1997) The philosophical glossary. http://www.visi.com/~thornley/david/philosophy/definitions.html

Tomasello, Michael (2003) *Constructing a Language: A Usage-Based Theory of Language Acquisition*. Cambridge, Mass.: Harvard University Press.

Topping, Donald M. (1973) *Chamorro Reference Grammar*. Honolulu: University of Hawai'i Press.

Tosco, Mauro (1991) *A Grammatical Sketch of Dahalo, including Texts and a Glossary.* Hamburg: Buske.

—— (1997) *Af Tunni: Grammar, Texts, and Glossary of a Southern Somali Dialect.* Cologne: Köppe.

—— (2001) *The Dhaasanac Language: Grammar, Text, Vocabulary of a Cushitic Language of Ethiopia.* Cologne: Köppe.

Toweett, Taaitta (1979) *A Study of Kalenjin Linguistics.* Nairobi: Kenya Literature Bureau.

Traill, Anthony (1985) *Phonetic and Phonological Studies of !XÓÕ Bushman.* Hamburg: Buske.

Trubetzkoy, N. S. (1939) *Grundzüge der Phonologie.* Travaux de Cercle Linguistique de Prague 7. English translation 1969: *Principles of Phonology.* Berkeley: University of California Press.

Trudgill, Peter (2002) Linguistic and social typology. In J. K. Chambers, et al. (eds.), *The Handbook of Language Variation and Change.* Malden, Mass.: Blackwell.

Tserdanelis, Georgios (2001) A perceptual account of manner dissimilation in Greek. In Hume and Johnson (2001b: 172–99).

Tuggy, David H. (1979) Tetelcingo Nahauatl. In Langacker (1979: 1–140).

Tuite, Kevin (1997) *Svan.* Munich: Lincom Europa.

Unbegaun, B. O. (1957) *Russian Grammar.* Oxford: Clarendon Press

Uyechi, Linda Ann N. (1996). *The Geometry of Visual Phonology.* Palo Alto, Calif.: CSLI.

Valdman, Albert (1976) *Introduction to French Phonology and Morphology.* Rowley, Mass.: Newbury House.

Vamarasi, Marit (2002) *Rotuman.* Munich: Lincom Europa.

van den Berg, René (1989) *A Grammar of the Muna Language.* Dordrecht: Foris.

van der Hulst, Harry (1995) The composition of handshapes. In *Working Papers in Linguistics* 23. Dept of Linguistics, University of Trondheim.

van Enk, Gerrit J., and Lourens de Vries (1997) *The Korowai of Irian Jaya.* New York: Oxford University Press.

van Klinken, Catharina Lumien (1999) *A Grammar of the Fehan Dialect of Tetun: An Austronesian Language of West Timor.* Canberra: Pacific Linguistics.

Van Knippenberg, A., and A. Dijksterhuis (1996) A posteriori stereotype activation: the preservation of stereotypes through memory distortion. *Social Cognition* 14: 21–53.

van Sambeek, W. F. (1966) *A Bemba Grammar.* Cape Town: Galvin & Sales.

Vance, Timothy J. (1987) *An Introduction to Japanese Phonology.* Albany, NY: State University of New York Press.

Vanoverbergh, Morice (1937) *Some Undescribed Languages of Luzon.* Nijmegen: Dekker & van de Vegt.

Vaux, Bert (1998) *The Phonology of Armenian.* Oxford: Clarendon Press.

—— (2002) Consonant epenthesis and the problem of unnatural phonology. Paper presented at Yale University Linguistics Colloquium.

Vennemann, Theo (1972) Phonetic analogy and conceptual analogy. In T. Vennemann and T. H. Wilbur (eds.), *Schuchardt, the Neogrammarians, and the Transformational*

Theory of Phonological Change: Four Essays (= *Linguistische Forschungen* 26). Frankfurt am Main: Athenäum, pp. 181–204.

—— (1974) Topics, subjects, and word order: from SXV to SVX via TVX. In Anderson J. M. and C. Jones (eds.), *Historical Linguistics*, vol. 2 (proceedings of the First International Conference on Historical Linguistics). Amsterdam: North-Holland, pp. 339–76.

Vihman, Marilyn May (1993) Variable paths to early word production. *Journal of Phonetics* 21: 61–82.

—— (1996) *Phonological Development: The Origins of Language in the Child.* Cambridge, Mass.: Blackwell.

—— and William Croft (2007) Phonological development: toward a "radical" templatic phonology. *Linguistics*: 683–725.

Vogt, Hans (1940) *The Kalispel Language: An Outline of the Grammar with Texts, Translations, and Dictionary.* Oslo: Dybwad.

Volker, Craig Alan (1982) Introduction to Rabaul Creole German (Unserdeutsch). Ph.D. dissertation, University of Queensland.

—— (1998) *The Nalik Language of New Ireland, Papua New Guinea.* New York: Lang.

Voorhis, Paul H. (1974) *Introduction to the Kickapoo Language.* Bloomington: Indiana University.

Voorhoeve, C. L. (1965) *The Flamingo Bay Dialect of the Asmat Language.* The Hague: Nijhoff.

Wali, Kashi, and Omkar N. Koul (1997) *Kashmiri.* New York: Routledge.

Walker, Willard (1975) Cherokee. In Crawford (1975: 189–96).

Wallon, H. (1945) *Les origines de la pensée chez l'enfant.* Paris Presses Universitaires de France.

Wang, Marilyn D., and Robert C. Bilger (1973) Consonant confusions in noise: a study of perceptual features. *Journal of the Acoustical Society of America* 54: 1248–66.

Wang, Yingxu, Dong Liu, and Ying Wang (2003) Discovering the capacity of human memory. *Brain and Mind* 4: 189–98.

Ward, Ida C. (1933) *The Phonetic and Tonal Structure of Efik.* Cambridge: Heffer.

Waters, Bruce E. (1989) *Djinang and Djinba: A Grammatical and Historical Perspective.* Canberra: Pacific Linguistics.

Watkins, Laurel J. (1984) *A Grammar of Kiowa.* Lincoln: University of Nebraska Press.

Watters, John Robert (1981) *A Phonology and Morphology of Ejagham, with Notes on Dialect Variation.* Ann Arbor: UMI.

Weber, David John (1983) *A Grammar of Huallaga (Huanaco) Quechua.* Ann Arbor: UMI.

Wedel, Andrew (2004) Self-organization and categorical behavior in phonology. Ph.D. dissertation, UC Santa Cruz.

Weidert, A., and B. Subba (1985) *Concise Limbu Grammar and Dictionary.* Amsterdam: Lobster.

Weijer, Jeroen M. van de (1995) Continuancy in Obstruents and in Liquids. *Lingua* 96: 45–61.

Werker, Janet F., and Richard C. Tees (1984) Phonemic and phonetic factors in adult cross-language speech perception. *JASA* 75: 1866–78.

Westerman, D., and H. J. Melzian (1974) *The Kpelle Language in Liberia*. Berlin: Reimer/Vohsen.

Westley, David O. (1991) *Tepetotutla Chinantec Syntax: Studies in Chinantec Languages*, vol. 5. Arlington: Summer Institute of Linguistics and the University of Texas at Arlington.

Wheeler, Alva, and Margaret Wheeler (1962) Siona phonemics (Western Tucanoan). In Elson (1962: 96–111).

Wheeler, Max (1979) *The Phonology of Catalan*. Oxford: Blackwell.

Whisler, Ronald (1992) Phonology of Sawai. In Burquest and Laidig (1992).

White, Robin Barbara Davis (1973) *Klamath Phonology*. University of Washington Studies in Linguistics and Language Learning vol. 12.

Whitney, William Dwight (1867) *Language and the Study of Language: Twelve Lectures on the Principles of Linguistic Science*. London: Trübner.

—— (1875) *The Life and Growth of Language: An Outline of Linguistic Science*. New York: Appleton.

Wichmann, Søren (1995) *The Relationship Among the Mixe-Zoquean Languages of Mexico*. Salt Lake City: University of Utah Press.

Wickelgren, W. A. (1965) Distinctive features and errors in short-term memory for English vowels. *Journal of the Acoustical Society of America* 38: 583–8.

—— (1966) Distinctive features and errors in short-term memory for English vowels. *Journal of the Acoustical Society of America* 39: 388–98.

Wiering, Elisabeth (1994) Tone patterns of nominals in Doyayo. In Wiering and Wiering (1994a: 85–115).

Wiering, Elisabeth, and Marinus Wiering (eds.) (1994a) *The Doyayo Language: Selected Studies*. Arlington, Tex.: Summer Institute of Linguistics.

—— and —— (1994b) Phonological description of Doyayo (Poli dialect). In Wiering and Wiering (1994a: 1–51).

Willett, Thomas Leslie (1988) *A Reference Grammar of Southeastern Tepehuan*. Ann Arbor: UMI.

Williamson, Kay (1965) *A Grammar of the Kolokuma Dialect of Ijo*. Cambridge: Cambridge University Press.

Wilson, Colin (2003) Experimental investigation of phonological naturalness. In G. Garding and M. Tsujimura (eds.), *WCCFL* 22. Somerville, Mass.: Cascadilla Press, pp. 533–46.

Wilson, W. A. A. (1961) *An Outline of the Temne Language*. London: SOAS.

Winfield, Revd. W. W. (1928) *A Grammar of the Kui Language*. Calcutta: Baptist Mission Press.

Woollams, Geoff (1996) *A Grammar of Karo Batak, Sumatra*. Canberra: Pacific Linguistics.

Xu, Shixuan (2001) *The Bisu Language*, trans. Cecilia Brassett. Munich: Lincom Europa.

Yadav, Ramawatar (1996) *A Reference Grammar of Maithili.* New York: Mouton de Gruyter.

Yallop, Colin (1977) *Alyawarra.* Canberra: Advocate Press.

Yi, Hyon-bok (1989) *Korean Grammar.* New York: Oxford University Press.

Yip, Moira (2004a) Lateral survival: an OT account. To appear in P. Boersma and J. Antonio Cutillas (eds.), *Advances in Optimality Theory,* special issue of *International Journal of English Studies,* 4.2: 25–51.

—— (2005) Variability in feature affiliations through violable constraints: The case of [lateral]. In M. van Oostendoorp and J. van de Weijer, eds. *The Internal Organization of Phonological Segments: Studies in Generative Grammar 77.* Berlin/New York: Mouton de Gruyter.

Zeshan, Ulrike (2005) Sign languages. In Haspelmath et al. (2005: 558–9).

Ziervogel, D. (1952) *A Grammar of Swazi.* Johannesburg: Witwatersrand University Press.

—— (1959) *A Grammar of Northern Transvaal Ndebele.* Pretoria: van Schaik.

Zimmermann, J. (1858) *A Grammatical Sketch and Vocabulary of the Akra- or Gā-Language.* Stuttgart: Gregg International.

Zvelebil, Kamil V. (1973) *The Irula Language.* Wiesbaden: Harrassowitz.

Language index

Feature index

Index

acoustic cues; *see* cues, acoustic
acquisition
  device; *see* language acquisition device
  emergence of structure and
  innate features and 23–5, 44–5, 62–3
  perception and 42–4
  unnatural sound patterns 107–8
  trivial 112
affricates, ambivalence of 71–2
ambiguity, phonetic 64, 71–3
ambivalence, phonological 56–77, 117, 137
  of affricates 72–3
  of lateral liquids 58–65, 68–73
  of nasals 62–8
analogy 88–90, 109–10; *see also*
    generalization
aphasia 24–5
Articulator Theories 28
attention 109–10, 188, 193
audition 109–10, 193

Bernoulli Principle 186
bilabials 124, 136
binarity 31–2
Blue Nile Ethiopian restaurant 1–2
Brownian motion 188
Buckeye Corpus 96

categorization 44, 109–11, 189
change; *see* diachrony
chickens 26
chinchillas 43
class
  concave 115–16, 130–3
  convex 129
  crazy 119–24
  definitions 2–3, 12–13, 48–9
  examples 13–15, 51–2, 118–33
  feature analysis 49–55
  idiosyncratic 4–5, 10
  L-shaped; *see* concave
  natural 12–3, 76, 161–3
  phonologically active
    accounting for 84–8
    emergence of 4, 7–9, 98–9

  recurrent 76–7
  in survey 47–55, 150–1
  predictions 4, 75–7, 84–5, 114–17, 152,
    159–61
  randomly-generated 150–1, 171
  survey; *see* survey of classes
  unnatural
    analysis of 163–5
    number of 59, 77, 118
    occurrence of 3–5, 115–16
    recurrent 143–6
    types of 118–33
clicks 178–9
clustering 169–71
coarticulation 41
  vowel harmony and 99–100, 108–11, 192–3
cognitive representation; *see*
    representation, cognitive
complexity
  cognitive 190–1
  representational 24
  social factors and 97
consonants
  class 148, 163–4
  clustering 169–70
  continuancy 62–5
  depressor 93–5
  perception 39, 44, 169–71
  substitution 37–8
  survey assumptions 49
constraints; *see* Optimality Theory
coordination 99, 108–10, 192
corner vowels; *see* vowels, corner
coronals, patterning of 62–4
correlates, phonetic; *see* features, phonetic
    correlates of
covert feature effects 80
cues, acoustic
  attention and 188–9
  salience 39, 41–2

deafness 18
Dependency Phonology 11, 74
development, language; *see* acquisition
devoicing, final 3, 42, 85

Genetic Change feedback loop 184–97
genome, human 183–6, 191
gestures
    development of sound patterns and 108
    mistiming 99, 187, 192
glottals
    consonant-tone interaction and 94
    patterning with labials and velars, 143–4
grammar
    transformational 32
    universal; *see* Universal Grammar

harmony; *see* vowel harmony
historical explanation; *see* diachrony
historical residue; *see* residue, historical

identity relation 11
implosives
    patterning independently of
        ejectives 166
    tone lowering and 93–5
impossible
    languages 180
    sound patterns 20–1
    speech sounds 25
Information Theory 31–2
information, sequential; *see* sequential
    information
innate feature theory; *see also* features,
    innate
    arguments against 15–34, 73, 77, 107–8,
        133
    description 3, 6, 29–30, 58, 103
    insights 10–2
    motivations for 32–4
    predictions of, 73–6, 114–17, 126
inventory, segment
    definitions and 12–13
    feature availability and 162
    survey and 49–51

labialization, contrastive 11, 34
labials
    markedness and 96
    patterning with velars and glottals, 143–4
    representation 105–8
labiovelars 124–5
language acquisition device 183–8, 194
language change; *see* diachrony
laryngeals 165–6
laterals
    continuancy of 56–77

patterning of 60–2
patterning compared to obstruents and
    nasals 62–6
patterning with nasals 126–7
variability, 68–70
Library of Congress 47
liquids 56; *see also* laterals

Macro Model 180–1
magnetoencephalography (MEG) 45–6
Major Articulator Theory 124
markedness 24, 96, 177
Markov chain 177–81
memory
    capacity 100
    taxation 30–1, 45, 100
Micro Model 181–2
modality
    differences 15–19, 38–9, 196
    Feature Geometry and 102
morphology 8, 177–8

nasalization
    of consonants 120, 135–40
    of vowels
        allophonic 137, 140
        development of 86
        natural classes and 85
nasals
    ambivalence of 65–8
    patterning of 62–8
    patterning with laterals 126–7, 133–5
    patterning with sibilants 127
    representation of 74
    sound change and 85
natural class; *see* class, natural
Natural Phonology 106–7
naturalness; *see* class, natural
Neogrammarians 88–9
neutralization, incomplete 42
No Line-Crossing 25
Noise in Transmission feedback
    loop 184–96
null hypothesis 21–3, 195–7

obstruents, voiceless, patterning with
    sonorants 144
oppositions 10–11, 30, 100
Optimality Theory
    antagonistic constraints in 115–16, 166–7
    apparent natural classes and 115–16
    cognitive representation and 112, 175